GUIDE TO
Marxist Literary
Criticism

GUIDE TO
Marxist Literary Criticism

Compiled by

Chris Bullock and David Peck

THE HARVESTER PRESS

For Kay and for Holly

First published in Great Britain in 1980 by
THE HARVESTER PRESS LIMITED
Publishers: John Spiers and Margaret A. Boden
16 Ship Street, Brighton, Sussex

© 1980 by Indiana University Press

ISBN 0-7108-0003-7

Manufactured in the United States of America

CONTENTS

Introduction   vii

1. Bibliographical Tools   1
2. General Collections   3
3. Journals   6
4. Marxist Criticism: General   8
5. Literary Genres: Drama   29
6. Literary Genres: Fiction   34
7. Literary Genres: Poetry   39
8. National Literatures: British   42

   A. General / 42
   B. Before 1800 / 45
   C. Nineteenth Century / 47
   D. Twentieth Century / 49
       i. general / 49
       ii. the 1930s / 50

9. National Literatures: United States   53

   A. General / 53
   B. Before 1900 / 55
   C. 1900-1930 / 57
   D. The 1930s / 57
   E. 1940- / 62

10. National Literatures: English-Canadian   65

    A. General / 65
    B. Twentieth Century / 67
        i. general / 67
        ii. the 1930s / 70

11. Individual Authors   72
12. Teaching English   129
13. Language, Linguistics, and Literacy   133
14. Literature & Society   139

Contents

15. Appendix: A Reading List on Mass Culture   148
  A. General / 148
      i. Journals / 148
      ii. Bibliographies and Collections / 148
      iii. Individual Studies / 151
  B. Film, Radio, Television / 157
  C. Other Media / 162

Index   169

INTRODUCTION

The *Guide* is a practical handbook for students and teachers who wish to learn more about the contributions Marxism has to make to the study of English and North American literatures. Its sections on these national literatures, on genres, and on individual authors are comprehensive; it also offers long listings on Marxist theory, language, teaching English, literature and society, and mass culture. We have tried to make the organization of our listings as clear and accessible as possible. An explanation of our format and criteria follows.

PRINCIPLES OF SELECTION

Since this is a bibliography of works available in English *on* English, Canadian, and U. S. literatures, works that are not yet translated from other languages, or works in English on subjects outside these areas (such as a Soviet or English Marxist analysis of Russian literature) are not listed. In all sections we have included some non-Marxist criticism (indicated by "NM") and some mixed collections ("M/NM"); the "Literature & Society; Sociology of Literature" section (14) contains non-Marxist items almost exclusively. Our principle in this matter has been to list non-Marxist items on Marxist works and writers (e.g., S. S. Prawer on *Karl Marx and World Literature*), and to include non-Marxist critics whose work has furthered the development of Marxist criticism (e.g., Ian Watt on the English novel).

Our attempt has been to include *all* forms of Marxist criticism in English. We have listed as Marxist writings by critics who deem themselves to be Marxists or whose work—on the basis of internal evidence—reveals basic Marxist principles or a Marxist orientation. We have not included Marxist history, economics, sociology, or philosophy; although such work is essential to an understanding of Marxism and Marxist criticism, we have necessarily limited ourselves in this *Guide* to the categories of literature and culture.

One strength of the current Marxist renaissance in literary studies is its range, and we have tried to be true to that range by listing items from all available Marxist journals and books in English. The exceptions are ephemeral items: book reviews are not generally noted (unless they deal in a significant way with books listed in the *Guide* itself), nor are simple reiterations of fixed Marxist positions. (Thus we have not catalogued every item, for example, from *Soviet Literature* or *Literature & Ideology*.)

The other exception to comprehension is the Appendix (section 15), "A Reading List on Mass Culture." Here a listing with pretensions to completeness would be almost as long as the rest of the *Guide*; what section 15 offers instead is a sampling of relevant material. (By "relevant" we mean related to mass culture defined as a profit culture designed for massified consumers; we do not include items solely devoted to art films, video experiments, folksong, and other examples of avant garde or popular culture.)

FORMAT

Sections

Each of the fifteen sections in the *Guide* (e.g., Drama, Language) is a self-contained survey of Marxist criticism on that particular area. The items *within* a section are ordered alphabetically and numbered consecutively. Within each individual critic's listing, items are chronological, first among books and then among articles. Criticism *on* a critic or author is designated by a lowercase letter following the item number (4.109*c* is an article *on* Lukács) and is ordered chronologically. The format of the Appendix follows that of the *Guide* as a whole.

Bibliographical Information

Section 1 is a listing of useful bibliographical tools. Individual items in the *Guide* that also contain useful bibliographies are marked by an asterisk (*) and are generally put at the beginning of sections. Where bibliographies on individual critics or authors exist (for example, Peter Murphy's 1976 listing for Lukács), we do *not* list earlier items on that writer already collected in such bibliographies.

Journals

Section 3 is a listing of journals (not exclusively Marxist) where numerous items of Marxist criticism can be found. (Those used most frequently in the *Guide* are abbreviated after the title.) In certain sections, we also list journals of relevance to that section in particular (e.g., *New Masses* in the American section, *This Magazine* in the Canadian section). Special issues of journals are listed throughout the *Guide* under the title of that particular issue. (The special Marxist issue of *Studies in Romanticism*, in other words, is listed in the nineteenth-century British subsection under the issue title, "Marxism and Romanticism.")

Cross-listing

Individual chapters in books and essays in collections of criticism are usually cross-listed in the particular sections where they belong. (While LeRoy's *Perplexed Prophets* is listed in the nineteenth-century British subsection, for example, his individual chapters on Arnold, Wilde, and others are listed under those writers in the "Individual Authors" section.) If a critic's articles are gathered into a collection, we cite the collection rather than the original articles, although the annotations to such collections generally spell out the individual contents in some detail. When a work is relevant to more than one section, it is listed in its major area and cross-listed under "Others" at the end of sections that pertain to it secondarily. Within section 11, multiple-author titles (e.g., "Emerson and Wordsworth") are fully cited under the name of the first author ("Emerson") and then listed by title and our entry number only for the other author(s) in the title ("Wordsworth"). "*S.a.*" after an individual author in section 11 directs the reader to "see also" selected items (generally less than article or chapter length) listed elsewhere in the *Guide*. In cross-references like these, we list our own entry number, page numbers (where applicable), and author's surname. (For further information on cross-listing, see "Index" below.)

Individual Entries

The format for individual entries follows the *MLA Handbook* with only minor changes. We list place of publication, publisher, and dates for books whenever possible, but we do not use "pp." for journal and volume entries, and we drop issue numbers of journals where we have the volume number and the exact date of publication. Whenever possible, and wherever relevant, we cite the original date of book publication and then refer readers to more recent or readily available editions. (Example: the entry for Trotsky's *Literature and Revolution* reads "1924; Ann Arbor: University of Michigan Press, 1960." The semicolon in this case precedes the reprint.)

Index

Readers should use the Index regularly, because a number of *critics* we list in the *Guide* appear in more than one section. (All the items for Lucien Goldmann, for instance, whose work appears throughout the *Guide*, can be found together only under "Goldmann" in the comprehensive Index.) Individual *authors*, like Shakespeare, on the other hand, only appear in section 11, and not in the Index. The Index also contains a number of key terms and topics (such as alienation, socialist realism, and utopian literature) that recur in entries in different sections of the *Guide*.

CONCLUSION

Our own classroom experience leads us to believe that the *Guide* will be useful to students and teachers in a number of fields—not only literature, but sociology, history, philosophy, and others as well. We hope that the *Guide* will arouse further interest in and commitment to Marxism as a critical discipline of thought and action and that it will inspire Marxist critics and scholars to explore areas of study as yet inadequately treated. Clearly, there are a number of areas (like literature and psychology) where Marxist criticism needs to continue its work. What we hope to make clear through the *Guide* is both how much work *has* been done and how much remains to be done.

Our working deadline for this edition of the *Guide* was July 1, 1979. However, we hope that a second edition may be possible, and we welcome suggestions regarding format and additional items from readers.

ACKNOWLEDGMENTS

We owe a great debt to Lee Baxandall, both for his pioneering work in Marxist bibliography and for his advice on the present project. Thanks for help on the *Guide* should also go to the following scholars: Fay Blake, Frank Davey, Sheila Delany, Todd Gitlin, Brent Harold, Dell Hymes, Marlene Kadar, Richard Ohmann, Paul Siegel, James Steele, Stephen Wolfe, Don Lazere, Gaylord LeRoy, David Margolies, Norman Rudich, George Woodcock, Steve Zelnick, and Jack Zipes; to research assistants Colin Morton and Elaine Young at Edmonton; and to the interlibrary loan staff at Long Beach. Needless to say, we hold only ourselves responsible for the final shape and content of the *Guide*.

GUIDE TO
Marxist Literary Criticism

- 1 -

Bibliographical Tools

1.1 AIMS *Newsletter.* New York: The American Institute for Marxist Studies, 1964– .
Bimonthly listing of books, articles, conferences, etc.

1.2 *Alternative Press Index.* Baltimore: Alternative Press Centre, 1969– .
Quarterly "index to alternative and radical publications."

1.3 Bathrick, David, et al., comps. "Bibliography." In 4.126, 157–72.
Includes "Anthologies and Bibliographies," "Individual Works."

1.4 Baxandall, Lee, comp. *Marxism and Aesthetics: A Selective Annotated Bibliography.* New York: Humanities Press, 1968.
The definitive international bibliography; lists works (in English only) from Africa to Yugoslavia.

1.5 Lawford, Paul, comp. *Marxist Aesthetics: A Short Bibliography of Works in English.* Keele: University of Keele, 1977.
Inclusive, but uncritical and unorganized.

1.6 *News from Neasden: A Catalogue of New Radical Publications* (London, 1975–).

1.7 Peck, David, comp. *American Marxist Literary Criticism, 1926–1941: A Bibliography.* New York: The American Institute for Marxist Studies, 1975.

1.8 _____ . "Marxist Literary Criticism in the United States, 1941–1966: A Bibliography." *Bulletin of Bibliography & Magazine Notes,* 35 (October–December 1978), 172–79.

1

1.9 _____ . "The New Marxist Criticism: A Bibliography." *The Minnesota Review*, Nos. 2-3 (Spring–Fall 1974), 127–32. "The New Marxist Criticism: A Bibliography, II." *MR,* No. 7 (Fall 1976), 100–105. "The New Marxist Criticism: A Bibliography, III." *MR*, No. 12 (Spring 1979), 50–58.

1.10 Raina, M. L., comp. "Marxism and Literature: A Select Bibliography." In 2.11, 308–14.

Sections on "Marxist Aesthetics," "Marxism and Literary Criticism," and "Applications."

Others: Solomon (2.15), Angenot (14.1), "Mass Culture, Political Consciousness and English Studies" (15.19), works throughout the *Guide* with asterisks.

-2-

General Collections

2.1 *Aesthetics and Politics*. London: New Left Books, 1978.
Thirties debates of Adorno, Bloch, Lukács, Brecht, Benjamin.
Afterword by Fredric Jameson. Reviewed by Terry Eagleton,
New Left Review, No. 107 (January–February 1978), 21–34.

2.2 Baxandall, Lee, ed. *Radical Perspectives in the Arts*. Baltimore:
Penguin, 1972.
An international range of critics; sections on "The Arts and
Capitalism," "The Arts and Socialism," and "The Future of
Culture."

2.3 Craig, David, ed. *Marxists on Literature: An Anthology*.
Baltimore: Penguin, 1975.
Selections from the 'classic' Marxist critics, from Marx to Ernst
Fischer, but few contemporaries. Reviewed by Jack Lindsay,
Meanjin Quarterly (Melbourne), 35 (1976), 339–46.

2.4 "Ideology and Literature." *New Literary History*, 4 (Spring
1973). (M/NM)
Special issue includes essays by American, Canadian, and
European critics.

2.5 Knight, Stephen, and Michael Wilding, eds. *The Radical
Reader*. Sydney: Wild & Woolley, 1977.
A collection of "new, hitherto unpublished radical criticism of
literary topics" by American and Commonwealth critics.

2.6 Lang, Berel, and Forrest Williams, eds. *Marxism and Art:
Writings in Aesthetics and Criticism*. New York: David McKay,
1972.

Includes "Sources" (Marx to Mao) and "Elements" (twenty-five critics in sections on theory, art history, genres, and critical practice).

2.7 LeRoy, Gaylord, and Ursula Beitz, eds. *Preserve and Create: Essays in Marxist Criticism*. New York: Humanities Press, 1973.
Essays from the U.S.S.R., Eastern Europe, on questions of partisanship, point of view, socialist realism, and related topics.

2.8 "Literature in Revolution." *TriQuarterly*, No. 23/24 (Winter/ Spring 1972). Ed. Charles Newman and George Abbott White. Rpt. *Literature in Revolution*. Boston: Holt, Rinehart and Winston, 1972. (M/NM)
Articles by critics from liberal to New Left, in sections on "The Responsibility of Literature," "Rereadings," "Popular Culture," and "Critical Consciousness."

2.9 "Marxism and Utopia." *The Minnesota Review*, No. 6 (Spring 1976), 51–139.
Special supplement includes Fredric Jameson, "Introduction/ Prospectus: To Reconsider the Relationship of Marxism to Utopian Thought," seven essays.

2.10 "Marxist Alternatives to the Traditions." *The Minnesota Review*, No. 5 (Fall 1975), 33–163.
Special supplement contains a dozen essays on genres, literary theory, and individual authors.

2.11 "Marxist Interpretations of Mailer, Woolf, Wright, and Others." *College English*, 34 (November 1972).

2.12 "A Phalanx from the Left." *College English*, 31 (March 1970). Includes articles on criticism and pedagogy (several collected in 12.18).

2.13 Rudich, Norman, ed. *Weapons of Criticism: Marxism in America and the Literary Tradition*. Palo Alto, Cal.: Ramparts Press, 1976.
"Part I: Criticism in History" contains theoretical essays; "Part II: Literature in History," essays on individual authors.

2.14 "Socio-Criticism." *Sub-stance*, No. 15 (1976).
Special issue has essays by both American and European critics on codes, myths, signs, and ideology.

2.15 Solomon, Maynard, ed. *Marxism and Art: Essays Classic and Contemporary.* New York: Random House, 1973.

Probably the most comprehensive anthology in the field; includes selections from Marx and Engels (fifty pages), as well as a wide range of twentieth-century critics. Reviewed by Tom Morris, *Telos*, No. 27 (Spring 1976), 218–29.

2.16 "Symposium on Marxist Aesthetic Thought." *Arts in Society,* 12 (Summer-Fall 1975), 216–41.

Symposium in "Art and Social Experience: Our Changing Outlook on Culture" issue reprints papers from 1973 meeting of the American Society for Aesthetics, commentary and discussion.

Others: Durand (9.4), Kampf and Lauter (12.18), Barker (14.5, 14.6), Burns (14.8), Laurenson (14.50), Routh and Wolff (14.66), other collections throughout the *Guide.*

–3–

Journals

3.1 *Alive* (Toronto, 1975–).
Formed from the merger of *Alive Magazine* and *Literature & Ideology* (both 1969–75).

3.2 *Artery: A Cultural and Political Journal for Left Unity* (London, 1974–).

3.3 *Arts in Society* (Madison, Wis., 1958–76).

3.4 *College English* (Urbana, Ill., 1939–). (*CE*)

3.5 *Ideology and Consciousness* (London, 1977–).

3.6 *Literature and History* (London, 1975–). (*L & H*)

3.7 *Literature & Ideology* (Montreal, 1969–75). (*L & I*)

3.8 *Marxism Today* (London, 1957–). (*MT*)
Journal for the Communist Party of Great Britain.

3.9 *Marxist Perspectives* (New York, 1978–).

3.10 *The Minnesota Review* (Bloomington, Ind., NS 1973–). (*MR*)

3.11 *New German Critique* (Milwaukee, Wis., 1974–). (*NGC*)

3.12 *New Left Review* (London, 1960–). (*NLR*)
Formed by the union of *Universities and Left Review* and *The New Reasoner*.

3.13 *New Literary History* (Charlottesville, Va., 1969–). (*NLH*)

3.14 *Praxis: A Journal of Radical Perspectives on the Arts* (Goleta, Cal., 1975–).

3.15 *Radical Teacher: A Newsjournal of Socialist Theory and Practice* (New York, 1975–). (*RT*)

3.16 *Red Letters: Communist Party Literature Journal* (London, 1976–). (*RL*)

3.17 *Science & Society: An Independent Journal of Marxism* (New York, 1936–). (*S&S*)

3.18 *Social Text* (Madison, Wis., 1979–).

3.19 *Studies on the Left* (Madison, Wis., New York, 1959–67). (*SOL*)

3.20 *Telos: A Quarterly Journal of Radical Thought* (St. Louis, 1968–).

3.21 *Working Papers in Cultural Studies* (Birmingham, England, 1971–). (*WPCS*)

3.22 *Zeitschrift fur Anglistik und Amerikanistik* (Berlin, 1953–). (*ZAA*)

Others: *Left Review* (8.95), *The Modern Quarterly* (London) (8.98), *The Modern Quarterly* (Baltimore) (9.56), *New Masses* (9.57), *Partisan Review* (9.59), *Canadian Dimension* (10.17), *Canadian Forum* (10.18), *The Marxist Quarterly* (10.29), *New Frontiers* (10.31), *This Magazine* (10.37), *Working Teacher* (10.44), *New Frontier* (10.54), *Shakespeare Jahrbuch* (11.189b), *Cineaste* (15.1), *Cine Tracts* (15.2), *Cultural Correspondence* (15.3), *Culture & Context* (15.4), *The Cultural Worker* (15.5), *Discourse* (15.6), *Jump Cut* (15.7), *Media Ecology Review* (15.8), *Open Secret* (15.9), *Screen* (15.10), *Toward Revolutionary Art* (15.11), *Wedge* (15.12).

–4–

Marxist Criticism: General

This section contains major examples and assessments of Marxist critical theory. Applied criticism appears in the sections on genre, national literatures, individual authors, and mass culture.

4.1 Adorno, Theodor. *Prisms: Cultural Criticism and Society.* 1955; London: Neville Spearman, 1967.
Individual studies on Huxley, jazz, Walter Benjamin, other topics.

4.2 Althusser, Louis. *Lenin and Philosophy and Other Essays.* London: New Left Books, 1971.
See "Ideology and Ideological State Apparatuses" (123–73), "A Letter On Art" (Appendix, 203–208), and "Cremonini" (Appendix, 209–20). Eagleton's *Criticism and Ideology* (4.39) is influenced by these essays.

4.3a Callinicos, Alex. *Althusser's Marxism.* London: Pluto Press, 1976.

4.3b Barker, Francis. "Althusser and Art." *RL*, No. 4 (Spring 1977), 7–12.
See also: David Margolies, "Some Further Thoughts on Althusser," *RL*, No. 5 (Summer 1977), 18–19.

4.4 Aronowitz, Stanley. "Culture and Politics." *Politics and Society*, 6, No. 3 (1976), 347–96.

4.5 _____ . "Critic as Star." *MR* No. 9 (Fall 1977), 71–111.

4.6 Arvon, Henri. *Marxist Esthetics*. Introd. Fredric Jameson. Ithaca, N.Y.: Cornell University Press, 1973.
Useful accounts of European Marxist criticism, Soviet literary history, Brecht versus Lukács, other topics.

4.7 Baxandall, Lee. "Introduction." In 2.16, 216-17.

4.8 _____ . "Literature and Ideology." In 2.13, 119-32.

4.9 _____ . "The Marxist Orientation to Art and Literature." *NGC*, No. 3 (Fall 1976), 163-80.
A thoughtful review of Craig (2.3), Lang and Williams (2.6), LeRoy and Beitz (2.7), "Literature in Revolution" (2.8), Solomon (2.15), Hawthorn (4.76), and Vasquez (4.180).

4.10 Beker, Miroslav. "Marxism and the Determinants of Critical Judgment." *Journal of Aesthetics and Art Criticism*, 29 (Fall 1970), 33-41.

4.11 Bell, Gene H. "Ideology and American Literary Criticism." *S&S*, 37 (Fall 1973), 300-25.

4.12 _____ . "Bruno's Castle, or Some Current Literary Misconceptions." *Praxis*, No. 1 (Spring 1975), 3-14.

4.13 Benjamin, Walter. *Illuminations*. Ed. Hannah Arendt. New York: Harcourt, Brace & World, 1968.
Includes "The Work of Art in the Age of Mechanical Reproduction" (also in 2.6, 2.15) and some of Benjamin's writings on Brecht and Baudelaire.

4.14 _____ . *Charles Baudelaire: A Lyric Poet in the Era of High Capitalism*. Ed. Harry Zohn. London: New Left Books, 1973.

4.15 _____ . *Reflections: Essays, Aphorisms, Autobiographical Writings*. Ed. Peter Demetz. New York: Harcourt Brace Jovanovich, 1978.
Includes "The Author as Producer" and other essays.

4.16 _____ . *One-Way Street and Other Writings*. Introd. Susan Sontag. London: New Left Books, 1979.
Essays on politics, aesthetics, language, literature.

4.17a Jacobs, Carol. "Walter Benjamin: Image of Proust." *Modern Language Notes*, 86 (December 1971), 910-32.

4.17b Witte, Bernd. "Benjamin and Lukács: Historical Notes on the Relationship Between Their Political and Aesthetic Theories." *NGC*, No. 5 (Spring 1975), 3-26.

4.17c Burns, Rob. "Understanding Benjamin." *RL*, No. 7 (1978), 16–33.

4.18 Birchall, Ian. "The Total Marx and the Marxist Theory of Literature." In *Situating Marx: Evaluations and Departures.* Ed. Paul Walton and Stuart Hall. London: Human Context Books, 1972, 118–45.

See also Stanley Mitchell, "Extended Note to Ian Birchall's Paper," 146–51, and Jerry Palmer, "Contribution to a Marxist Theory of Artistic Creativity," 152–65, both of which are commentaries on Birchall's essay.

4.19 ———. "Marxism and Literature." In 14.66, 92–108.

4.20 Bisztray, George. *Marxist Models of Literary Realism.* New York: Columbia University Press, 1978.

An analysis from Marx, Engels, and Lenin to Lukács, Garaudy, and Fischer.

4.21 ———. "Literary Sociology and Marxist Theory: The Literary Work as a Social Document." In 14.70, 47–56.

4.22 Buck-Morss, Susan. *The Origins of Negative Dialectics: Theodor Adorno, Walter Benjamin and the Frankfurt School.* New York: The Free Press, 1977. Reviewed by Peter U. Hohendahl, *Telos*, No. 34 (Winter 1977–78), 185–87.

4.23 Burniston, Steve, and Chris Weedon. "Ideology, Subjectivity and the Artistic Text." *WPCS*, No. 10 (Spring 1977), 203–33.

WPCS No. 10 is a special issue on ideology that includes other articles on Lukács, Gramsci, Althusser, and related topics.

4.24 Caudwell, Christopher. *Illusion and Reality: A Study of the Sources of Poetry.* 1937; New York: International Publishers, 1963.

The most serious British Marxist critic of the 1930s, Caudwell's work is a mixture of insight and crude shorthand.

4.25 ———. *Romance and Realism: A Study in English Bourgeois Literature.* Ed. Samuel Hynes. Princeton, N.J.: Princeton University Press, 1970.

A previously unpublished section of *Illusion and Reality*.

4.26 ———. *Studies and Further Studies in a Dying Culture.* New York: Monthly Review Press, 1972.

A combined reissue of *Studies in a Dying Culture* (1938), with essays on Lawrence, Shaw, Wells, Freud, and related figures, and *Further Studies in a Dying Culture* (1949), which has essays on aesthetics, history, psychology, and philosophy.

*4.27a Margolies, David N. *The Function of Literature: A Study of Christopher Caudwell's Aesthetics*. New York: International Publishers, 1969.

4.27b Mulhern, Francis. "The Marxist Aesthetics of Christopher Caudwell." *NLR*, No. 85 (May–June 1974), 37-58.

4.27c Sypher, Eileen. "Towards a Theory of the Lyric: Georg Lukács and Christopher Caudwell." *Praxis*, No. 3 (1976), 173-83.

4.27d Pradhan, S. V. "Caudwell's Theory of Poetry: Some Problems of a Marxist Synthesis." *British Journal of Aesthetics*, 17 (Summer 1977), 266-74.

4.27e Thompson, E. P. "Caudwell." In *The Socialist Register 1977*. Ed. Ralph Miliband and John Saville. London: The Merlin Press, 1977, 228-76.

4.27f Draper, Michael. "Christopher Caudwell's Illusions." In 8.97, 78-102.

4.28 Coste, Didier. "Politextual Economy: In Defence of an Unborn Science." In 2.5, 37-53.
An attempt to develop a theory of political/economic reading of literary texts.

4.29 Craig, David. "Toward Laws of Literary Development." In 14.70, 11-30. Rpt. in 2.3, 134-60.

4.30 Craig, David, and Michael Egan. "Can Literature Be Evidence?" *MR*, No. 4 (Spring 1975), 85-105.

4.31 _____ . "The Literature of Revolution." *Praxis*, No. 2 (Winter 1976), 29-57.

4.32 Crews, Frederick. "Do Literary Studies Have an Ideology?" *PMLA*, 85 (May 1970), 423-28. Rpt. in *Out of My System: Psychoanalysis, Ideology and Critical Method*. New York: Oxford University Press, 1975. (NM)

4.33 Cultural Theory Panel attached to the Central Committee of the Hungarian Socialist Workers' Party. "Of Socialist Realism." In 2.2, 240-66.

4.34 Della Volpe, Galvano. *Critique of Taste.* 1960; London: New Left Books, 1978.

4.35 Demetz, Peter. *Marx, Engels and the Poets: Origins of Marxist Literary Criticism.* Chicago: University of Chicago Press, 1967.
An invaluable scholarly (if anti-Marxist) account of Marx and Engels as literary critics, Plekhanov, Mehring, Lukács, and "Marxist Criticism Past and Present."

4.36 ———. "Marxist Literary Criticism Today." *Survey,* 18 (Winter 1972), 63–72. (NM)
On European Marxist criticism since 1963.

4.37 Di Salvo, Jackie. "This Murder: New Criticism and Literary Scholarship." *NUC-MLC Newsletter,* 1, No. 3 (1969), 11.

4.38 Dunham, Barrows. *The Artist in Society.* New York: Marzani & Munsell, 1960.
Marxist aesthetics.

4.39 Eagleton, Terry. *Criticism and Ideology: A Study in Marxist Literary Theory.* London: New Left Books, 1976.
A major text in which Eagleton attempts to outline a scientific materialist criticism. Reviewed by Francis Mulhern, *NLR,* No. 108 (March–April 1978), 77–87.

4.40 ———. *Marxism and Literary Criticism.* Berkeley: University of California Press, 1976.
An excellent introduction to Marxist criticism, focussing on four topics: literature and history, form and content, the writer and commitment, and the author as producer.

4.41 ———. "Marxism and Form." *Poetry Nation,* 1 (1973), 59-61.

4.42 ———. "Ideology and Literary Form." *NLR,* No. 90 (March–April 1975), 81–109. Rpt. in 4.39.
See also Francis Mulhern, "Ideology and Literary Form: A Comment," *NLR,* No. 91 (May–June 1975), 80–87, for a sharp critique of Eagleton; reply by Eagleton in No. 92 (July–September 1975), 107–108. Further: Arnold Kettle, "Literature and Ideology," *RL,* No. 1 (Spring 1976), 3–5; Alan Hunt, "Discussion: Ideology and Its Role in Marxist Theory," *RL,* No. 2 (Summer 1976), 11–12.

4.43 ———. "Marxist Literary Criticism." In *Contemporary Approaches to English Studies.* Ed. Hilda Schiff. London: Heinemann, 1977, 94–103.

4.44 ———. "Marxist Literary Criticism." In 14.66, 85–91.
4.45 ———. "Liberality and Order: The Criticism of John Bayley." *NLR,* No. 110 (July–August 1978), 29–40.
4.46 Ellis, Kate. "Women, Culture, and Revolution." *RT,* No. 2 (June 1976), 3–8.
See Ellen Cantarow's response, which immediately follows the article (9–10).
4.47 Fekete, John. *The Critical Twilight: Explorations in the Ideology of Anglo-American Literary Theory from Eliot to McLuhan.* Boston: Routledge & Kegan Paul, 1978. Reviewed by Lynne Layton, *Telos,* No. 34 (Winter 1977–78), 187–96.
4.48 ———. "Reflections on Literary Theory and Culture." *Praxis,* No. 1 (Spring 1975), 25–36.
4.49 Ferrier, Carol. " 'The Inadequacy of the Imagination': Towards a Feminist Literary Criticism." In 2.5, 193–206.
4.50 Finkelstein, Sidney. *Art and Society.* New York: International Publishers, 1947.
A "layman's approach to aesthetic problems." See 1.4, 176–77, 179, for controversy over book.
4.51 ———. "The Artistic Expression of Alienation." In *Marxism and Alienation: A Symposium.* Ed. Herbert Aptheker. New York: Humanities Press, 1965, 26–57.
4.52 ———. "Beauty and Truth." In 2.13, 51–73.
4.53 Fischer, Ernst. *The Necessity of Art: A Marxist Approach.* 1959; London: Penguin, 1978.
Particularly good on the origins and functions of art.
4.54 ———. *Art Against Ideology.* 1966; New York: Braziller, 1969.
4.55 Fokkema, D. W., and Elrud Kunne-Ibsch. *Theories of Literature in the Twentieth Century: Structuralism, Marxism, Aesthetics of Reception.* New York: St. Martin's Press, 1978. (NM)
See Chapter 4, "Marxist Theories of Literature."
4.56 Garaudy, Roger. *Literature of the Graveyard.* New York: International Publishers, 1948.
On Sartre, Mauriac, Malraux, and Koestler.
4.57 ———. "Marxism and Art." In *Marxism in the Twentieth Century.* New York: Scribner's, 1970, 164–97.
4.58 Girnus, Wilhelm. "On the Problem of Ideology and Literature." In 2.4, 483–500.

4.59 Goldmann, Lucien. *The Hidden God: A Study of Tragic Vision in the Pensées of Pascal and the Tragedies of Racine.* 1955; London: Routledge & Kegan Paul, 1964.

4.60 *The Human Sciences and Philosophy.* 1966; London: Jonathan Cape, 1969.
Very useful general analysis of means and ends in literary, sociological, and philosophical investigations.

*4.61 _____. *Cultural Creation in Modern Society.* Introd. William Mayrl. 1971; St. Louis: Telos Press, 1976.
Essays on dialectics, mass media, "potential consciousness," contemporary literature and industrial society.

4.62 _____. "Ideology and Writing." *TLS*, September 28, 1967, 903–905.

4.63 _____. "The Sociology of Literature: Status and Problems of Method." In 14.71, 493–516; rpt. in 14.2.

4.64 _____. "Criticism and Dogmatism in Literature." In *The Dialectics of Liberation.* Ed. David Cooper. Baltimore: Penguin, 1968, 128–49.

4.65 _____. "Marxist Criticism." In *The Philosophy of the Enlightenment.* Cambridge, Mass.: MIT Press, 1973, 86–97.

4.66 _____. "Dialectical Materialism and Literary History." *NLR*, No. 92 (July–August 1975), 39–51.
See also Francis Mulhern, "Introduction to Goldmann," 34–38.

*4.67a Rodriguez, Ileana, and Marc Zimmerman, comps. "Lucien Goldmann: A Bibliography." In 4.61, 148–75.

4.67b Rudich, Norman. "The Marxism of Lucien Goldmann in *The Philosophy of the Enlightenment.*" *Praxis*, No. 3 (1976), 205–17.

4.67c Leenhardt, Jacques. "Toward a Sociological Aesthetic: An Attempt at Constructing the Aesthetic of Lucien Goldmann." In 2.14, 94–104.

4.67d Routh, Jane. "A Reputation Made: Lucien Goldmann." In 14.66, 150–62.

4.68 Goode, John. "Women and the Literary Text." In *The Rights and Wrongs of Women.* Ed. Juliet Mitchell and Ann Oakley. Harmondsworth: Penguin, 1976, 217–55.

4.69 Gramsci, Antonio. *The Modern Prince and Other Writings.* London: Lawrence and Wishart, 1957.

Includes "Marxism and Modern Culture," other influential essays from the twenties and thirties.

4.70 _____ . *Selections from the Prison Notebooks of Antonio Gramsci.* Ed. Quintin Hoare and Geoffrey Nowell Smith. New York: International Publishers, 1971.

Much contemporary discussion of ideology and hegemony is indebted to the original theory found in "The Formation of the Intellectuals," "The Organization of Education and Culture," and other essays here.

*4.71a Boggs, Carl. *Gramsci's Marxism.* London: Pluto Press, 1976.

4.71b Thibaudeau, Jean. "Preliminary Notes on the Prison Writings of Gramsci: The Place of Literature in Marxist Theory." *Praxis*, No. 3 (1976), 3–29.

4.71c Davidson, Alistair. "The Literary Criticism of Antonio Gramsci: An Introduction." In 2.5, 55–71.

4.71d Mercer, Colin. "Culture and Ideology in Gramsci." *RL*, No. 8 (1978), 19–40.

4.72 Gross, David. "On Writing Cultural Criticism." *Telos*, No. 16 (Summer 1973), 38–60.

*4.73 Hall, Stuart. "Marxism and Culture." *Radical History Review*, 18 (Fall 1978), 5–14.

A discussion of the intellectual's role and "history from below." Good bibliography.

4.74 Harap, Louis. *The Social Roots of the Arts.* New York: International Publishers, 1949.

Explores "the roots of the arts in social forces"; chapters on "Production as Foundation," "Class and Audience," "Art and Social Action," related topics.

4.75 Harrington, Michael. "A Marxist Approach to Art." *The New International,* 22 (Spring 1956), 41–49.

4.76 Hawthorn, Jeremy. *Identity and Relationship: A Contribution to Marxist Theory of Literary Criticism.* London: Lawrence and Wishart, 1973.

An argument for seeing the literary work "in as many different contexts as are possible." Reviewed by James Kavanagh, *Praxis*, No. 2 (Winter 1976), 239–47.

4.77 Hess, Hans. "Is There a Theory of Art in Marx?" *MT*, October 1973, 306–14.

4.78 ———. "Art and Social Function." *MT*, August 1976, 245–52.

4.79 Hohendahl, Peter U. "The Use Value of Contemporary and Future Literary Criticism." *NGC*, No. 7 (Winter 1976), 3–20.
A helpful examination of the institutional context of literary criticism at the present time and in possible futures.

4.80 ———. "Introduction to Reception Aesthetics." *NGC*, No. 10 (Winter 1977), 29–63.

4.81 ———. "Prolegomena to a History of Literary Criticism." *NGC*, No. 11 (Spring 1977), 151–63.
The need to see literary criticism as part of literary history and as a social institution; discusses Saintsbury, Wellek.

4.82 James, C. Vaughan. *Soviet Socialist Realism: Origins and Theory*. New York: St. Martin's Press, 1973.
Appendixes contain Lenin's "Party Organization and Party Literature," "On Proletarian Culture (draft resolution)," and other relevant documents in the development of socialist realism in the twenties and thirties.

4.83 Jameson, Fredric. *Marxism and Form: Twentieth Century Dialectical Theories of Literature*. Princeton, N.J.: Princeton University Press, 1971.
Substantial accounts of Adorno, Benjamin, Bloch, Lukács, Marcuse, Sartre. "Towards Dialectical Criticism" (306–416) is a seminal discussion of how a dialectical criticism should move between form and content. Reviewed by Bart Grahl, *Telos*, No. 12 (Summer 1972), 155–60.

4.84 ———. *The Political Unconscious: Studies in the Ideology of Form*. Ithaca, N.Y.: Cornell University Press, 1979.

4.85 ———. "Notes Toward a Marxist Cultural Politics." Introduction to 2.10, 35–39.

4.86 ———. "Criticism in History." In 2.13, 31–50.

4.87 Jauss, Hans Robert. "The Idealist Embarrassment: Observations on Marxist Aesthetics." *NLH*, 7 (Autumn 1975), 191–208.

4.88 Jay, Martin. *The Dialectical Imagination: A History of the Frankfurt School and the Institute of Social Research, 1923–1950*. Boston: Little, Brown, 1973. (NM)

4.89 Kampf, Louis. *On Modernism: The Prospects for Literature and Freedom*. Cambridge, Mass.: MIT Press, 1967.

4.90 Kettle, Arnold, and V. G. Hanes. *Man and the Arts: A Marxist Approach.* New York: The American Institute for Marxist Studies, 1968.

Pamphlet contains title essay by Kettle and Hanes's article on Frye (11.71b), both of which originally appeared in *Horizons: The Marxist Quarterly* (Toronto).

4.91 Kogan, P. "The Fascist Premises of Archetypal Criticism." *L&I,* No. 6 (1970), 17–30.

4.92 _____. "Obscurantist Trends in American Criticism." *L&I,* No. 12 (1972), 37–44.

4.93 _____. "On Dogmatic Criticism." *L&I,* No. 16 (1974), 29–36.

4.94 Köpeczi, Bela. "A Marxist View of Form in Literature." *NLH,* 3 (Winter 1972), 355–72.

4.95 Laing, Dave. *The Marxist Theory of Art.* Atlantic Highlands, N. J.: Humanities Press, 1978.

Chapters on socialist realism, "The German Debates," "Marxism and Popular Culture," "British and American Developments."

4.96 Lenin, V. I. *On Culture and Cultural Revolution.* Moscow: Progress Publishers, 1966.

4.97 _____. *On Literature and Art.* Moscow: Progress Publishers, 1967.

Includes "Party Organization and Party Literature" (also in 2.6, 2.15, 4.82).

4.98 _____. *Not By Politics Alone: The Other Lenin.* Ed. Tamara Deutscher. London: Allen & Unwin, 1973.

Includes Lenin on culture, other writers on Lenin and culture.

4.99a Morawski, Stefan. "Lenin as Literary Theorist." *S&S,* 29 (Winter 1965), 3–25.

4.100 LeRoy, Gaylord. *Marxism and Modern Literature.* New York: The American Institute for Marxist Studies, 1967.

On "the cognitive function of art," form, realism, modernism, socialist realism, and related topics.

4.101 LeRoy, Gaylord, and Ursula Beitz. "The Marxist Approach to Modernism." *Journal of Modern Literature,* 3 (July 1974), 1158–74.

4.102 Lifshitz, Mikhail. *The Philosophy of Art of Karl Marx.* 1933; London: Pluto Press, 1973.
Reprint of the "best study in English of Marx's cultural views" (1.4).

4.103 Lindsay, Jack. *Decay and Renewal: Critical Essays on Twentieth Century Writing.* Sydney: Wild & Woolley, 1976.
Includes "The Role of the Individual in Art," "Towards a Marxist Aesthetic," other essays on Lukács, European and Australian writers.

4.104 Long, Michael. "Marxism and Criticism: Contribution to a Discussion." *MT*, November 1966, 341–50.
Marxist literary critics can learn from writers like Pound and Fenollosa, Lawrence and Eliot, and from 'unorthodox' Marxist critics like John Berger and Ernst Fischer.

4.105 Lukács, Georg. *Realism In Our Time: Literature and the Class Struggle.* 1957; New York: Harper & Row, 1964.
Published in Britain as *The Meaning of Contemporary Realism* (1962), this pivotal Lukács work is divided into chapters on "The Ideology of Modernism," "Franz Kafka or Thomas Mann?" and "Critical Realism and Socialist Realism."

4.106 _____. *Writer and Critic and Other Essays.* Ed. Arthur D. Kahn. New York: Grosset & Dunlap, 1971.
Includes "Marx and Engels on Aesthetics," other literary essays.

4.107 _____. *Marxism and Human Liberation: Essays on History, Culture and Revolution.* Ed. E. San Juan, Jr. New York: Dell, 1973.
Fifteen essays in sections on "Theory and Practice," "Aesthetics and Literary Criticism," and "Problems and Perspectives."

4.108 _____. "Introduction to a Monograph on Aesthetics." *New Hungarian Quarterly*, 5 (Summer 1964), 57–72. Lukács's *Aesthetics*, left incomplete at his death in 1971, has not yet been fully translated into English.

*4.109a Murphy, Peter, comp. *Writings By and About Georg Lukács: A Bibliography.* New York: The American Institute for Marxist Studies, 1976.

4.109b Lowy, Michael. *Georg Lukács—From Idealism to Bolshevism.* London: New Left Books, 1979.

4.109c Schmidt, James. "The Concrete Totality and Lukács' Concept of Proletarian *Bildung*." *Telos*, No. 24 (Summer 1975), 2–40.

4.109d Markus, Gyorgy. "The Soul and Life: The Young Lukács and the Problem of Culture." *Telos*, No. 32 (Summer 1977), 95–115.

4.109e Orr, John. "Georg Lukács." In 14.66, 109–30.

4.110 Lunacharsky, Anatoli V. *On Literature and Art.* Moscow: Progress Publishers, 1965.
Collection of articles on European writers by the first Soviet Commissar of Education.

4.111a Lebedev, Alexander. "The Purpose of Literary Criticism: Coercion Can't Create." *American Dialog*, 5 (Winter 1968–69), 13–15.
Mainly on Lunacharsky.

4.111b Vásquez, Adolfo Sánchez. "Lunacharsky: The Paradoxes of Art and Revolution." *Praxis*, No. 2 (Winter 1976), 107–16.

4.112 Macherey, Pierre. *A Theory of Literary Production.* 1966; Boston: Routledge & Kegan Paul, 1978.
Represents "a development of Althusser's account of the relationship between literature and ideology."

4.113 ———. "The Problem of Reflection." In 2.14, 6–20; rpt. in 14.5.

4.114 ———. "The Image in the Mirror." *RL*, No. 8 (1978), 4–16.

4.115a Eagleton, Terry. "Pierre Macherey and the Theory of Literary Production." In 2.10, 134–44.

4.115b Mercer, Colin, and Jean Radford. "An Interview with Pierre Macherey." *RL*, No. 5 (Summer 1977), 3–9.

4.116 MacDiarmid, Hugh. *Selected Essays.* London: Jonathan Cape, 1969.

4.117 Mao Tse-Tung. *On Literature and Art.* Peking: Foreign Language Press, 1967.
Includes "Talks at the Yenan Forum on Literature and Art," "On 'Let a Hundred Flowers Blossom...'," other talks and essays.

4.118 Marcuse, Herbert. *The Aesthetic Dimension: Toward a Critique of Marxist Aesthetics.* Boston: Beacon Press, 1978. Reviewed by Annette T. Rubinstein, *S&S*, 42 (Winter 1978–79), 503–505; Lee Baxandall, *MR*, No. 12 (Spring 1979), 108–10.

4.119 _____ . "The Affirmative Character of Culture." In *Negations: Essays in Critical Theory*. Boston: Beacon Press, 1968, 88–133.

4.120 _____ . "The New Sensibility." In *An Essay on Liberation*. Boston: Beacon Press, 1969, 23–48.

4.121 _____ . "Art as a Form of Reality." In *On the Future of Art*. Ed. Edward F. Fry. New York: Viking Press, 1970, 123–34.

4.122 _____ . "Art and Revolution." In *Counterrevolution and Revolt*. Boston: Beacon Press, 1972, 79–128.

4.123 _____ . "Art in the One-Dimensional Society." In 2.2, 53–67.

4.124a Goldmann, Lucien. "Understanding Marcuse." *Partisan Review*, 38, No. 3 (1971), 247–62.

4.124b Schoolman, Morton. "Marcuse's Aesthetics and the Displacement of Critical Theory." *NGC*, No. 8 (Spring 1976), 54–79.

4.125 Markiewicz, Henryk. "Marxist Theories of Social Differentiation." In *Actes du VIe Congrès de l'Association Internationale de Littérature Comparée*. Ed. Michel Cadot, et al. Stuttgart: Bieber, 1975, 41–47.
On social class in literature.

4.126 *Marx & Engels on Literature & Art: A Selection of Writings*. Ed. Lee Baxandall and Stefan Morawski. St. Louis: Telos Press, 1973.
Best brief collection of original Marxist statements on the arts.

4.127 *Marx/Engels on Literature and Art*. Moscow: Progress Publishers, 1976.
Recent and comprehensive anthology of original documents on aesthetics.

4.128 Mayer, Hans. *Steppenwolf and Everyman: Outsiders and Conformists in Contemporary Literature*. Ed. Jack D. Zipes. New York: Crowell, 1971.
Includes "Literature and Daily Life: Everyman in the Soviet Union and the United States," "Steppenwolf and Everyman: Literary Types of the Outsider," nine essays on European literature.

4.129 Mehring, Franz. "Karl Marx and Metaphor." In *Karl Marx and Friedrich Engels*. 1927; New York: Monthly Review Press, 1973, 95–101.

4.130 Mercer, Colin, and Chris Nawrat. "Culture, Ideology and Criticism: A Review of Recent Developments." *RL*, No. 6 (1977-78), 53-59.

Comments on WPCS No. 10 (4.23), *Ideology and Consciousness* (3.5), *Wedge* (15.12), and other journals.

4.131 Mitchell, Stanley. "The 18th Brumaire and the Construction of a Marxist Aesthetics." In 14.6, 22-26.

4.132 Morawski, Stefan. *Inquiries Into the Fundamentals of Aesthetics.* Cambridge, Mass.: MIT Press, 1974.

Reviewed by Louis Harap, *S&S*, 40 (Fall 1976), 341-51; Russell Berman, *NGC*, No. 16 (Winter 1979), 169-73.

4.133 _____. "The Aesthetic Views of Marx and Engels." *Journal of Aesthetics and Art Criticism*, 28 (Spring 1970), 301-14.

An expanded version of this essay appears as the introduction to 4.126.

4.134 _____. "Politicians Versus Artists." *Arts in Society*, 10 (Fall-Winter 1973), 8-18.

4.135 _____. "Censorship Versus Art: Typological Reflections." *Praxis* (Zagreb), 10 (1974), 153-67.

4.136 _____. "Challenge and Paradox of the Recent Avant-Garde." In 2.16, 226-29.

4.137 _____. "Art, Censorship and Socialism." *Praxis*, No. 1 (Spring 1975), 38-47.

4.138 _____. "Contemporary Approaches to Aesthetic Inquiry: Absolute Demands and Limited Possibilities." *Critical Inquiry*, 4 (Autumn 1977), 55-83.

4.139 _____. "Historicism and the Philosophy of Art." *Praxis*, No. 4 (1978), 71-85.

4.140 Morris, William. *On Art and Socialism: Essays and Lectures.* London: J. Lehmann, 1947.

E. P. Thompson makes a persuasive case for Morris as an original contributor to Marxist thought (11.150a).

4.141 Naumann, M. "Literary Production and Reception." *NLH*, 8 (Autumn 1976), 107-26.

4.142 Neilson, Frank P. "The Philosophical Premises of Structuralist Criticism." *L&I*, No. 17 (1974), 31-38.

4.143 Plekhanov, George. *Art and Social Life.* London: Lawrence and Wishart, 1953.

4.144 ———— . *Unaddressed Letters. Art and Social Life.* Moscow: Progress Publishers, 1957.

Plekhanov is one of the classic Marxist contributors to the subject. His essays on the social basis of style and the art-for-art's-sake ideology are frequently authologized (as in 2.6).

4.145a Baxandall, Lee. "Marxism and Aesthetics: A Critique of the Contribution of George Plekhanov." *Journal of Aesthetics and Art Criticism*, 25 (Spring 1967), 267–79.

4.146 Prawer, S. S. *Karl Marx and World Literature.* Oxford: The Clarendon Press, 1976. (NM)

An historically organized survey of Marx's comments on and uses of literature, including his introduction of the terminology and concepts of literary criticism into his general analysis. Reviewed by Lee Baxandall, *MR*, No. 9 (Fall 1977), 149–53.

4.147 Rader, Melvin. "Marx's Interpretation of Art and Aesthetic Value." *British Journal of Aesthetics*, 7 (July 1967), 237–49. (NM)

4.148 Richter, Dieter. "History and Dialectics in the Materialist Theory of Literature." *NGC*, No. 6 (Fall 1975), 31–47.

4.149 Rieser, Max. "The Aesthetic Theory of Socialist Realism." *Journal of Aesthetics and Art Criticism*, 16 (December 1957), 237–48. (NM)

In part an analysis and critique of Lukács's views.

4.150 Robinson, Lillian S. *Sex, Class, and Culture.* Bloomington: Indiana University Press, 1978.

Contains a number of essays published over the last decade, including "Criticism—Who Needs It?" (also in 14.19), and "Criticism—and Self-Criticism" (in 2.13).

4.151 Rodriguez, Ileana, and Marc Zimmerman. "First Aesthetic Meditation on *Capital*." In 2.14, 160–86.

4.152 Rose, Margaret A. *Reading the Young Marx and Engels: Poetry, Parody and the Censor.* Totowa, N.J.: Rowman and Littlefield, 1978.

Textual criticism, philosophy, and social history are linked here "to an understanding of the relationship between context, language and theory in Marx's early German language works."

4.153 "Round Table on the Arts." *The Marxist Quarterly* (Toronto), No. 9 (Spring 1964).

Special issue has brief articles on art, aesthetics, and revolution.

4.154 Rudich, Norman. "The Value of the Aesthetic in Marxism." In 2.16, 218–21.

4.155 Rühle, Jürgen. *Literature and Revolution: A Critical Study of the Writer and Communism in the Twentienth Century.* 1960; New York: Praeger, 1969. (NM)
Almost exclusively on European literature.

4.156 Sanders, Scott. "Towards a Social Theory of Literature." *Telos*, 18 (Winter 1973–74), 107-21.
Important analysis of left-wing criticism in the thirties, New Criticism, Goldmann, and beyond.

4.157 San Juan, E. "Art Against Imperialism." *Praxis*, No. 1 (Spring 1975), 15–18.
Also collected in 2.16, 222–25; a longer version appears in 2.13, 147–60.

4.158 Sartre, Jean-Paul. *What Is Literature?* 1949; New York: Harper, 1965.
From *Situations*, II. Sartre, in this pre-Marxist phase, discusses the question of commitment.

4.159 _____ . *Literary and Philosophical Essays.* 1955; New York: Collier Books, 1962.
Essays from *Situations* I and III on Faulkner, Dos Passos, Giraudoux, Camus, and others.

4.160 _____ . *The Problem of Method.* New York: Knopf, 1963.
Published in England as *Search for a Method* (London: Methuen, 1963).

4.161 _____ . *Situations.* New York: George Braziller, 1965.
Translation of *Situations* IV includes essays on Gide, Camus, Nizan, and others.

4.162 _____ . *Essays in Aesthetics.* Freeport, N.Y.: Books for Libraries Press, 1970.

4.163 _____ . *Politics and Literature.* London: Calder & Boyars, 1973.
Five essays from the sixties on language, theater, revolution and the intellectual.

4.164 _____ . *Between Existentialism and Marxism.* New York: Pantheon Books, 1974.

4.165 Sartre, Jean-Paul, et al. "Symposium on the Question of Decadence." In 2.2, 225–39.
1965 discussion with Ernst Fischer, Edouard Goldstucker, Milan Kundera.

*4.166a Willcox, Richard, comp. *Sartre: An International Bibliography.* Edmonton: University of Alberta Press, 1975.

4.166b Chiodi, Pietro. *Sartre and Marxism.* Atlantic Highlands, N.J.: Humanities Press, 1976.

4.166c Lawler, James. *The Existential Marxism of Jean-Paul Sartre.* Amsterdam: Gruner, 1976.

4.166d Aronson, Ronald. *Jean-Paul Sartre—The Politics of Imagination.* London: New Left Books, 1979.

4.166e McGuigan, Jim. "The Literary Sociology of Sartre." In 14.66, 163–80.

4.167 Scanlan, James P. "The Impossibility of a Uniquely Authentic Marxist Aesthetics." *British Journal of Aesthetics,* 16 (Spring 1976), 128–36. (NM)

4.168 Shor, Ira. "Notes on Marxism and Method" and "Questions Marxists Ask About Literature." In 2.11, 173–77, 178–79.

4.169 Steiner, George. "Marxism and Literature." In *Language and Silence.* New York: Atheneum, 1967, 303–92. (NM)
Seven essays on Lukács, Trotsky, "Marxism and the Literary Critic," related topics.

4.170 Swingewood, Alan. "Literature and *Praxis*: A Sociological Commentary." *NLH,* 5 (Autumn 1973), 169–76.

4.171 _____. "Marxism and Literary Theory." *L&H,* 2 (October 1975), 45–59.

4.172 _____. "Marxist Approaches to the Study of Literature." In 14.66, 131–49.

4.173 Tax, Meredith. "Introductory: Culture Is Not Neutral, Whom Does It Serve?" In 2.2, 15–29.

4.174 Thomson, George. "Marxism and Spiritual Values." *MT,* August 1961. 234–40.

4.175 Trotsky, Leon. *Literature and Revolution.* 1924; Ann Arbor: University of Michigan Press, 1960.
Chapters on Russian literature (Blok, Futurism) as well as theoretical discussions of proletarian culture and socialist art.

4.176 ———. *On Literature and Art.* Ed. Paul N. Siegel. New York: Pathfinder Press, 1970.
Includes sections on "Critical Theory" and "Essays in Literary Criticism." See Siegel's introduction, 7–26.

4.177a Deutscher, Isaac. " 'Not By Politics Alone...'." In *The Prophet Unarmed: Trotsky 1921–1929.* London: Oxford University Press, 1959, 164–200.

4.177b Barker, Francis. "Some Problems in Trotsky's Literary Criticism." In 14.5, 174–79.

4.177c Geras, Norman. "Literature of Revolution." *NLR*, Nos. 113–14 (January–April 1979), 3–41.
An analysis of Trotsky as a writer.

4.178 Truitt, Willis. "Art for the People." In *The Arts in a Democratic Society.* Ed. Dennis A. Mann. Bowling Green, Ohio: Popular Press, 1977, 58–69.

4.179 Truitt, Willis, and Sheila M. Meehan. "A Note on Revolutionary Art and Ideology." *Praxis*, No. 2 (Winter 1976), 81–90.

4.180 Vasquez, Adolfo Sanchez. *Art and Society: Essays in Marxist Aesthetics.* 1965; New York: Monthly Review Press, 1973.
On "the hostility of capitalist production to art" and other basic Marxist questions.

*4.181 Von Staden, Heinrich. "Greek Art and Literature in Marx's Aesthetics." *Arethusa*, 8 (Spring 1975), 119–44. (NM)
This special "Marxism and the Classics" issue of *Arethusa* also includes Robert Padgug, "Select Bibliography on Marxism and the Study of Antiquity," 201–25, and other essays on art and culture.

4.182 ———. "Nietzsche and Marx on Greek Art and Literature: Case Studies in Reception." *Daedalus*, 105 (Winter 1976), 79–96. (NM)

4.183 Wartofsky, Marx W. "Art as Humanizing Praxis." *Praxis*, No. 1 (Spring 1975), 56–65.

4.184 Wasson, Richard. "The New Marxist Criticism: Introduction." In 2.11, 169–72.

4.185 ———. "From Priest to Prometheus: Culture and Criticism in the Post-Modernist Period." *Journal of Modern Literature*, 3 (July 1974), 1188–1202.

4.186 _____ . "'The True Possession of Time': Paul Nizan, Marxism, and Modernism." *Boundary 2,* 5 (Winter 1977), 395–410.

4.187 Weber, Shierry M. "Aesthetic Experience and Self-Reflection as Emancipatory Processes: Two Complementary Aspects of Critical Theory." In *On Critical Theory.* Ed. John O'Neill. New York: The Seabury Press, 1976, 78–103.

4.188 Weimann, Robert. *Structure and Society in Literary History.* Charlottesville: University Press of Virginia, 1976.
Chapters on "Past Significance and Present Meaning in Literary History" (also in 2.7), "Structuralism and Literary History" (also in 2.4), the theory of literary history, and American practice. Reviewed by Gaylord LeRoy, *MR,* No. 9 (Fall 1977), 153–56.

4.189 _____ . "Reception Aesthetics and the Crisis in Literary History." *CLIO,* 5 (Fall 1975), 3–35.

4.190a Lennox, Sara. "Robert Weimann and GDR Literary Theory." *NGC,* 11 (Spring 1977), 164–70.

4.191 Werckmeister, O. K. "Marx on Ideology and Art." In 2.4, 501–19.

4.192 Widmer, Kingsley. "The End of Criticism: Some Reflections on Radical Practice." *Praxis,* No. 1 (Spring 1975), 88–97.

4.193 Williams, Raymond. *Reading and Criticism.* London: Muller, 1950. (NM)

4.194 _____ . *Culture and Society, 1780–1950.* London: Chatto and Windus, 1958.
See "Marxism and Culture" (258–75) for useful comments on Marx, Lenin, English Marxist criticism of the thirties, and related topics.

4.195 _____ . *The Long Revolution.* London: Chatto and Windus, 1961.
The 'long revolution' is the democratic, industrial, and cultural transformations in modern Britain. Chapters on analysis of culture, growth of the reading public, growth of the popular press, and related topics.

4.196 _____ . *Keywords: A Vocabulary of Culture and Society.* New York: Oxford University Press, 1976.

4.197 ———— . *Marxism and Literature.* New York: Oxford University Press, 1977. Reviewed by Michael Scrivener, *Telos,* No. 38 (Winter 1978–79). 190–98.

4.198 ———— . *Politics and Letters.* London: New Left Books, 1979. A "volume of interviews with Williams, conducted by *NLR,* that is designed to bring into clear focus the major theoretical and political issues posed by his work."

4.199 ———— . "Ideas of Nature." *TLS,* December 4, 1970, 1419–21.

4.200 ———— . "An Introduction to Reading and Culture in Society." In 14.42, 125–41.

4.201 ———— . "Literature and Sociology: In Memory of Lucien Goldmann." *NLR,* No. 67 (May–June 1971), 3–18.

4.202 ———— . "Literature *in* Society." In *Contemporary Approaches to English Studies.* Ed. Hilda Schiff. London: Heinemann, 1977, 24–37.

4.203 ———— . "Post-war British Marxism." *NLR,* No. 100 (November 1976–January 1977), 81–94.

Contains a rather veiled defense of his own work against the criticism levelled at it by Eagleton (4.204c) and others.

4.204a Kettle, Arnold. "Culture and Revolution: A Consideration of the Ideas of Raymond Williams and Others." *MT,* October 1961, 301–307.

4.204b Siegmund-Schultze, Dorothea. "Raymond Williams' Concept of Culture." *ZAA,* 22 (1974), 131–45.

4.204c Eagleton, Terry. "Criticism and Politics: The Work of Raymond Williams." *NLR,* No. 95 (January–February 1976), 3–23. Rpt. as Chapter 1 of 4.39.

See also Raymond Barnett, "Raymond Williams and Marxism: A Rejoinder to Terry Eagleton," *NLR,* No. 99 (September–October 1976), 47–64.

4.204d Watkins, Evan. "Raymond Williams and Marxist Criticism." *Boundary 2,* 4 (Spring 1976), 933–46. Rpt. in *The Critical Act: Criticism and Community.* New Haven, Conn.: Yale University Press, 1978, 141–57. (NM)

4.205 Zimmerman, Marc. "Polarities and Contradictions: Theoretical Bases of the Marxist-Structuralist Encounter." *NGC,* No. 7 (Winter 1976), 69–90.

4.206 _____ . "Marxism, Structuralism and Literature: Orientations and Schemata." *Ideologies and Literature*, 2 (March–April 1978), 27–53.

4.207 _____ . "Exchange and Production: Structuralist and Marxist Approaches to Literary Theory." *Praxis*, No. 4 (1978), 151–68.

–5–

Literary Genres: Drama

5.1 Althusser, Louis. "The 'Piccolo Teatro': Bertolazzi and Brecht: Notes on a Materialist Theatre." In *For Marx*. 1965; London: New Left Books, 1977, 129–51.
In the 'latent structure' of Bertolazzi's *El Nost Milan*, we find elements also present in Brecht's greatest plays.

5.2 Barker, Clive. "From Fringe to Alternative Theatre." *ZAA*, 26 (1978), 48–62.

5.3 Baxandall, Lee. "Beyond Brecht: the Happenings." *SOL*, 6, No. 1 (1966), 28–36.

5.4 _____ . "Spectacles and Scenarios: A Dramaturgy of Radical Activity." In 2.2, 371–88.
A defense of the radical adoption of the dramatic style in politics.

5.5 _____ . "The San Francisco Mime Troupe Perform Brecht." *Praxis*, No. 1 (Spring 1975), 116–21.
Baxandall's critique of the Mime Troupe raises important questions regarding dramatic performance and revolutionary culture. See rebuttal by Ira Shor, 122–29.

5.6 Beck, Julian, et al. "The New Repertories and Revolutionary Theater." *SOL*, 4 (Spring 1964), 39–62.

5.7 Blankfort, Michael. "Facing the New Audience: Sketches Toward an Aesthetic for the Revolutionary Theatre." *New Theatre*, June 1934, 11–12; July–August, 14–15; November, 25–27.

Insists on credible psychology, denouements of broad implica-
tion. Many examples.

5.8 Bradby, David, and John McCormick. *People's Theatre.*
Totowa, N. J.: Rowman and Littlefield, 1978.

A broad introductory study of the individuals and groups
important to the development of people's theatre.

5.9 Brecht, Bertolt. *Brecht on Theatre: The Development of an
Aesthetic.* Ed. John Willett. New York: Hill and Wang, 1964.

"Contains every significant essay available in English" (1.4),
together with useful notes. Brecht's writings are more notes
toward a theory than the theory itself, but they make a vital
contribution to the debate about Marxism's attitude toward the
avant-garde, experimental form, modernism.

5.10 _____. *The Messingkauf Dialogues.* London: Methuen, 1965.
"Discussions of theatre practice" (1.4).

5.11a Benjamin, Walter. *Understanding Brecht.* 1966; London:
New Left Books, 1973.

5.11b Lunn, Eugene. "Marxism and Art in the Era of Stalin and
Hitler: A Comparison of Brecht and Lukács." *NGC*, No. 3 (Fall
1974), 12–44.

5.11c Hermand, Jost. "Brecht on Utopia." In 2.9, 96–113.

5.11d Zimmerman, Marc. "Brecht and the Dynamics of Production." *Praxis*, No. 3 (1976), 115–37.

5.11e Bruggemann, Heinz, "Bertolt Brecht and Karl Korsch: Questions of Living and Dead Elements Within Marxism." *Praxis,*
No. 4 (1978), 287–96.

5.12 Caute, David. *The Illusion: An Essay on Politics, Theatre and
the Novel.* New York: Harper & Row, 1972.

On commitment, modernism, alienation, and the development
of a dialectical theater and a dialectical novel.

5.13 Davis, R. G. *The San Francisco Mime Troupe: The First 10
Years.* Palo Alto, Cal.: Ramparts Press, 1978.

5.14 _____ . "Radical Theatre vs. Institutional Theatre." *SOL*, 4
(Spring 1964), 28–38.

Argues that creativity flourishes when companies are not funded
by bureaucracies and therefore are forced to economize on
space. Evidence: the work of the San Francisco Mime Troupe.

5.15 Figes, Eva. *Tragedy and Social Evolution.* London: John Calder, 1976. (NM)

5.16 Gorky, Maxim. "Observations on the Theatre." *English Review,* April 1924, 496–98.

5.17 Grotwoski, J. *Towards a Poor Theatre.* New York: Simon & Schuster, 1968.

5.18 Gurvitch, George. "The Sociology of the Theatre." In 14.8, 71–81. (NM)
Affinities between society and theater. Branches of the sociology of theater consist of analysis of audience, performance, play-content, social functions of theater.

5.19 Hays, Michael. "Theater History and Practice: An Alternative View of Drama." *NGC,* No. 12 (Fall 1977), 85–97.
Drama encompasses much more than the text; dramatic analysis must also consider space, architecture, stage procedures, audience relations, and so on.

5.20 Heinemann, Margot. "Popular Drama and Leveller Style—Richard Overton and John Harris." In 8.2, 69–92.

5.21 Klein, Maxine. *Theatre for the 98%.* Boston: South End Press, 1978.
A study of people's theater.

5.22 Lawson, John Howard. *Theory and Practice of Playwriting.* 1936; New York: Hill and Wang, 1960.
Lawson was a major figure in radical American theater in the twenties and thirties.

5.23 Lindsay, Jack. *The Clashing Rocks: A Study of Early Greek Religion and Culture and the Origins of Drama.* London: Chapman and Hall, 1965.

5.24 Littlewood, Joan. "Plays for the People." *World Theatre,* 8 (Winter 1959–60), 283–90.

5.25 Lukács, Georg. "The Sociology of Modern Drama." *Tulane Drama Review,* 9 (Summer 1965), 146–70. Rpt. in *Theory of the Modern Stage.* Ed. Eric Bentley. Baltimore: Penguin, 1968.
An early (1909) essay, abridged in the Bentley reprint.

5.26 _____ . "Marx and Engels on Problems of Dramaturgy." *International Theatre,* No. 2 (1934), 11–14.

5.27 ———. "Approximation to Life in the Novel and the Play." In 6.19, 150–77.

5.28 Mayer, Hans. "Culture, Property and Theatre." In 2.2, 301–23.

5.29 Meyerhold, Vsevelod. *Meyerhold on Theatre*. Ed. Edward Braun. New York: Hill and Wang, 1969.
A comprehensive selection of writings on theater and film by the experimental Russian director and theorist.

5.30 Miller, Arthur. *The Theater Essays of Arthur Miller*. Ed. Robert A. Martin. Harmondsworth: Penguin, 1968. (NM)
Includes the important "On Social Plays," originally the preface to *A View from the Bridge*.

5.31 Mittenzwei, Werner. "Contemporary Drama in the West." In 2.7, 105–37.

5.32 O'Casey, Sean. *Blasts and Benedictions: Articles and Stories*. London: St. Martin's Press, 1967.

5.33 ———. "Two Letters." In *The Socialist Register 1965*. Ed. Ralph Miliband and John Saville. New York: Monthly Review Press, 1965.
Attacks on Zhdanov-style socialist realism by the radical Irish playwright.

5.34 Paterson, Doug. "Popular Theatre and Political Content." *The Insurgent Sociologist*, 7 (Fall 1977), 43–48.
Practical plans for a new theater.

5.35 Piscator, Irwin. "The Theatre of the Future." *Tomorrow*, February 1942, 14–19.
The radical German director on Epic Theater and other topics.

5.36 Sartre, Jean-Paul. *Sartre on Theater*. Ed. Michel Contat and Michel Rybalka. New York: Pantheon Books, 1976.
Sections: "Documents, Lectures and Conversations on the Theater" (includes "Epic Theater and Dramatic Theater," 77–121); "Documents and Interviews on [Sartre's] Plays."

5.37 Suvin, Darko. "Modes of Political Drama." *Massachusetts Review*, 13, No. 2 (1972), 309–24.

5.38 Thomson, George. *Aeschylus and Athens: A Study in the Social Origins of Drama*. London: Lawrence and Wishart, 1949.

5.39 Williams, Raymond. *Drama in Performance*. 1954; Harmondsworth: Penguin, 1972.

Text and Performance in *Antigone, Antony and Cleopatra, The Seagull;* experimental drama, "Bergman's *Wild Strawberries,* and other topics.

5.40 _____. *Modern Tragedy.* London: Chatto and Windus, 1966.
A history and criticism of concepts of tragedy is followed by analyses of authors (Miller, Williams, O'Neill, Lawrence, Eliot, European authors) embodying various aspects of modern tragedy.

5.41 _____. *Drama from Ibsen to Brecht.* London: Chatto and Windus, 1968.
An expanded version of *Drama from Ibsen to Eliot* (1952/1964). Includes analysis of the late nineteenth-century masters, Irish dramatists, alternative drama, social and political drama, recent drama.

5.42 _____. *Drama in a Dramatised Society.* Cambridge: Cambridge University Press, 1975.

5.43 _____. "The Social History of Dramatic Forms." In 4.195, 271–99.

5.44 Zipes, Jack. Introd. to *Political Plays for Children.* St. Louis: Telos Press, 1973.
A discussion of the principles of the Berlin GRIPS theater company prefaces a selection of their plays.

Others: Sartre (4.163), Cornforth (8.2), *Life and Literature* (8.9), Goldstein (8.34), Szenczi and Ferenczi (8.44), Williams (8.66), Egri (8.69), Jones (8.71, 8.93), Kettle (8.74), Thomas (8.104), Galassi (9.20), Zipes (9.31), M. M. (10.53).

–6–

Literary Genres: Fiction

6.1 Brake, Mike. "The Image of the Homosexual in Contemporary English and American Fiction." In 14.50, 177–96.

6.2 Bromley, Roger. "Natural Boundaries: the Social Function of Popular Fiction." *RL*, No. 7 (1978), 34–60.

6.3 Burgum, Edwin Berry. *The Novel and the World's Dilemma.* 1947; New York: Russell & Russell, 1963.
On "Social Forces and Fiction," Joyce, Proust, Mann, and other European and American novelists. Burgum's attempt to integrate psychological categories into Marxist criticism of the novel is spoiled by a certain inflexibility.

6.4 _____. "Science Fiction." *New Foundations*, 7 (Spring 1954), 30–35.

6.5 _____. "Freud and Fantasy in Contemporary Fiction." *S&S*, 29 (Spring 1965), 224–31.

6.6 "Change, SF and Marxism: Open or Closed Universe?" *Science-Fiction Studies*, 1 (Fall 1973), 84–94.
Contributors to this symposium (continued in later issues) include Frank Rottensteiner, Bruce Franklin, and others.

6.7 Diakonova, Nina. "Notes on the Evolution of the *Bildungsroman* in English." *ZAA*, 16 (1968), 341–51.

6.8 Ehrlich, Bruce. "Social Action and Literary Fable: Some Openings for Dialogue." In 2.10, 40–52.
Concerned with developing a Marxist methodology for the novel.

6.9 Fitting, Peter. "The Modern Anglo-American SF Novel: Utopian Longing and Capitalist Cooptation." *Science-Fiction Studies*, 6 (March 1979), 59–76.

An excellent survey, and one of a number of Marxist analyses that can be found in the pages of this journal (like 6.6 above).

6.10 Fruchter, Norman. "A Realist Perspective." *SOL*, 4 (Spring 1964), 110–34.

An attempt to start from but go beyond Lukács's use of realism as a critical tool in the analysis of novels by Gogol, Lessing, Mary McCarthy, Uwe Johnson.

6.11 Goldmann, Lucien. *Towards a Sociology of the Novel*. 1964; London: Tavistock Publications, 1975.

Argues that the novel and its social context can be seen to have homologous structures. A key work in the development of Marxist criticism of the novel; discusses Malraux, the *noveau roman*.

6.12 Harold, Brent. "The Intrinsic Sociology of Fiction." *Modern Fiction Studies*, 23 (1977–78), 593–99.

6.13 Jameson, Fredric. "Magical Narratives: Romance as Genre." *NLH*, 7 (Autumn 1975), 135–63.

6.14 Johnson, Roy. "The Proletarian Novel." *L&H*, No. 2 (October 1975), 84–95.

Argues that belief that proletarian culture is a "hidden gem" waiting to be discovered is false, since it ignores determination of the superstructure by the base. Proust as example; survey of British proletarian novels.

6.15 Knight, Everett. *A Theory of the Classical Novel*. New York: Barnes and Noble, 1970.

Study of Dickens, Balzac, Flaubert, Stendhal, and Zola that argues that the identity given characters in the classical novel is an ideological device to resolve the contradictions bourgeois society imposes on personality. Reviewed by James Kavanagh, *Praxis*, No. 2 (Winter 1976), 239–47.

6.16 Levine, George. "Politics and the Form of Disenchantment." *CE*, 36 (December 1974), 422–35.

Novels by Scott, Eliot, Pynchon are used as a springboard for evolving a political criticism of the development and implications of the novel form.

6.17 Lukács, Georg. *The Soul and the Forms.* 1910; London: Merlin Press, 1974.

Predates Lukács's conversion to Marxism, but contains reflections on the novel that remain influential in his later work.

6.18 ———. *The Theory of the Novel: A Historico-Philosophical Essay on the Forms of Great Epic Literature.* 1920; London: Merlin Press, 1971.

Written in 1914–15 under the influence of Dilthey, Simmel, Weber, and romantic anticapitalism, as Lukács's 1962 "Preface" (11–23) points out. An important attempt at a typology of the novel form, and a major influence upon Goldmann's work.

6.19 ———. *The Historical Novel.* 1937; London: Merlin Press, 1962.

Traces the historical novel from its classic stage in Scott, through its decline into a special genre, to its modern possibilities.

6.20 ———. *Studies in European Realism.* 1950; New York: Grosset & Dunlap, 1964.

Essays (1939–44) on Balzac, Zola, Russian literary criticism, Tolstoy. Defines Lukács's concept of realism.

6.21 ———. "The Intellectual Physiognomy of Literary Characters." *International Literature*, 1936, No. 8, 56–83. Rpt. in 2.2, 89–141, and 4.106, 149–88.

6.22a Fehér, Ferenc. "Is the Novel Problematic?" *Telos*, No. 15 (Spring 1973), 47–74.

Comments on Lukács's *Theory of the Novel* (6.18). See Andrew Feenberg, "Aesthetics as Social Theory: Introduction to Fehér's 'Is the Novel Problematic?'," 41–46.

6.22b Birchall, Ian. "Georg Lukács and the Novels of Emile Zola." In 14.50, 92–108.

6.22c Crow, Dennis. "Form and the Unification of Aesthetics and Ethics in Lukács's *Soul and Forms.*" *NGC*, No. 15 (Fall 1978), 159–77.

6.23 Pascal, Roy. "The Autobiographical Novel and the Autobiograpy." *Essays in Criticism*, 9 (April 1959), 134–50.

Chief examples are *Villette, Sons and Lovers, Portrait of the Artist as a Young Man.*

6.24 Sanders, Scott. "Marxism and the Writing of Fiction." In 2.10, 98–103.

6.25 Schwartz, Larry. "On the Problem of Criticizing Political Fiction." *Polit*, 1 (Fall 1977), 109–19.

6.26 Shor, Ira Neil. "The Novel in History: Lukács and Zola." *CLIO*, 2 (October 1972), 19–41.
Useful as an introduction to Lukács's views on the novel. After analysis, these views are tested by the case of Zola.

6.27 Siegel, Paul. *Revolution and the Twentieth-Century Novel.* New York: Pathfinder Press, 1979.
"It seeks to give a Marxist analysis of ten novels concerned with the concept of social revolution and to show what they contribute to an understanding of the world revolution taking place in our time." Analyses of Bennett, Orwell, London, Koestler, Mailer, Wright, and four European novelists.

6.28 Suvin, Darko. *Metamorphoses of Science Fiction: On the Poetics and History of a Literary Genre.* New Haven: Yale University Press, 1979.

6.29 Swingewood, Alan. *The Novel and Revolution.* London: Macmillan, 1975.
Theoretical section is followed by studies of individual novelists (including Gissing, Conrad, Koestler). Reviewed by Terry Eagleton, *MR*, No. 7 (Fall 1976), 117–20.

6.30 _____. "Hegemony, Praxis, and the Novel Form." *Praxis*, No. 1 (Spring 1975), 98–110.

6.31 Watt, Ian. *The Rise of the Novel: Studies in Defoe, Richardson and Fielding.* London: Chatto and Windus, 1957. (NM)
Still the best study of the relationship between the novel's distinctive features and the rise of the middle class. See especially "Realism and the Novel Form" (9–35) and "The Reading Public and the Rise of the Novel" (36–61).

6.32 Weimann, Robert. "Point of View in Fiction." In 2.7, 54–75.

6.33 _____. "Rhetoric and Structure in 'Point of View': Towards a Critique of Formalist Concepts of Perspective in Fiction." In *Actes du VIe Congrès de l'Association Internationale de Littérature Comparée.* Ed. Michel Cadot, et al. Stuttgart: Bieber, 1975, 275–79.

6.34 Williams, Raymond. "Realism and the Contemporary Novel."
In 4.195, 300–16.

6.35 Zipes, Jack. "Breaking the Magic Spell: Politics and the Fairy
Tale." *NGC*, No. 6 (Fall 1975), 116–35.

Others: Caudwell (4.25), Lukács (4.105), Caute (5.12), Southall
(8.17), Williams (8.22), Ter-Abramova (8.45), Howard (8.52),
Kettle (8.53), Musselwhite (8.60), Williams (8.65), Fox (8.87),
Burgum (9.77), Angenot (14.1), Girard (14.24), Howe (14.35),
Van Ghent (14.74).

–7–

Literary Genres: Poetry

7.1 Adorno, Theodor W. "Lyric Poetry and Society." *Telos,* No. 20 (Summer 1974), 56–71.

7.2 Bold, Alan. Introd. to *Penguin Book of Socialist Verse.* Harmondsworth: Penguin, 1970, 33–58.

7.3 Brecht, Bertolt. "On Rhymeless Verse with Irregular Rhythms." In 5.9, 115–20; rpt. in 2.3, 429–34.

7.4 Bronowski, Jacob. *The Poet's Defence.* Cambridge: Cambridge University Press, 1939. (NM)
A "materialist" discusses the critical writings of Sidney, Shelley, Dryden, Wordsworth, Coleridge, Swinburne, Housman, Yeats.

7.5 Burgum, Edwin Berry. "The Cult of the Complex in Poetry." *S&S,* 15 (Winter 1951), 31–48.
Attack on Empson, proposal of alternative approach.

7.6 Cudjoe, Selwyn R. "Revolutionary Struggle and Poetry." *Freedomways,* 18, No. 2 (1978), 70–83.

7.7 Graff, Gerald R. *Poetic Statement and Critical Dogma.* Evanston, Ill.: Northwestern University Press, 1970. (NM)
Useful counterstatement to New Critical position on poetry and referentiality.

7.8 Laska, P. J. "Political Poetry & The Politicalization of Art." *The Unrealist: A Left Literary Magazine* (1978), 17–24.

7.9 Lindsay, Jack. *Perspective for Poetry.* London: Fore Publications, 1944.

7.10 ———— . *The Troubadors and Their World of the Twelfth and Thirteenth Centuries.* London: Frederick Muller, 1976.
The originators of European vernacular literature are linked to their social context; examples of their verse follow.

7.11 ———— . "Anti-clerical Poets of the Twelfth Century." *Life and Letters To-Day,* 19 (September 1938), 35–46.
On Latin and Provençal poets.

7.12 ———— . "Neglected Aspects of Poetry." *Poetry and the People* (London), Nos. 1–7 (1938–39), passim.
Essays in this periodical cover "Austrialian populist verse ... old Tyne songs; Carmina Burana; English political broadsides" (1.4).

7.13 ———— . "Politics and the Poet." *MT,* February 1958, 49–54.

7.14 Markov, Dmitri. "On the Theoretical Foundations of the Poetics of Socialist Realism." *Soviet Literature,* 1976 No. 7, 120–26.

7.15 Matthews, G. M. "Sex and the Sonnet." *Essays in Criticism,* 2 (April 1952), 119–37.

7.16 Mayakovsky, V. *How Are Verses Made?* 1926; London: Jonathan Cape, 1970.
Reflections by the experimental and revolutionary Russian poet.

7.17a Berger, John, and Anya Bostock. "Mayakovsky: Language and Death of a Revolutionary Poet." *Praxis,* No. 1 (Spring 1975), 48–55.

7.18 Mitchell, Roger. "A Polemic for Poetry." *MR,* No. 8 (Spring 1977), 119–22.

7.19 Morton, A. L. "On the Nature of the Ballad." In 8.10, 1–11.

7.20 Raban, Jonathan. *The Society of the Poem.* London: Harrap, 1971. (NM)

7.21 Richmond, William Kenneth. *Poetry and the People.* London: Routledge, 1947.
The effect upon language of class division in English society; popular poetry.

7.22 Schlauch, Margaret. *Modern English and American Poetry: Techniques and Ideologies.* London: C. A. Watts, 1956.

7.23 Siegel, Paul. "The Petrarchan Sonneteers and Neo-Platonic Love." *Studies in Philology*, 42 (April 1945), 164–80.
Differences between Italianate and neo-Platonic sonnets reflect their differing class origins.

7.24 Thompson, Denys. *The Uses of Poetry*. Cambridge: Cambridge University Press, 1978. (NM)
Account of the social functions of poetry from ancient times to the present.

7.25 Thomson, George Derwent. *Marxism and Poetry*. London: Lawrence and Wishart, 1945.
Argues that poetry derives from the labor process. Examples from English, Irish, Greek poetry. Chapters on speech and magic; rhythm and labor; improvisation and inspiration; epic; drama; tragedy; the future.

'7.26 ———. "The Art of Poetry." In *Studies in Ancient Greek Society: The Prehistoric Aegean*. London: Lawrence and Wishart, 1954. Rpt. in 2.3, 47–75.

7.27 Trotsky, Leon. "The Formalist School of Poetry and Marxism." In 4.175, 162–83.

7.28 Vicinus, Martha. "The Study of Ninteenth-Century British Working-Class Poetry." In 12.19, 322–53.

7.29 Yevtushenko, Evgenii. "Poetry and the Canons." *Soviet Studies in Literature*, 13 (Winter 1976–77), 12–21.

Others: Caudwell (4.24), Sypher (4.27c), Pradhan (4.27d), Barrell (8.1), *Life and Literature* (8.9), Pearson (8.15), Southall (8.17), Szenczi and Ferenczi (8.44), Turner (8.46), Day-Lewis (8.83), Henderson (8.92), Spender (8.101).

–8–

National Literatures: British

A. GENERAL

8.1 Barrell, John, and John Bull. Introd. to *The Penguin Book of English Pastoral Verse*. Harmondsworth: Penguin, 1974, 1–9.
"At the outset, the Pastoral is a *mythical* view of men in society, at the service of those who control the political, economic and cultural strings of society." From Elizabethan pastoral to W. B. Yeats.

8.2 Cornforth, Maurice, ed. *Rebels and Their Causes: Essays in Honour of A. L. Morton*. London: Lawrence and Wishart, 1978.
Includes essays on popular theater and individual English authors, as well as historical and political essays.

8.3 Craig, David. *The Real Foundations: Literature and Social Change*. London: Chatto and Windus, 1973.
Sections: "Industrial Culture" (from industrial songs to D. H. Lawrence), "Poetry and Modern Life" (Eliot to MacDiarmid), "The New Wave" (Sillitoe and others).

8.4 Egbert, Donald Drew. "Radicalism, Marxism and the Theory and Practice of Art in England." In 14.13, 381–580.

8.5 Jackson, T. A. *Old Friends to Keep: Studies in English Novels and Novelists*. London: Lawrence and Wishart, 1950.
Revised versions of articles written for the *Daily Worker* on authors from Defoe to Conan Doyle. Sketchy, popular treatments.

8.6 Kettle, Arnold. *Introduction to the English Novel*. 2 vols. 1951; New York: Harper & Row, 1960.

Chapters on "Life and Pattern," "Realism and Romance," as well as individual novels and novelists.

8.7 _____ . "The Progressive Tradition in Bourgeois Culture." In *Essays in Socialist Realism and the British Cultural Tradition.* London: Fore Publications, n.d. Rpt. *Masses & Mainstream,* 7 (January 1954), 9–20.

Marlowe, Shakespeare, Cervantes, Fielding, and the implications for later realism.

8.8 LeRoy, Gaylord. "Romanticism and Modernism: The Marxist View." In *Marxism and Democracy.* Ed. Herbert Aptheker. New York: Humanities Press, 1965, 59–70.

8.9 *Life and Literature of the Working Class: Essays in Honor of William Gallacher.* Berlin: Humboldt University, 1966.

Essays on British authors from Henryson to Sillitoe, Scottish vernacular poetry and folk song, workers' theater, other topics.

8.10 Morton, A. L. *The Language of Men.* London: Cobbett Press, 1945.

Chapters on English authors from Bacon to Forster, ballads, popular writers.

8.11 _____ . *The English Utopia.* 1952; London: Lawrence and Wishart, 1969.

More, Bacon, 'levellers,' Defoe, Swift, Butler, Morris, Wells, Huxley, Orwell, other writers of Utopian literature.

8.12 _____ . *The Matter of Britain: Essays in a Living Culture.* London: Lawrence and Wishart, 1966.

8.13 O'Flinn, Paul. *Them and Us in Literature.* London: Pluto Press, 1975.

Essays in 'popular' language on English authors from Shakespeare to Orwell; "Women in the 19th Century"; other topics.

8.14 Orwell, George. *Critical Essays.* London: Secker and Warburg, 1946. (NM)

Essays on Dickens, Wells, Kipling, Yeats, Koestler, Wodehouse, and others.

8.15 Pearson, Gabriel. "Romanticism and Contemporary Poetry." *NLR,* No. 16 (1962), 47–75.

Initiated useful debate on romanticism, socialism, and poetry. Critiques of Pearson were made by David Craig, "The New

Poetry of Socialism," No. 17, 73–84, and Stanley Mitchell, "Romanticism and Socialism," No. 19, 56–68.

8.16 Rubinstein, Annette T. *The Great Tradition in English Literature: From Shakespeare to Shaw.* 1953; 2 vols. New York: Monthly Review Press, 1969.

8.17 Southall, Raymond. *Literature, the Individual and Society: Critical Essays on the 18th and 19th Centuries.* London: Lawrence and Wishart, 1977.

Essays on "The Novel and the Isolated Individual," pastoral poetry, and English authors from Swift to George Eliot.

8.18 Ussher, Arland. "Irish Literature." *ZAA,* 14 (1966), 30–55.

A useful survey.

8.19 West, Alick. *Crisis and Criticism.* London: Lawrence and Wishart, 1936.

On Read, Joyce, Richards, T. S. Eliot, Heslop, and general topics, including Romanticism, language, idiom, value, others.

8.20 ———. *The Mountain in the Sunlight.* London: Lawrence and Wishart, 1958.

On English authors from Bunyan to Priestley.

8.21 ———. *Crisis and Criticism and Selected Literary Essays.* London: Lawrence and Wishart, 1975.

Reprints 8.19 entire, except for Heslop chapter; essays on Bunyan, Defoe, and Pater from 8.20; plus new essays on Swift and Lawrence.

8.22 Williams, Raymond. *The English Novel: From Dickens to Lawrence.* London: Chatto and Windus, 1970.

Dickens, the Brontës, Eliot, Hardy, Conrad, city novels, Lawrence.

8.23 ———. *The Country and the City.* London: Chatto and Windus, 1973.

A study of country and city as subject and theme in literature from Marvell to Lawrence that is also a polemic against a 'loss of the organic society' view of historical development.

8.24 ———. "Interregnum." In 4.194, 166–95.

Gissing, Shaw, Hulme, others.

Others: Caudwell (4.24, 4.25), Barrell (11.43a), Empson (14.14), Filmer (14.18), Ingle (14.41), Moers (14.63), Showalter (14.69), Van Ghent (14.74).

B. BEFORE 1800

8.25 Boyer, C. V. "Three Poets and the Agrarian Revolution." *The Modern Quarterly* (Baltimore), 3 (October–December 1925), 56–68.

Reactions to the agrarian revolution of Goldsmith, Crabbe, and Ebenezer Elliott.

8.26 Cantarow, Ellen. "A Wilderness of Opinions Confounded: Allegory and Ideology." In 2.11, 215–53.

On *The Faerie Queene, Piers Plowman,* and *Pilgrim's Progress.* "Comment" on article by Nancy Hoffman, 253–55.

8.27 Colley, John Scott. *"Fulgens and Lucres*: Politics and Aesthetics." *ZAA*, 23 (1975), 322–30.

8.28 Craig, David. *Scottish Literature and the Scottish People 1680–1830.* London: Chatto and Windus, 1961.

8.29 Danby, John E. *Poets on Fortune's Hill: Studies in Sidney, Shakespeare, Beaumont and Fletcher.* London: Faber, 1952. Rpt. as *Elizabethan and Jacobean Poets.* London: Faber, 1964.

8.30 Delany, Sheila. "The Late Medieval Attack on Analogical Thought: Undoing Substantial Connection." In 14.59, 37–58.

8.31 ———. "Substructure and Superstructure: The Politics of Allegory in the Fourteenth Century." *S&S*, 38 (Fall 1974), 257–80.

8.32 Delany, Sheila, and Vahan Ishanian. "Theocratic and Contractual Kingship in *Havelok the Dane*." *ZAA*, 22 (1974), 290–302.

8.33 Eagleton, Terry. "Ecriture and Eighteenth Century Fiction." In 14.5, 55–58.

8.34 Goldstein, Leonard. "On the Transition from Formal to Naturalistic Acting in the Elizabethan Theatre." *Bulletin of the New York Public Library*, 60 (July 1958), 330–49.

8.35 Hill, Christopher. *Puritanism and Revolution.* London: Secker and Warburg, 1958.

Includes articles on Richardson, Marvell, and other topics.

8.36 Krapp, Robert Martin. "Class Analysis of a Literary Controversy." *S&S*, 10 (Winter 1946), 80–92.

On the dispute between wit and sense in seventeenth-century literature.

8.37 Lawton, David. "English Poetry and English Society, 1370–1400." In 2.5, 145–68.

8.38 Schlauch, Margaret. *English Medieval Literature and Its Social Foundations.* 1956; New York: Cooper Square Publishers, 1971.

8.39 _____. *Antecedents of the English Novel: 1400-1600.* London: Oxford University Press,1963.

8.40 _____. "Themes of English Fiction, 1400-1600: Some Suggestions for Future Research." *Kwartalnik Neofilologiczny* (Warsaw), 6 (1959), 339-42.

8.41 _____. "Realism and Convention in Medieval Literature." *Kwartalnik Neofilologiczny,* 11 (1964), 3-12.

*8.42a Niecko, Jacek. "List of Publications [by Margaret Schlauch]." In *Studies in Language and Literature in Honour of Margaret Schlauch.* Warsaw: PWN-Polish Scientific Publications, 1966, 9-20.

Non-Marxist essays on *Beowulf,* Chaucer, Malory, Milton, other authors and topics.

8.43 Southall, Raymond. *Literature and the Rise of Capitalism: Essays Mainly on the Sixteenth and Seventeenth Centuries.* London: Lawrence and Wishart, 1973.

On English authors from More to Samuel Johnson.

8.44 Szenczi, Miklós, and László Ferenczi, eds. *Studies in Eighteenth Century Literature.* Budapest: Akademin Kiado, 1974.

Includes essays on the crisis in English comedy, English poetry, Milton and Shakespeare, and other European topics.

8.45 Ter-Abramova, V. G. "Thomas Holcroft and the English Democratic Novel at the End of the Eighteenth Century." *ZAA,* 26 (1978), 293-304.

8.46 Turner, James. *The Politics of Landscape: Rural Scenery and Society in English Poetry, 1630-1660.* Oxford: Basil Blackwell, 1979.

Sophisticated discussion of the role of class, ideology, and literary text in creating views of landscape.

8.47 Weston, Jack. "Revising the Canon of British Eighteenth-Century Literature." *RT,* No. 2 (June 1976), 25-29.

8.48 _____. "The Period Course: Eighteenth Century British Literature." In 12.8, 6-11.

This article (in the "Guide to Marxist Teaching" issue of *RT*) also provides an excellent brief Marxist introduction to British literature from 1660 to 1800; valuable notes.

Others: Knights (14.45), Loftis (14.54), McRobbie (14.59).

C. NINETEENTH CENTURY

8.49 Ashraf, Mary. "The New Literature of the Eighteen-Thirties." *ZAA*, 24 (1976), 22–36.

8.50 Beardon, Sue. "Women in Victorian Poetry." *RL*, No. 1 (Spring 1976), 6–9.

8.51 Hicks, Granville. *Figures of Transition: A Study of British Literature at the End of the Nineteenth Century.* 1939; Westport, Conn.: Greenwood Press, 1969.
On individual British authors from Morris to Kipling.

8.52 Howard, David B., John Lucas, and John Goode, eds. *Tradition and Tolerance in Nineteenth-Century Fiction: Critical Essays on Some English and American Novels.* London: Routledge & Kegan Paul, 1966. (M/NM)

8.53 Kettle, Arnold *The Novel in the Mid-Nineteenth Century.* Milton Keynes: Open University Press, 1973.

8.54 ———. "The Early Victorian Social-Problem Novel." In *From Dickens to Hardy.* Vol. 6. The Pelican Guide to English Literature. Ed. Boris Ford. Harmondsworth: Penguin, 1958, 169–87.
Godwin, Disraeli, Mrs. Gaskell, Charles Kingsley.

8.55 Klingender, Francis. *Art and the Industrial Revolution.* 1947; London: Paladin, 1972.
Refers to literature as well as the visual arts.

8.56 LeRoy, Gaylord. *Perplexed Prophets: Six Nineteenth Century British Authors.* Philadelphia: Temple University Press, 1953.
Chapters on authors from Carlyle to Wilde.

8.57 Lucas, John, ed. *Literature and Politics in the Nineteenth Century.* London: Methuen, 1971. (M/NM)
Essays on individual British authors, the 1880s, politics and poetry in the 1830s.

8.58 "Marxism and Romanticism." *Studies in Romanticism*, 16 (Fall 1977), 409–561.

This special issue includes David Punter on Blake, Paul Breines on Lukács and Romanticism, Leonard Wessell on "Marx's Romantic Poetry and the Crisis of Romantic Lyricism," and other topics in European Romanticism.

8.59 Mitchell, Jack. "Aesthetic Problems of the Development of the Proletarian-Revolutionary Novel in Nineteenth Century Britain." *ZAA*, 11 (1963), 248–64. Rpt. in 2.3, 245–66.

Explaining failure of novels of Chartists Thomas Wheeler, Ernest Jones, and others.

8.60 Musselwhite, David. "The Novel as Narcotic." In 14.6, 207–24.

8.61 Thompson, E. P. "Class Consciousness." In *The Making of the English Working Class*. 1963; New York: Vintage, 1968, 711–832.

On radical writing in nineteenth-century England, especially Cobbett.

*8.62 Vicinus, Martha. *The Industrial Muse: A Study of Nineteenth Century Working Class Literature*. New York: Barnes & Noble, 1974.

Contains chapters on street ballads and broadsides, literature as propaganda, Chartist poetry and fiction, self-educated poets, dialect literature of the industrial North, and music halls; bibliography.

8.63 West, Alick. "Romantic Criticism," "Marx and Romanticism," "Continuation of Romanticism." In 8.20, 2–30, 68–72, 73–74.

A defense of the Romantic movement that rests on the movement's interest in the social origins of art.

8.64 Williams, Raymond. "A Nineteenth Century Tradition." In 4.194, 23–161.

8.65 ———— . "Forms of English Fiction in 1848." In 14.6, 277–90.

8.66 ———— . "Social Environment and Theatrical Environment: The Case of English Naturalism." In *English Drama: Forms and Development*. Ed. Marie Axton and Raymond Williams. Cambridge: Cambridge University Press, 1977, 203–23.

Others: Vicinus (7.28), LeRoy (8.8), Pearson (8.15), Southall (8.17), Barker (14.6), James (14.43).

D. TWENTIETH CENTURY
i. General

8.67 Craig, David, and Michael Egan. "Decadence and Crack-Up: Literature and Society in the Twenties and Thirties." In 2.5, 11–36.

8.68 Eagleton, Terry. *Exiles and Emigrés: Studies in Modern Literature.* New York: Schocken Books, 1970.

8.69 Egri, Peter. "Anger and Form." *ZAA*, 11 (1963), 269–80. British theater in revolt in the 1950s.

8.70 Gray, Nigel. *The Silent Majority: A Study of the Working Class in Post-War British Fiction.* London: Vision Press, 1973. (NM) Chapters on individual authors from Hines to Naughton.

8.71 Jones, Leonard Abraham. "The Workers Theatre Movement in the Twenties." *ZAA*, 14 (1966), 259–81.

8.72 Katona, Anna. "The Decline of the Modern in Recent British Fiction." *ZAA*, 13 (1965), 35–44.
Rather sketchy argument concerning the return to social commitment in Amis, Lessing, Sillitoe, Wain, and Angus Wilson.

8.73 Kettle, Arnold. "Rebels and Causes: Some Thoughts on the Angry Young Men." *MT*, March 1958, 65–72.

8.74 ———. "Our Theatre in the Sixties." *MT*, September 1962, 276–81.
On absurdist theater, Pinter, Osborne, Wesker.

8.75 Kocmanová, Jessie. "Scottish Literature and Hugh MacDiarmid." *Labour Monthly* (London), 61 (January 1979), 17–21.
Discussion of MacDiarmid is prefaced by useful comments on historical reasons for democratic orientation of Scottish writing and culture.

8.76 Mathews, J. H. "Surrealism and England." *Comparative Literature Studies*, 1, No. 1 (1964), 55–72.

8.77 Mitchell, Jack. "The Struggle for the Working-Class Novel in Scotland, 1900–1939." *ZAA*, 21 (1973), 384–413.

8.78 Raskin, Jonah. *The Mythology of Imperialism.* New York: Random House, 1971.
Chapters on individual British authors from Kipling to Orwell.

8.79 Sanders, Scott. "The Left-Handedness of Modern Literature." *Twentieth Century Literature*, 23 (December 1977), 417–36.

An explanation of and partial justification for the emphasis on the nonrational in English and other modern writers.

8.80 Wall, Alan. "Little Magazines: Notes Toward a Methodology." In 14.4, 105–17.

8.81 Williams, Raymond. "Twentieth-Century Opinions." In 4.194, 199–284.

Others: Caudwell (4.26), Mulhern (11.116a), Bradbury (14.7), Harrison (14.29).

ii. The 1930s

8.82 Brown, Stuart Gerry. "Three English Radical Poets." *New Masses*, July 3, 1934, 33–36.

This review of Auden, Day-Lewis, and Spender, and the response by Genevieve Taggard (September 25, 18–20), raise interesting questions about the possible romanticism of thirties radical poetry.

8.83 Day-Lewis, Cecil. *A Hope for Poetry*. 1933/1935; Westport, Conn.: Greenwood Press, 1976.

8.84 ———. *Revolution in Writing*. London: The Hogarth Press, 1935.

Pamphlet contains lectures to young people on the writer and morals, and Communist demands on art.

8.85 ———, ed. *The Mind in Chains: Socialism and the Cultural Revolution*. London: Frederick Muller, 1937.

The best-known collection of British Marxist critical writing of the 1930s consists of generally lightweight essays. On literature: Edward Upward, "Literature"; Edgell Rickword, "Culture, Progress and the English Tradition."

8.86 Dupee, F. W. "The English Literary Left." *Partisan Review*, 5 (August–September 1938), 11–21.

8.87 Fox, Ralph. *The Novel and the People*. 1937; New York: International Publishers, 1945.

Aspects of the history and form of the novel discussed in a simple, straightforward way.

8.88 ———. *Ralph Fox: A Writer in Arms*. Ed. John Lehmann, T. A. Jackson, and C. Day-Lewis. London: Lawrence and Wishart, 1937.

Includes "Marxism and Literature" (from 8.87), 185–92, section of Fox's writing as "The Literary Critic," 211–52.

8.89 Harris, Henry. "The Symbol of the Frontier in the Social Allegory of the 'Thirties." *ZAA*, 14 (1966), 127–40.

8.90 Henderson, Philip. *Literature and a Changing Civilization*. London: John Lane, 1935.

8.91 ———. *The Novel Today: Studies in Contemporary Attitudes*. London: John Lane, 1936.

8.92 ———. *The Poet and Society*. 1939; Folcroft, Pa.: Folcroft Press, 1969.

8.93 Jones, Len. "The Worker's Theatre in the Thirties." *MT*, September 1974, 271–80. Rpt. in *ZAA*, 23 (1975), 300–13.

8.94 Klaus, H. Gustav. "Socialist Fiction of the 1930s: Some Preliminary Observations." *Renaissance and Modern Studies*, 20 (Fall 1976), 14–38. Rpt. in 8.97, 13–41.

8.95 *Left Review* (1934–38). Ed. Montague Slater, et al. Contributors on literature included: Edgell Rickword, Rex Warner, Douglas Garman, R. D. Charques, T. A. Jackson, Philip Henderson.

8.96 Lewis, John, ed. *The Modern Quarterly Miscellany No. 1*. London: Lawrence and Wishart, 1947.

Includes essays on beauty, Shakespeare, Ossian, Emily Brontë, Dostoevsky, and Lewis's "What is Marxist Criticism?" (3–10).

8.97 Lucas, John, ed. *The 1930s: A Challenge to Orthodoxy*. New York: Barnes & Noble, 1978, (M/NM)

Interview with Edgell Rickword, poems and a play by Randall Swingler and Montagu Slater, articles on Waugh, James Boswell, left journals, half a dozen individual authors of the period.

8.98 *The Modern Quarterly* (1938–39; NS, 1945–53).

Contributors on literature included Christopher Caudwell. See 8.96 above.

8.99 Rolfe, Edwin. "Poetry." *Partisan Review*, 2 (April–May 1935), 32–51.

Comments on the direction of poetry in the thirties; mention of Eliot, Auden, others.

8.100 Spender, Stephen. *The Destructive Element: A Study of Modern Writers and Beliefs*. London: Jonathan Cape, 1935.

8.101 _____ . *Life and the Poet*. London: Secker and Warburg, 1942.

8.102 Strachey, John. *Literature and Dialectical Materialism*. New York: Covici, Friede, 1934.

8.103 "The Thirties: A Special Number." *The Review: A Magazine of Poetry & Criticism*, No. 11–12 (1964). (M/NM)
Includes conversations with Edgell Rickword and Edward Upward; brief articles on Auden, the Spanish Civil War, and related topics.

8.104 Thomas, Tom. "The Worker's Theatre Movement: Memoirs and Documents." *History Workshop*, No. 4 (Autumn 1977), 102–42.

Others: Williams (4.194), Johnson (6.14), Hynes (14.40), Ingle (14.41), Maxwell (14.61).

-9-

National Literatures: United States

A. GENERAL

9.1 Ames, Russell. "Protest and Irony in Negro Folksong." *S&S*, 14 (Summer 1950), 192–213; "Implications of Negro Folk Song." *S&S*, 15 (Spring 1951), 163–73.

*9.2 Blake, Fay. *The Strike in the American Novel.* Metuchen, N. J.: The Scarecrow Press, 1972. (NM)
Includes analysis of thirties Marxist theory and practice and synopses of dozens of American strike novels in annotated bibliography.

9.3 Calverton, V. F. *The Liberation of American Literature.* 1932; New York: Octagon Books, 1973.
Traces "the development of American literature in relationship with... social forces, expressed in the form of class content," from the colonial period through the 1920s.

9.4 Durand, Regis, ed. *Myth and Ideology in American Culture.* Villaneuve d'Ascq: Université de Lille, 1976. (M/NM)
Part I contains articles on "Super-Realism," James, and selected individual authors; Part II, articles on Toomer, McKay, and other black writers. Durand's introduction intelligently discusses the Marxist approach to ideology.

9.5 Egbert, Donald Drew. *Socialism and American Art: In the Light of European Utopianism, Marxism, and Anarchism.* Princeton, N.J.: Princeton University Press, 1967. (NM)
Revised, expanded paperback edition of the concluding essay in the first volume of Egbert and Stow Persons, eds., *Socialism and American Life* (Princeton, 1952).

9.6 Finkelstein, Sidney. *Existentialism and Alienation in American Literature.* New York: International Publishers, 1965.

Discusses O'Neill, Camus, Fitzgerald, Balzac, Faulkner, Sartre, Baldwin, and Purdy, among other authors. See debate on book in *American Dialog*, 3 (March–April 1966), 7–14, with John Howard Lawson, Jack Lindsay, others; Finkelstein's reply, 3 (November–December 1966), 34–38.

9.7 Franklin, H. Bruce. *The Victim as Criminal and Artist: Literature from the American Prison.* New York: Oxford University Press, 1978.

Chapters on slave narratives, Melville, nineteenth- and twentieth-century prison literature.

9.8 Hicks, Granville. *The Great Tradition: An Interpretation of American Literature Since the Civil War.* 1933/1935; Chicago: Quadrangle Books, 1969.

With Calverton (9.3), one of the oft-cited examples of the mechanistic, class-conscious Marxist literary criticism of the thirties.

9.9 Martin, Wendy. "Seduced and Abandoned in the New World: The Image of Women in American Fiction." In *Woman in Sexist Society: Studies in Power and Powerlessness.* Ed. Vivian Gornick and Barbara K. Moran. New York: NAL, 1972, 329–46.

From *Charlotte Temple* to *The Company She Keeps.*

9.10 Nikolyukin, A. N. "Past and Present Discussions of American National Literature." In 2.4, 575–90.

9.11 "The Origins of Left Culture in the U.S.: 1880–1940." Ed. Paul Buhle. Combined special issue of *Cultural Correspondence* #6–7 and *Green Mountain Irregulars* #6 (Spring 1978).

9.12 Parrington, Vernon L. *Main Currents in American Thought.* 3 vols. 1927–30; New York: Harcourt, Brace & World, 1958.

Includes *The Colonial Mind (1620–1800)* and *The Romantic Revolution in America (1800–1860),* both published in 1927, and *The Beginnings of Critical Realism (1860–1920),* published in fragmentary and posthumous form in 1930.

*9.13 Rideout, Walter, B. *The Radical Novel in the United States, 1900–1954.* Cambridge, Mass.: Harvard University Press, 1956. (NM)

Comprehensive and useful survey, especially on the proletarian novel of the thirties. Appendix: "American Radical Novels," 292–300.

9.14 Rubinstein, Annette T. "A Note on American Literary Independence." *S&S*, 40 (Fall 1976), 352–55.
Anglo-American literary relations since 1776.

9.15 Smith, Bernard. *Forces in American Criticism: A Study in the History of American Literary Thought.* 1939; New York: Cooper Square Publishers, 1971.
Survey of American literary criticism from the Puritans through the nineteenth century to the major figures of the early twentieth century.

9.16 *20th Century American Literature: A Soviet View.* Moscow: Progress Publishers, 1976.
Analyses and reviews of all genres of American literature, classic and popular writers.

Others: Weimann (4.188).

B. BEFORE 1900

9.17 Barnett, Louise K. *The Ignoble Savage: American Literary Racism, 1790–1890.* Westport, Conn.: Greenwood Press, 1975. (NM)
This study of "white American attitudes toward Indians" includes chapters on Hawthorne and Melville.

9.18 Charvat, William. "American Romanticism and the Depression of 1837." *S&S*, 2 (Winter 1937), 67–82.
See also George Mayberry's response to Charvat, "In Defense of Emerson," 2 (Spring 1938), 257–58.

9.19 Franklin, H. Bruce. " 'A' Is for Afro-American: A Primer on the Study of American Literature." In 2.10, 53–64.
An earlier version of Chapter 1 of 9.7, on slave narratives.

9.20 Galassi, Frank. "The Acquisitive Sense in American Drama." *Praxis*, No. 2 (Winter 1976), 149–55.

9.21 Henderson, Harry B. *Versions of the Past: The Historical Imagination in American Fiction.* New York: Oxford University Press, 1974.

Discusses social and historical elements often neglected in studies of Cooper, Hawthorne, Melville, Twain, and other (mostly nineteenth-century) American novelists.

9.22 Howe, Irving. "Anarchy and Authority in American Literature." In 14.37, 93–111.

9.23 LeRoy, Gaylord C. "American Innocence Reconsidered." *The Massachusetts Review*, 4 (Summer 1963), 623–46.

9.24 Miller, James E., Jr. "The 'Classic' American Writers and the Radicalized Curriculum." In 2.12, 565–70.

9.25 Matthiessen, F. O. *American Renaissance: Art and Expression In the Age of Emerson and Whitman*. New York: Oxford University Press, 1941. (NM)
This classic study has long sections on Thoreau, Melville, Hawthorne, etc.

9.26a White, George Abbott. "Ideology and Literature: *American Renaissance* and F. O. Matthiessen." In 2.8, 431–500.

9.27 Pfaelzer, Jean. "American Utopian Fiction 1888–1896: The Political Origins of Form." In 2.9, 114–17.

9.28 Reilley, John M. "Beneficent Roguery: The Detective in the Capitalist City." *Praxis*, No. 3 (1976), 154–63.
The interactions of history, ideology, and literature in late nineteenth-century America.

9.29 Simpson, Louis P. "The Symbolism of Literary Alienation in the Revolutionary Age." *Journal of Politics*, 38 (August 1976), 79–100. (NM)
On Freneau, Brackenridge, Charles Brockden Brown.

9.30 Zipes, Jack. *The Great Refusal: Studies of the Romantic Hero in German and American Literature*. Frankfurt: Bad Homburg, 1970.
Deals with Melville, Cooper, Poe, Hawthorne.

9.31 ———. "Dunlap, Kotzebue, and the Shaping of American Theater: A Reevaluation from a Marxist Perspective." *Early American Literature*, 8 (Winter 1974), 272–84.

Others: Howard (8.52), Geismar (14.22).

C. 1900-30

9.32 Bland, Edward. "Social Forces Shaping the Negro Novel." *The Negro Quarterly*, 1 (Fall 1942), 241-48.
In the 1920s.

9.33 Bonosky, Phillip. "The Background to American Progressive Literature." *ZAA*, 9 (1961), 253-60.

9.34 Calverton, V.F. *The Newer Spirit: A Sociological Criticism of Literature.* 1925; New York: Octagon Books, 1974.
Essays on Sherwood Anderson, "Proletarian Art," other topics.

9.35 Cowley, Malcolm. *Exile's Return: A Narrative of Ideas.* 1934; New York: The Viking Press, 1951.
The first edition of this study of twenties writers has several radical sections cut out of later versions; "Art Tomorrow" epilogue is recovered in 9.43.

9.36 ———— , ed. *After the Genteel Tradition: American Writers 1910-1930.* 1937; Carbondale: Southern Illinois University Press, 1964.
Includes "Foreword: The Revolt Against Gentility," "Postscript: Twenty Years of American Literature," "A Literary Calendar: 1911-1930," and fifteen essays (mostly from *The New Republic*) on individual American writers of the period.

9.37 Sinclair, Upton. *Mammonart: An Essay in Economic Interpretation.* Pasadena, Cal.: Upton Sinclair, 1925.
Analyzes the arts "from the point of view of the class struggle."

9.38 Whipple, T. K. *Spokesmen.* 1928; Berkeley: University of California Press, 1963.
The success or failure of ten writers from Henry Adams to O'Neill is linked to the possibilities in "The American Situation."

Others: Craig and Egan (8.67), Wilson (9.70), Geismar (14.20), Maglin (14.60).

D. THE 1930s

9.39 Aaron, Daniel. *Writers on the Left.* New York: Harcourt, Brace & World, 1961. (NM)

Comprehensive but unsympathetic, anecdotal survey of American radical literary history, particularly the thirties.

9.40 Burke, Kenneth. *The Philosophy of Literary Form: Studies in Symbolic Action.* 1941; Berkeley: University of California Press, 1973.

Contains many of Burke's best essays from the 1930s, a period in which he was developing some of his more important critical ideas.

9.41a Jameson, Fredric. "The Symbolic Inference: or, Kenneth Burke and Ideological Analysis." *Critical Inquiry,* 4 (Spring 1978), 507–23.

See response by Burke, "Methodological Repression and/or Strategies of Containment," 5 (Winter 1978), 400–16; Jameson's answer, "Ideology and Symbolic Action," 417–22.

9.42 Calverton, V. F. "Literature Goes Left." *Current History,* 41 (December 1934), 316–20.

One of dozens of essays by this prolific Marxist critic of the decade.

9.43 Cowley, Malcolm. *Think Back On Us...A Contemporary Chronicle of the 1930s.* Ed. Henry Dan Piper. 2 vols. Carbondale: Southern Illinois University Press, 1967.

Cowley's most important essays and reviews from the thirties are reprinted here.

9.44 Farrell, James T. *A Note on Literary Criticism.* New York: The Vanguard Press, 1936.

Farrell's attack on Stalinist critics here was part of the polemical border wars that defined so much of the Marxist literary criticism of the 1930s.

9.45 Fraina, Louis. [Pseud.: Lewis Corey] "Human Values in Literature and Revolution." *Story,* May 1936, 4–6, 8.

9.46a Baxandall, Lee. "The Marxist Aesthetic of Louis C. Fraina." In 9.54, 195–203.

Discusses an unjustly neglected American Marxist critic who wrote from the early years of the century into the 1930s.

9.47 Freeman, Joseph. *An American Testament: A Narrative of Rebels and Romantics.* 1936; New York: Octagon Books, 1973.

The best memoir-history to come out of the radical thirties.

9.48 Gilbert, James Burkhart. *Writers and Partisans: A History of Literary Radicalism in America.* New York: Wiley, 1968. (NM) A sympathetic history of *Partisan Review* and Rahv, Phillips, and other critics close to it in the 1930s.

9.49 Gold, Michael. *Mike Gold: A Literary Anthology.* Ed. Michael Folsom. New York: International Publishers, 1972. The best essays and reviews of this critic-activist, from 1920 to 1940.

9.50 Hart, Henry, ed. *American Writers' Congress.* New York: International Publishers, 1935. Includes papers given at the 1st Congress by Burke, Cowley, Farrell, Dos Passos, Freeman, Hicks, two dozen others.

9.51 ———, ed. *The Writer in a Changing World.* New York: International Publishers, 1937. Papers from the 2nd American Writers' Congress by Freeman, Newton Arvin, Cowley, Burke, Hicks, Hemingway, MacLeish, and others.

9.52 Hicks, Granville. *Granville Hicks in the 'New Masses'.* Ed. Jack Alan Robbins. Port Washington, N.Y.: Kennikat Press, 1974. Collects Hicks's most important work in the decade, from "The Crisis in American Criticism" (1933) through dozens of reviews.

9.53 Hicks, Granville, et al., eds. *Proletarian Literature in the United States: An Anthology.* New York: International Publishers, 1935. Includes Introduction by Freeman; sections of fiction, poetry, drama, reportage; essays in the "Literary Criticism" section by Gold, Cowley, Hicks, Phillips and Rahv, Bernard Smith, others.

9.54 Madden, David, ed. *Proletarian Writers of the Thirties.* Carbondale: Southern Illinois University Press, 1968. (NM) Articles on proletarian poetry, the proletarian novel, related topics; critical appraisals of Gold and other proletarian writers.

9.55 Mangione, Jerre. *The Dream and the Deal: The Federal Writers' Project, 1935–1943.* New York: Little, Brown, 1972. (NM)

9.56 *The Modern Quarterly* (1923–40). Ed. V. F. Calverton. Most of the better literary pieces in this journal (known as *The Modern Monthly* from 1933 to 1938) were by Calverton himself.

9.57 *New Masses* (1926–48). Ed. Mike Gold, et al.

Contributors in criticism included Hicks, Freeman, others. (See 9.58.)

9.58 North, Joseph, ed. *New Masses: An Anthology of the Rebel Thirties*. New York: International Publishers, 1969.

Includes essays and reviews by Gold, Dos Passos, Richard Wright, John Howard Lawson, Hart, and others who wrote for this influential radical journal in the 1930s.

9.59 *Partisan Review* (1934–). Ed. Philip Rahv, William Phillips, et al.

Contributors in the early Marxist phase of this journal included Newton Arvin, Edmund Wilson, others.

9.60 Pells, Richard H. *Radical Visions and American Dreams: Culture and Social Thought in the Depression Years*. New York: Harper & Row, 1973. (NM)

One of the more serious analyses of thirties Marxist criticism to date; see Chapter 4, "Literary Theory and the Role of the Intellectual," 151–93.

9.61 Phillips, William, and Philip Rahv. "Criticism." *Partisan Review*, 2 (April–May 1935), 16–31.

Discussion of the function and value of Marxist criticism; includes responses from Hicks, Obed Brooks, Newton Arvin.

9.62 ———. "Some Aspects of Literary Criticism." *S&S*, 1 (Winter 1937), 212–20.

9.63 Rahv, Philip. *Literature and the Sixth Sense*. Boston: Houghton Mifflin, 1970.

Collects some of Rahv's best criticism from the period.

9.64 Ruland, Richard. *The Rediscovery of American Literature: Premises of Critical Taste, 1900–1940*. Cambridge, Mass.: Harvard University Press, 1967. (NM)

Includes useful accounts of thirties Marxist criticism and the work of F. O. Matthiessen.

9.65 Salzman, Jack, with Barry Wallenstein, eds. *Years of Protest: A Collection of American Writings of the 1930's*. New York: Pegasus, 1967.

The best anthology of the decade's literature; includes criticism by Gold, Calverton, Hicks, Cowley, and others.

9.66 Sutton, Walter. *Modern American Criticism.* Englewood Cliffs, N.J.: Prentice-Hall, 1963. (NM)
Chapter 4, "Liberal and Marxist Criticism," is a balanced and useful analysis of several key Marxist essays from the 1930s.

9.67 Whipple, T. K. *Study Out the Land.* Berkeley: University of California Press, 1943.
Thirties essays on Dos Passos, "Literature as Action,""Literature in the Doldrums," other topics.

9.68 Wilson, Edmund. *Axel's Castle.* 1931; New York: Scribner's, 1961.
This "Study in the Imaginative Literature of 1870–1930" reveals the roots of Wilson's thirties Marxism. Chapters on "Symbolism," "Axel and Rimbaud," six modern writers.

9.69 _____ . *The Triple Thinkers: Twelve Essays on Literary Subjects.* 1938; New York: Oxford University Press, 1948.
Later edition collects both "Marxism and Literature"(1937) and "The Historical Interpretation of Literature" (1940), two of Wilson's more important essays from the decade.

9.70 _____ . *The Shores of Light: A Literary Chronicle of the Twenties and Thirties.* 1952; New York: Vintage, 1961.
Contains some of Wilson's best criticism from the decade, but omits several crucial Marxist pieces.

9.71 Zabel, Morton D., ed. *Literary Opinion in America.* 2 vols. 1937; New York: Harper & Row, 1962.
Both editions include several Marxist essays from the 1930s.

9.72 Zimmerman, Michael, ed. *Sociological Criticism of the 1930's.* New York: Harper & Row, 1974.
This "Harper Studies in Language and Literature" pamphlet collects essays by Gold, Hicks, Farrell, Cowley, Allen Tate, and the Russian I. Kashkeen.

Others: Peck (1.7), Sanders (4. 156), Lawson (5.22), Craig and Egan (8.67), Blake (9.2), Calverton (9.3), Hicks (9.8), Rideout (9.13), Smith (9.15), Cowley (9.36), Clecak (9.79), LeRoy (9.92), Matthiessen (9.94), Potamkin (15.128).

E. 1940–

9.73 Bonosky, Phillip. "Against the Schematic in Culture." *Political Affairs,* September 1972, 27–39.
Critique is answered by Gaylord LeRoy and Ursula Beitz, "Conscious Direction in Culture," 40–53.

9.74 Breslow, Paul. "The Support of the Mysteries." *SOL,* 1 (Fall 1959), 15–28.
"A Look at the Literary Prophets of the Beat Middle Class"— Cozzens, Kerouac, Salinger, other fifties writers.

9.75 Brown, Lloyd L. "Which Way for the Negro Writer?" *Masses & Mainstream,* 4 (March, April 1951), 53–63, 50–59.

9.76 Brown, Margaret J. "The Treatment of Money in American Fiction." *L&I,* No. 4 (Winter 1969), 69–84.
On Kosinski, O'Hara, Oates, Bellow, Robbins, Auchincloss, Susann.

9.77 Burgum, Edwin Berry. "Literary Form: Social Forces and Innovations." *Sewanee Review,* 49 (July–September 1941), 325–38.
On the new "open" literary form of the contemporary novel and drama.

9.78 _____ . "Art in War Time: The Revival of the Heroic Tradition." *S&S,* 6 (Fall 1942), 331–51.
On "the use of art as propaganda."

9.79 Clecak, Peter. "Marxism, Literary Criticism, and the American Academic Scene." *S&S,* 31 (Summer 1967), 275–301.
Includes a brief history of American Marxist criticism from the thirties to the sixties.

9.80 Farrell, James T. "American Literature Marches On." *The New International,* September, October 1946, 218–23, 243–47.

9.81 Fast, Howard. *Literature and Reality.* New York: International Publishers, 1950.
Most rigid, limited kind of political-literary criticism.

9.82 Finkelstein, Sidney. "The New Criticism." *Masses & Mainstream,* 3 (December 1950), 76–86.

9.83 Geismar, Maxwell. "The American Short Story Today." *SOL,* 4, No. 2 (1964), 21–27. (NM)

9.84 ——— . "American Literature and the Cold War." *American Dialog*, 3 (March–April 1966), 3–6.

9.85 Graff, Gerald. *Literature Against Itself: Literary Ideas in Modern Society.* Chicago: University of Chicago Press, 1978. (NM)
In part, "about the social context of literature and criticism," but also an attack on current Marxist approaches. Best essays are on the New Criticism and "Post-Modern American Fiction."

9.86 Green, Gerald. "Back to Bigger." In 9.54, 26–45.
What has happened to the social realist form of the novel since the 1930s.

9.87 Howe, Irving. "Mass Society and Post-Modern Fiction." In 14.37, 77–97.

9.88 Jameson, Fredric. "The Great American Hunter, or, Ideological Content in the Novel." In 2.11, 180–97.
On Mailer, Dickey, and the Marxist analysis of contemporary literature; comment on article by Sol Yurick, 198–99.

9.89 Jerome, V. J. *Culture in a Changing World: A Marxist Approach.* New York: New Century Publishers, 1947.

9.90 Langford, Howard D. "The Imagery of Alienation." In *Marxism and Alienation: A Symposium.* Ed. Herbert Aptheker. New York: Humanities Press, 1965, 58–89.
Examples from contemporary American literature.

9.91 Lawson, John Howard. *The Hidden Heritage: A Rediscovery of the Ideas and Forces That Link the Thought of Our Time With the Culture of the Past.* New York: Citadel, 1950.
Cultural history that deals mainly with medieval and Renaissance periods.

9.92 LeRoy, Gaylord. "Proletarian Literature in the U.S.—the Problem of Continuity with the 30s." *ZAA*, 25 (1977), 227–32.
See also Hanna Behrand, "The Problem of Continuity with the 30s," a "Reply" to LeRoy, *ZAA*, 26 (1978), 160–65.

9.93 Maltz, Albert. *The Citizen Writer: Essays in Defense of American Culture.* New York: International Publishers, 1950.
Seven essays, including the title piece and "The Writer as Conscience of the People."

9.94 Matthiessen, F. O. *The Responsibilities of the Critic.* New York: Oxford University Press, 1952.
See title essay in particular. Collection also includes appraisals of a number of Marxist works from the 1930s.

9.95 _____ . "Marxism and Literature." *Monthly Review*, 4 (March 1953), 398–400.

9.96 Mulyarchik, Alexander. "Facing the Present: Soviet Studies of Post-War U. S. Literature." *Soviet Literature*, 1976 No. 7, 152–57.

9.97 Newman, Charles. "Little Rumble Through the Remnants of Literary Culture." *TriQuarterly*, 26 (Winter 1973), 3–41. (NM) An essay that raises a number of Marxist questions about the production and distribution of literature in the U.S.

9.98 Proffer, Carl R., ed. *Soviet Criticism of American Literature in the Sixties: An Anthology.* Ann Arbor, Mich.: Ardis, 1972. Collection of Soviet reviews and articles on twentieth-century American literature, as well as surveys of their own criticism; see "Introduction: American Literature in the Soviet Union."

9.99 Riche, James. "Decadence in Contemporary American Fiction." *L&I*, 3 (Fall 1969), 21–30.

9.100 Shaftel, Oscar. "The Social Content of Science Fiction." *S&S*, 17 (Spring 1953), 97–118.

9.101 Siegel, Paul N. "The Drama and the Thwarted American Dream." *Lock Haven Review*, No. 7 (1965), 52–62.
Dissatisfaction of man in modern society, as viewed through American plays from Odets to Hansberry and Albee.

9.102 Slochower, Harry. *No Voice Is Wholly Lost... Writers and Thinkers in War and Peace.* 1945; rpt. as *Literature and Philosophy Between Two Wars.* New York: Citadel, 1964.

9.103 Zlobin, Georgi. "New Publications of American Writers." *Soviet Literature*, 1976 No. 7, 144–52.

9.104 Zollman, Sol. "Social Relations in Modern American Poetry." *L&I*, No. 5 (1970), 1–18.

Others: Peck (1.8, 1.9), Fruchter (6.10), Geismar (14.23).

-10-

National Literatures: English-Canadian

A. GENERAL

10.1 Cappon, Paul, ed. *In Our Own House: Social Perspectives on Canadian Literature*. Toronto: McClelland and Stewart, 1978.
Contents: Steele on Atwood (11.6b), Endres on Marxist literary criticism and English Canadian literature, Mathews on "Developing a Language of Struggle...," Fraser on "The Production of Canadian Literature," Marchand on a "(Hinterland Sociologist's) View of Anglo-Canadian Literature." With general introduction and other introductions by Paul Cappon.

10.2 Clark, J. Wilson. "Distortions of Canadian History in Criticism." *L&I*, No. 9 (1971), 45–50.
Main object of attack is D. G. Jones's *Butterfly on Rock: A Study of Themes and Images in Canadian Literature* (1970).

10.3 Fairley, Margaret. "Our Cultural Heritage." *New Frontiers*, 1 (Winter 1952), 1–7.
Discussion of the radical tradition in Canadian writing, art, and life. Critique of the Massey report.

10.4 ———. "The Cultural Worker's Responsibility to the People." *Horizons: The Marxist Quarterly*, No. 25 (Spring 1968), 4–6.
Obituaries for Margaret Fairley appear in the same issue, 1–4.

10.5 Fine, Charles. "U.S. Threat to Canadian Culture." *New Frontiers*, 1 (Winter 1952), 37–39.

10.6 Hopwood, V. G. "Have We a National Literature?" *New Frontiers*, 5, No. 1 (1956), 12–17.

10.7 Mandel, Elias Wolf, ed. *Contexts of Canadian Criticism.* Chicago: University of Chicago Press, 1971. (NM) Relevant: Robert L. McDougall, "The Dodo and the Cruising Auk: Class in Canadian Fiction," rpt. from *Canadian Literature*, 18 (Autumn 1963), 6–20; Dorothy Livesay, "The Documentary Poem: A Canadian Genre."

10.8 Mathews, Robin. *Canadian Literature: Surrender or Revolution.* Ed. Gail Dexter. Toronto: Steel Rail, 1978. Contains essays on individual Canadian authors, "The Social Political Novel," Canadian poetry, "The Universities and Liberal Ideology." Mathews's thesis is that Canadian literature is distinguished by its emphasis on community, as opposed to the ideology of individualism in American literature and life. Reviewed by Peter Hunt, *Canadian Forum*, August 1978, 31–32; Dennis Cooley, *Canadian Dimension*, 3 (November–December 1978), 48–51.

10.9 Rashley, R. E. *Poetry in Canada: The First Three Steps.* Toronto: Ryerson Press, 1958. (NM) Early and important attempt to relate Canadian poetry to Canadian life, focusing on pioneer poetry, poetry of the 1860s, poetry of the 1930s. Treatment of last reveals Rashley's anti-Marxism (see 150–51).

10.10 Sandwell, B. K. "Social Function of Fiction." *Queens Quarterly*, 49, No. 4 (1942), 322–32. (NM) Fiction must speak to the age/place it is in.

10.11 Stephen, A. M. "Canadian Poets and Critics." *New Frontier,* 1 (September 1936), 20–22. A survey of Canadian poetry establishing its links with Canadian history and arguing that it is not better known because of criticism that either claims too much or is aesthetically feeble and confused.

10.12 Sutherland, John. "Introduction: The Old and the New." In *Other Canadians: An Anthology of the New Poetry in Canada 1940-1946*. Montreal: First Statement Press, 1947. Rpt. in his *Essays, Controversies and Poems*. Ed. Miriam Waddington. Toronto, 1972, 48–62. Also rpt. in Louis Dudek and Michael Gnarowski, eds. *The Making of Modern Poetry in Canada.*

Toronto, 1967. In this historically important statement, Sutherland argues that poets of the forties have rejected the assumption that poetry should be a religion or a religion of art, and so have been able to come to terms with their environment in a way that augurs well for a distinctively Canadian socialism.

10.13 Watt, Frank W. "Literature of Protest." In *The Literary History of Canada*. Ed. Carl F. Klinck. Toronto: University of Toronto Press, 1965, 457–73. (NM)

Scholarly survey of radical writing in Canada from 1867 onwards. Watt's position is that the rediscovery of this literature helps the 'dialectic' between radicalism and conservatism, out of which literature grows.

B. TWENTIETH CENTURY

i. General

10.14 [*Alive* collective]. "James Reid and Sharon Stephenson: Revolutionary Poets Serving the Working Class." *Alive*, No. 41 (1975), 10.

These two poets have moved from *Tish*-type poetry (see 10.32 below) to revolutionary poetry, which is distinguished by revolutionary content, not so-called revolutionary form.

10.15 ———. "The Canadian Periodical Publishers Association." *Alive*, No. 45 (November 1975), 11–15.

An interview with Sheryl Munro.

10.16 ———. "Jack David: Editor, Essays in Canadian Writing." *Alive*, No. 49 (May 1976), 12–15.

Interview is the source of useful comments on the present state of Canadian writing.

10.17 *Canadian Dimension* (Winnipeg, 1963–).

A socialist journal that sometimes contains critical reviews of Canadian literature.

10.18 *Canadian Forum* (Toronto, 1920–).

A left-liberal journal occasionally carrying brief literary reviews.

10.19 Castro, Nils. "The Stormy History of *El Corno Emplumado*." *Open Letter*, 2nd Series, No. 3 (Fall 1972), 5–21.

An interview with the editors of the radical magazine that brought together Canadian, U.S., and Latin American poets during the 1960s.

10.20 Clark, J. Wilson. "Literature for an Independent Canada." *L&I*, No. 11 (1972), 1–12.

10.21 _____. "Two Lines in Canadian Literary History." *L&I*, No. 15 (1973), 27–36.

S. D. Clark, Northrop Frye, and Margaret Atwood (*Survival*) are attacked for ignoring the role of class in Canadian literary history.

10.22 _____. "National Identity and Class Struggle in Canadian Writing." *L&I*, No. 17 (1974), 1–8.

10.23 Duran, Gillian. "In Search of English-Canadian Theatre." *L&I*, No. 16 (1973), 19–28. Rpt. *Alive*, No. 41 (1975), 30–31.

10.24 Kennedy, Leo. "The Future of Canadian Literature." *The Canadian Mercury*, 1, Nos. 5–6 (April–May 1929), 99–100. Canadian literature will have no future until it overcomes "infantile paralysis" in the Victorian era.

10.25 _____. "Direction for Canadian Poets." *New Frontier*, 1 (June 1936), 21–24.

Official Canadian poetry gives the impression that "a colony of shoddy late-Tennysonian poets has been miraculously preserved here in all the drab bloom of their youth...." Canadian poets need to confront life, not simply landscape.

10.26 King, Carlyle. "Some Recent Canadian Fiction." *Canadian Dimension*, 1, Nos. 1–2 (1963), 22–23. (NM)

Canadian novelists are not yet concerned with social issues, but with the bewilderment and anxiety of individuals. Examples.

10.27 Kirsch, Martin. "Canadian Theatre In For the Long Haul." *This Magazine,* 10 (November–December 1976), 3–8.

On current Canadian theater, focusing on Toronto.

10.28 LeMoyne, Charles M. "The Ideology of Comparative Canadian Literature." *L&I*, No. 15 (1973), 7–16.

The development of comparative Canadian literature programs is a device to maintain Quebec's oppression.

10.29 *The Marxist Quarterly* (1962–66). Became *Horizons: The Marxist Quarterly* (1966–69).

10.30 Mundweiler, Leslie. "Toward a 'Poetic' Politics." *Open Letter*,

2nd Series, No. 1 (Winter 1971–72), 20–28.

"Comparatively few contemporary poets in Canada and the U.S. have really come to terms with the problem of how expression is to be the concernful projection of understanding and action." The need for poetry to connect with community politics.

10.31 *New Frontiers* (1952–56).

10.32 Richardson, Keith. *Poetry and the Colonized Mind: Tish.* Oakville, Ont.: Mosaic Press, 1976. (NM)

A study of *Tish*, a Vancouver poetry publication (1961–69), which provides a case study in colonization. *Tish* ignored Canadian poetics and social philosophy and adopted Black Mountain poetics and politics.

10.33 Roddan, S. "Writing in Canada." *Canadian Forum*, 26 (September 1966), 137.

The vested interests of colonial puritanism (like the vested interests of capitalistic society) keep Canadian writing immature.

10.34 Scott, F. R. "New Poems for Old: I. The Decline of Poesy." *Canadian Forum*, 11 (May 1931), 296–98; "II. The Revival of Poetry." 11 (June 1931), 337–39.

Scott's defense of modernism; mainly European/American examples.

10.35 Sheps, G. David. "Four Novels: A Review Article." *Canadian Dimension*, 2 (January–February 1965), 15–17.

Canadian fiction is still personal, empirical, pragmatic; little radical awakening of life's submerged possibilities. Discusses Ludwig, McCourt, Richler, Peter.

10.36 Stanley, George. "Political Poetry." *Open Letter*, 2nd Series, No. 1 (Winter 1971–72), 5–14.

Political poetry fails if it doesn't reflect the confusions out of which political awareness grows. Scott Wilson's *Vancouver Poem* makes a start at this; Diane diPrima's *Revolutionary Letters* offers only abstract rhetoric.

10.37 *This Magazine* (Toronto, 1973–). Formerly *This Magazine Is About Schools* (1966–73).

10.38 Waddington, Miriam. "Canadian Tradition and Canadian Literature." *Journal of Commonwealth Literature*, No. 8 (De-

cember 1969), 125–41. (NM)
Sees two major trends in Canadian criticism: the "apocalyptic-mythic" and the "historical-social." The first (represented by Northrop Frye, Malcolm Ross, Roy Daniells, and James Reaney) avoids the "risk of change" and the "necessity for political action." On the "historical-social" side are E. K. Brown, John Sutherland, Carl Klinck, Frank W. Watt, John P. Mathews, Desmond Pacey, and A. M. Klein.

10.39 Wayman, Tom. Introd. to *Beaton Abbot's Got the Contract: An Anthology of Working Poems.* Edmonton: Newest Press, n.d., n.p.

10.40 _____. "The Limits of Realism." *This Magazine*, 11 (May–June 1977), 25–29. Rpt. *NMFG* (Vancouver), No. 18 (1977), n.p.
Argues for a New Realism in Canadian literature. Reactions from Brian Fawcett, Stan Persky in rpt.

10.41 Weaver, R. L. "On the Novel: A Sociological Approach to Canadian Fiction." *Here and Now*, 2 (June 1949), 12–15. (NM)
On novelists with social themes: Ross, Grove, Callaghan, MacLennan.

10.42 _____. "Economics of Our Literature." *Queens Quarterly*, 60 (Winter 1954), 476–85. (NM)

10.43 Wilson, Edmund. *O Canada: An American's Notes on Canadian Culture.* New York: Farrar, Straus & Giroux, 1965. (NM)
Articles originally appearing in *The New Yorker* (November 14, 21, and 28, 1964), on Morley Callaghan, nationalistic literature, Quebec literature, other topics.

10.44 *Working Teacher* (Vancouver, 1977–).

10.45 Zwicker, Barrie. "Back at the Shop It's Still a Very Unequal Struggle." *Alive*, No. 42 (1975), 6.
The situation in Canadian periodical publishing and the effect of American magazines. Statistics given.

ii. The 1930s

10.46 Birney, Earl. "Proletarian Literature: Theory and Practice." *Canadian Forum*, 17 (May 1937), 58–60.

10.47 _____. "To Arms with Canadian Poetry." *Canadian Forum*, 19 (January 1940), 322–24.
Birney ironically berates Canadian poets for failing to support the war effort.

10.48 ———— . "Advice to Anthologists." *Canadian Forum*, 21 (February 1942), 338–40.

Attack on anthologies of patriotic writing.

10.49 Calmer, Alan. "A Hope for Canadian Poetry." *New Frontier*, 1 (October 1936), 28–29.

W. E. Collins's *The White Savannahs* and the Preface to the *New Provinces* collection chart the new realism that has improved Canadian poetry. But it is a realism not yet rooted in the specific detail of Canadian life.

10.50 Endres, Robin. Introd. to *Eight Men Speak and Other Plays from the Canadian Worker's Theatre*. Ed. Richard Wright and Robin Endres. Toronto: New Hogtown Press, 1976, vii–xxxvi.

10.51 Livesay, Dorothy. "Poet's Progress." *New Frontier*, 2 (June 1937), 23–24.

10.52 McKenzie, Ruth. "Proletarian Literature in Canada." *Dalhousie Review*, 19 (April 1939), 49–64. (NM)

Considers whether there is a proletarian movement in Canadian writing by reviewing Canadian periodicals, poetry, fiction, and drama for examples of "literature which describes the life of the working class from a class-conscious and revolutionary point of view." Main discoveries: Dorothy Livesay, A. M. Klein, Jack Parr.

10.53 M. M. and V. L. J. "Worker's Theater: Quebec in the 1830's; Ontario in the 1930's." *New Frontiers*, 3 (Summer 1954), 27–30.

10.54 *New Frontier: Canadian Literature and Social Criticism* (1936–37).

10.55 *New Provinces: Poems of Several Authors*. 1936; Toronto: University of Toronto Press, 1976.

See F. R. Scott's Preface to the 1936 volume, and A. J. M. Smith's "A Rejected Preface" in the 1976 edition. Together, these prefaces emphasize the need for new, socially aware techniques and content. See Michael Gnarowski's account of the history of the preface-writing for this collection in the 1976 edition.

10.56 Pressman, David. "The Drama Festival." *New Frontier*, 2 (June 1937), 26.

Review of Dominion Drama Festival indicates the distance between Canadian theater and a national people's theater.

–11–

Individual Authors

Readers should also consult the general literary histories, listed above under national literatures, which often include discussions of individual authors (e.g., David Craig in 8.28 for Scottish writers).

Adams, Henry

11.1a Whipple, T. K. "Henry Adams." In 9.38, 23–44.

11.1b Johnson, Edgar. "Henry Adams: The Last Liberal." *S&S*, 1 (Spring 1937), 362–77.

S.a. Howe (14.35)

Albee, Edward

11.2a Bigsby, C. W. E. *Albee*. Edinburgh: Oliver and Boyd, 1969. (NM)

Makes an interesting argument about the social orientation of Albee's 'existentialism.'

11.2b Baxandall, Lee. "The Theatre of Edward Albee." *Tulane Drama Review*, 9 (Summer 1965), 19–40. Rpt. in *The Modern American Theatre*. Ed. Alvin B. Kernan. Englewood Cliffs, N.J.: Prentice-Hall, 1967.

Establishes a useful typology of action and character in the plays.

11.2c Finkelstein, Sidney. "Cold War, Religious Revival and Family Alienation: William Styron, J. D. Salinger and Edward Albee." (11.206b)

11.2d _____ . "The Existential Trap: Norman Mailer and Edward Albee." (11.133a)

11.2e Duplessis, Rachel Blau. "In the Bosom of the Family: Contradiction and Resolution in Edward Albee." *MR*, No. 8 (Spring 1977), 133–45.

Considers the "evasions" in Albee in relation to "larger social issues and to American society at the time the plays were written and performed."

S.a. Siegel (9.101)

Alger, Horatio

11.3a Cohn, Jan. "A Marxist Analysis of Horatio Alger's *Ragged Dick.*" *Proceedings of the Sixth Annual Convention of the Popular Culture Association, Chicago, Illinois, April 22–24, 1976.* Comp. Michael T. Marsden. Bowling Green, Ohio: Bowling Green State University Popular Press, 1976. Microfilm.

Anderson, Sherwood

11.4a Calverton, V. F. "Sherwood Anderson: A Study in Sociological Criticism." In 9.34, 52–118.

11.4b Whipple, T. K. "Sherwood Anderson." In 9.38, 115–38.

11.4c Geismar, Maxwell. "Sherwood Anderson: Last of the Townsmen." In 14.20, 223–84.

Arnold, Matthew

11.5a LeRoy, Gaylord C. "Matthew Arnold." In 8.56, 40–85.

11.5b Williams, Raymond. "J. H. Newman and Matthew Arnold." In 4.194, 120–36.

Devoted almost exclusively to Arnold.

11.5c Harper, Susan, and Brendan Kenny. "Browning and Arnold as Cultural Critics." (11.24a)

S.a. Goode (11.44a)

Atwood, Margaret

11.6a Mathews, Robin. "Margaret Atwood: Survivalism." In 10.8, 119–30.

11.6b Steele, James. "The Literary Criticism of Margaret Atwood." In 10.1, 73–81.

11.6c Salutin, Rick. "A Note on the Marxism of Atwood's *Survival.*" *This Magazine*, 11 (December 1977), 22–23.

Survival is a "sort of prolegomenon to a Marxist criticism of Canadian literature."

S.a. Clark (10.21)

Auden, W. H.

11.7a Scarfe, Francis. *W. H. Auden.* Monaco: The Lyrebird Press, 1949.

Sensitive to social issues and social context; a good introductory study of the early Auden.

11.7b Hoggart, Richard. *Auden: An Introductory Essay.* 1951; London: Chatto and Windus, 1965.

11.7c ———. "The Long Walk: W. H. Auden." In 14.31 (Vol. 2), 56–94.

11.7d Gregory, Horace. "The Liberal Critics and W. H. Auden." *New Masses*, April 20, 1937, 25–27.

11.7e Rickword, Edgell. "Auden and Politics." *New Verse*, Nos. 26–27 (November 1937), 21–22.

The only really radical assessment in the Auden Double Number of *New Verse*; Rickword provides a terse but pointed description of weaknesses in Auden's development, notably his loss of "sensuous consciousness" of social change. Brief articles also by Isherwood, Spender, MacNeice, Grigson, Allott; "16 Comments on Auden" and "Writings by W. H. Auden: A Checklist...."

11.7f Greenberg, Samuel. "Auden: Poet of Anxiety."*Masses & Mainstream*, 1 (June 1948), 38–50.

11.7g Ohmann, Richard. "Auden's Sacred Awe." In *Auden: A Collection of Critical Essays.* Ed. Monroe K. Spears. Englewood Cliffs, N.J.: Prentice-Hall, 1964, 172–78.

11.7h Hardy, Barbara. "The Reticence of W. H. Auden." In 8.103, 54–64.

11.7i Harris, Henry. "The Symbols and Imagery of Hawk and Kestrel in the Poetry of Auden and Day-Lewis in the Thirties." *ZAA*, 13 (1965), 276–85.

11.7j Repogle, Justin. "Auden's Marxism." *PMLA*, 80 (December 1965), 584–95. (NM)

11.7k Eagleton, Terry. "A Note on Auden." In 8.68, 179–90.

11.7l Paulin, Tom. "*Letters from Iceland*: Going North." In 8.97, 59–77.

S.a. Brown (8.82), Dupee (8.86), Rolfe (8.99), Hynes (14.40), Maxwell (14.61).

Austen, Jane

11.8a Hookham, Kutty. "Jane Austen and Her Class." *University Forward*, 1 (October 1940), 12–16.

11.8b Kettle, Arnold. "Jane Austen: *Emma.*" In 8.6, 98–113.

11.8c Van Ghent, Dorothy. "On Pride and Prejudice." In 14.74, 99–111.

11.8d Southall, Raymond. "The Social World of Jane Austen." In 8.17, 105–39.

11.8e Lovell, Terry. "Jane Austen and Gentry Society." In 14.5, 118–32.

11.8f ———— . "Jane Austen and the Gentry: A Study in Literature and Ideology." In 14.50, 15–37.

11.8g Newton, Judith Lowder. "*Pride and Prejudice*: Power, Fantasy and Subversion in Jane Austen." *Feminist Studies*, 4 (February 1978), 27–42.

Bach, Richard

11.9a Broughton, Paul L. "Contemporary Abstract Symbolism in *Jonathan Livingston Seagull.*" *Alive*, No. 45 (November 1975), 9–10.

S.a. 20th Century American Literature (9.16)

Bacon, Francis

11.10a Lunacharsky, A. "Bacon in Shakespearian Surroundings." *International Literature*, 1936, No. 1, 85–99.

11.10b Morton, A. L. "Bacon's New Atlantis." In 8.10, 12–20.

11.10c ———— . "Francis Bacon—Philosopher of Nature." In 8.11, 53–58.

Baraka, Imamu [Leroi Jones]

11.11a Stratman, David G. "Culture and the Tasks of Criticism." In 2.13, 105–17.

Discussion of *The Slave* "in terms of class ideology."

Barrie, James

11.12a Rickword, Edgell. "Sir James Barrie." In *Scrutinies*. Vol. 1. London: Wishart, 1928, 1–13. Rpt., rev. "James Barrie." *Daily Worker* (London), June 21, 1937, 5.

Beaumont, Francis, and John Fletcher

11.13a Danby, J. E. "Beaumont and Fletcher: Jacobean Absolutists," and "*The Maid's Tragedy.*" In 8.29, 152–83, 184–206.

Behan, Brendan

11.14a Gray, Nigel. "Every Tinker Has His Own Way of Dancing: *Borstal Boy*, Brendan Behan (1958)." In 8.70, 75–99. (NM)

Bellamy, Edward

11.15a Beauchamp, Gorman. "*The Iron Heel* and *Looking Backward*: Two Paths to Utopia." (11.123h)

Bellow, Saul

11.16a Tanner, Tony. *Saul Bellow*. Edinburgh: Oliver and Boyd, 1965. (NM)

A pioneering study that is sensitive to the links between form and society in Bellow's work.

11.16b Geismar, Maxwell. "Saul Bellow: Novelist of the Intellectuals." In 14.23, 210–24.

11.16c Landor, M. "Centaur-Novels." In 9.98, 28–61.

On Bellow, Updike, Styron, and Trilling.

11.16d Finkelstein, Sidney. "The Anti-Hero of Updike, Bellow and Malamud." (11.218a)

11.16e Howe, Irving. "Down and Out in New York and Chicago: Saul Bellow, Professor Herzog, and Mr. Sammler." In 14.38, 121–36.

11.16f Bullock, C. J. "On the Marxist Criticism of the Contemporary Novel in the United States: A Re-evaluation of Saul Bellow." *Praxis*, No. 2 (Winter 1976), 189–98.

Argues that Bellow should be understood as a critical realist rather than as a modernist.

S. a. Brown (9.76), Mendelson (11.218c)

Bennett, Arnold.

11.17a Kettle, Arnold. "Arnold Bennett: The Old Wives' Tale." In 8.6, 87–91.

11.17b Siegel, Paul N. "Revolution and Evolution in Bennett's *The Old Wives' Tale*." *CLIO*, 4 (February 1975), 159–72.

Berger, John

11.18a Craib, Ian. "Sociological Literature and Literary Sociology: Some Notes on *G* by John Berger." *Sociological Review*, 22, No. 3 (1974), 321–32. (NM)

Blake, William

11.19a Lindsay, Jack. *William Blake: Creative Will and the Poetic*

Image. 2nd ed. London: Franfrolico Press, 1929.

11.19b ———— . *William Blake: His Life and Work.* New York: George Braziller, 1979.

11.19c Bronowski, Jacob. *William Blake: A Man Without a Mask.* 1943; New York: Haskell House, 1967. (NM)
This book revolutionized Blake studies, according to Solomon (2.15).

11.19d ———— . *William Blake and the Age of Revolution.* New York: Harper & Row, 1965. (NM)

11.19e Erdman, David. *Blake: Prophet Against Empire.* Princeton, N.J.: Princeton University Press, 1954. (NM)
Examination of Blake's attitudes toward the history of his time.

11.19f Morton, A. L. *The Everlasting Gospel: A Study in the Sources of William Blake.* London: Lawrence and Wishart, 1958.

11.19g Sabri-Tabrizi, G. R. *The 'Heaven' and 'Hell' of William Blake.* London: Lawrence and Wishart, 1973.

11.19h Glen, Heather. "The Poet in Society: Blake and Wordsworth on London." *L&H*, No. 3 (March 1976), 2–28.

11.19i Whitehead, Fred. "William Blake and Radical Tradition." In 2.13, 191–214.

11.19j Punter, David. "Blake: Creative and Uncreative Labour." In 8.58, 535–61.

11.19k ———— . "Blake, Marxism and Dialectic." *L&H*, No. 6 (Autumn 1977), 219–42.

11.19l Fauvet, Paul. "Mind-Forg'd Manacles: Blake and Ideology." *RL*, No. 6 (1978), 16–39.
Discussion: Edward Larrisy, "Blake and Ideology," *RL*, No. 8 (1978), 63–66.

Brierley, Walter

11.20a Johnson, Roy. "Walter Brierley: Proletarian Writing." *RL*, No. 2 (Summer 1976), 5–8.
Brierley, like many other working-class writers, accepts middle-class values uncritically. This argument is criticized by Carol Snee, "Walter Brierley: A Test Case," *RL*, No. 3 (Autumn 1976), 11–13.

Brontë, Charlotte, and Emily Brontë

*11.21a Eagleton, Terry. *Myths of Power: A Marxist Study of the Brontës.* London: Macmillan, 1975.

Eagleton's notes contain useful bibliographical suggestions; see 139–43. Reviewed by Deborah Rosenfelt, *MR*, No. 7 (Fall 1976), 114–17.

11.21b Hobday, C. H. "The Brontës After a Century: Those Subversive Sisters." *Our Time* (London), 7 (August 1947), 7–8.

11.21c Wilson, David. "Emily Brontë: First of the Moderns." In 8.96, 94–115.

Emily Brontë considered in the "light of her relationship to people of her time." Concludes with claim for her as possible source of the proletarian novel.

11.21d Kettle, Arnold. "Emily Brontë: *Wuthering Heights.*" In 8.6, 152–70.

11.21e Morton, A. L. "Genius on the Border." *Marxist Quarterly* (London), 2 (July 1955), 157–72.

11.21f Williams, Raymond. "Charlotte and Emily Brontë." In 8.22, 60–74.

11.21g Ohmann, Carol. "Emily Brontë in the Hands of Male Critics." *CE*, 32 (May 1971), 906–13.

A Marxist-feminist case about male critical misunderstanding of Emily Brontë.

11.21h Hardwick, Elizabeth. "The Brontës." In *Seduction and Betrayal: Women and Literature.* New York: Random House, 1974, 1–30. (NM)

The attempt to escape the misery awaiting genteel poor females is seen as central to the Brontës, especially Charlotte.

11.21i Gubar, Susan. "The Genesis of Hunger, According to *Shirley.*" *Feminist Studies,* 3 (Spring–Summer 1976), 5–21.

Shirley exposes the starvation and sexism produced by mercantile capitalism; its problems reflect the difficult relation between tradition and women's voice.

11.21j Musselwhite, David. "*Wuthering Heights*: The Unacceptable Text." *RL*, No. 2 (Summer 1976), 3–5. Rpt. in 14.5, 154–60.

For a critique of this article, see Francis Barker, "*Wuthering Heights* and the Real Conditions," *RL*, No. 3 (Autumn 1976), 10–11.

11.21k Showalter, Elaine. "Feminine Heroes. "Charlotte Brontë and George Eliot." In 14.69, 100–32.

11.21l Frankenburg, Ronald. "Styles of Marxism; Styles of Criticism. *Wuthering Heights*: A Case Study." In 14.50, 109–44.

11.21m Marxist-Feminist Collective. "Women's Writing: *Jane Eyre, Shirley, Villette, Aurora Leigh*." In 14.6, 185–206. Rpt. in *Ideology and Consciousness*, No. 3 (Spring 1978), 27–48.

11.21n Stoneman, Patsy. "The Brontës and Death: Alternatives to Revolution." In 14.6, 185–206.

S.a. Pascal (6.23)

Brooks, Van Wyck

11.22a Smith, Bernard. "Van Wyck Brooks." In 9.36, 57–66.

Browning, Elizabeth Barrett

11.23a Marxist-Feminist Collective. "Women's Writing: *Jane Eyre, Shirley, Villette, Aurora Leigh*." (11.21m)

Browning, Robert

11.24a Harper, Susan, and Brendan Kenny. "Browning and Arnold as Cultural Critics." In 14.5, 161–73.

Bryant, William Cullen.

11.25a Sillen, Samuel. Introd. to *William Cullen Bryant*. New York: International Publishers, 1945, 7–28.

11.25b Glicksberg, Charles I. "William Cullen Bryant and Communism." *The Modern Monthly*, 8 (July 1934), 353–59.

Bunyan, John

11.26a Lindsay, Jack. *John Bunyan: Maker of Myths*. 1937; New York: A. M. Kelley, 1969.

11.26b West, Alick. "John Bunyan." In 8.20, 11–57; rpt. in 8.21, 131–77.

11.26c Southall, Raymond. "The Popularity of *The Pilgrim's Progress*." In 8.43, 133–43.

S.a. Kettle (8.6), Cantarow (8.26)

Burke, Edmund

11.27a Reid, Chris. "Language and Practice in Burke's Political Writing." *L&H*, No. 6 (Autumn 1977), 203–18.

Burns, Robert

11.28a Campbell, J. R. *Robert Burns the Democrat*. Glasgow, 1959.

11.28b MacDiarmid, Hugh. "The Bicentenary of Robert Burns."

MT, January 1959, 11–15.

Burroughs, William

11.29a Adam, Ian W. "Society as Novelist." *Journal of Aesthetics and Art Criticism,* 25 (Summer 1967), 375–86.
Form and society in Burroughs and Thackeray.

Butler, Samuel

11.30a Cole, G. D. H. *Samuel Butler and 'The Way of All Flesh'.* London: Home and Van Thal, 1947.

11.30b ———. *Samuel Butler.* 1952; rev. ed. London: Longmans, 1961.
Cole's later pamphlet on Butler lays greater emphasis on *Erewhon.*

11.30c Hicks, Granville. "Samuel Butler, Cautious Rebel." In 8.51, 145–76.

11.30d Kettle, Arnold. "Samuel Butler: *The Way of All Flesh.*" In 8.6, 35–49.

S.a. Morton (8.11)

Byron, George Gordon

11.31a Lunacharsky, A. "Byron and Byronism." *International Literature,* 1938, No. 1, 71–77.

11.31b Erdman, D. V. "Bryon and Revolt in England." *S&S,* 11 (1947), 234–48.

11.31c Diakonova, Nina. "Byron and the English Romantics." *ZAA,* 18 (1970), 144–67.

Callaghan, Morley

11.32a Wilson, Edmund. "Morley Callaghan of Toronto." In 10.43, 9–31. (NM)

11.32b Zollman, Sol. "Fascist and Obscurantist Propaganda in Morley Callaghan." *L&I,* No. 3 (Fall 1969), 14–20.

11.32c Mathews, Robin. "Morley Callaghan: The New Colonialism." In 10.8, 91–107.

S.a. Weaver (10.41)

Cantwell, Robert

11.33a Conroy, Jack. "Robert Cantwell's *Land of Plenty.*" In 9.54, 74–84.

Capote, Truman

11.34a Baxandall, Lee. "The New Capote and the Old Soviet

Advice." *SOL*, 6 (March–April 1966), 92–100.

Capote's documentary method in *In Cold Blood* fulfills a Communist precept formulated years before the book came out.

Carlyle, Thomas

11.35a LeRoy, Gaylord. "Thomas Carlyle." In 8.56, 13–39.

11.35b Williams, Raymond. "Thomas Carlyle." In 4.194, 85–98.

11.35c Beer, Gillian. "Carlyle and *Mary Barton*: Problems of Utterance." In 14.6, 242–55.

Carroll, Lewis

11.36a Eagleton, Terry. "Alice and Anarchy." *New Blackfriars*, 53 (October 1972), 447–55.

Cary, Joyce

11.37a Kettle, Arnold. "Joyce Cary: *Mister Johnson*." In 8.6, 186–92.

11.37b Raskin, Jonah. "Forster and Cary: Old and New," *Mister Johnson*: On the Road," "The End: Neo-Colonialism," and "Works of Passion and Imagination." In 8.78, 222–41, 294–309, 310–18, 319–31.

Cather, Willa

11.38a Whipple, T. K. "Willa Cather." In 9.38, 139–60.

11.38b Hicks, Granville. "The Case Against Willa Cather." *The English Journal*, 22 (November 1933), 703–10.

11.38c Trilling, Lionel. "Willa Cather." In 9.36, 48–56.

11.38d Geismar, Maxwell. "Willa Cather: Lady in the Wilderness." In 14.20, 153–220.

Chapman, George

11.39a Goldstein, Leonard. "George Chapman and the Decadence in Early Seventeenth Century Drama." *S&S*, 27 (Winter 1963), 23–48.

Thoughtful and detailed definition of decadence.

11.39b ———— . "Some Aspects of Marriage and Inheritance in Shakespeare's *The Merry Wives of Windsor* and Chapman's *All Fools*." *ZAA*, 12 (1964), 375–86.

Chaucer, Geoffrey

11.40a Schlauch, Margaret. *Chaucer's Constance and Accused Queens*. New York: New York University Press, 1927.

11.40b Delany, Sheila. *Chaucer's House of Fame: The Poetics of*

Skeptical Fideism. Chicago: University of Chicago Press, 1972.

11.40c _____ . "Sexual Economics, Chaucer's Wife of Bath, and *The Book of Margery Kempe.*" In 2.10, 104–15.

11.40d _____ . "Techniques of Alienation in *Troilus and Criseyde.*" In 14.19, 77–95.

11.40e Rattenbury, Arnold. "Geoffrey Chaucer: The Poet in Society." *Our Time* (London), 4 (August 1944), 6–7, 18.

11.40f Krieger, Elliott. "Re-reading Allegory: *The Clerk's Tale.*" *Paunch*, No. 40–41 (April 1975), 116–35.

11.40g Knight, Stephen. "Politics and Chaucer's Poetry." In 2.5, 169–92.

11.40h Strohm, Paul. "Chaucer's Audience." *L&H*, No. 5 (Spring 1977), 26–41.

Chesterton, G. K.

11.41a Morton, A. L. "Chesterton: Man of Thermidor." In 8.10, 72–77.

Churchill, Charles

11.42a Morton, A. L. "Charles Churchill: The Bear with the Ragged Staff." In 8.10, 41–48.

Clare, John

11.43a Barrell, John. *The Idea of Landscape and the Sense of Place 1730-1840: An Approach to the Poetry of John Clare.* Cambridge: Cambridge University Press, 1972.

Clare's work provides a springboard for an examination of a subject important for the study of both the Augustans and the Romantics.

Clough, Arthur

11.44a Goode, John. "1848 and the Strange Disease of Modern Love." In 8.57, 45–76.

Clough, the Arnolds, and their varying reactions to 1848.

Cobbett, William

11.45a Thompson, E. P. "William Cobbett." In 8.61, 746–62.

11.45b Rickword, Edgell. "William Cobbett's *Twopenny Trash.*" In 8.2, 141–50.

Coleridge, Samuel Taylor

11.46a Colmer, John. *Coleridge: Critic of Society.* Oxford: The Clarendon Press, 1959. (NM)

11.46b Lindsay, Jack. "Samuel Taylor Coleridge [I]." *Arena*, 2 (February–March 1951), 36–49; "Samuel Taylor Coleridge [II]." *Arena*, 2 (April–May 1951), 29–43.

11.46c Wojcik, Manfred. "The Mimetic Orientation of Coleridge's Aesthetic Thought." *ZAA*, 17 (1969), 344–91.

11.46d ———. "Coleridge and the Problem of Transcendentalism." *ZAA*, 18 (1970), 30–58.

11.46e ———. "Coleridge: Symbol, Organic Unity, and Modern Aesthetic Subjectivism." *ZAA*, 18 (1970), 355–90.

11.46f ———. "Coleridge: Symbolization, Expression, and Artistic Creativity." *ZAA*, 19 (1971), 117–54.

11.46g Rudich, Norman. "Coleridge's 'Kubla Khan': His Anti-Political Vision." In 2.13, 215–41.

11.46h Southall, Raymond. "The Romanticism of Coleridge." In 8.17, 140–58.

11.46i Kroeber, Karl. "Coleridge's 'Fears': Problems in Patriotic Poetry." *CLIO*, 7 (Spring 1978), 359–73.

S.a. Bronowski (7.4)

Common, Jack

11.47a Webb, Igor. " 'What Culture Is Appropriate to the Worker?': Two English Working-Class Novelists: Robert Tressell and Jack Common." (11.214e)

Conrad, Joseph

11.48a Kettle, Arnold. "The Greatness of Joseph Conrad." *Modern Quarterly*, 3 (Summer 1948), 63–81.

11.48b ———. "Joseph Conrad: *Nostromo*." In 8.6, 68–83.

11.48c Howe, Irving. "Conrad: Order and Anarchy." In 14.35, 76–113.

11.48d Pavlov, Grigor. "Two Studies of Bourgeois Individualism by Joseph Conrad." *ZAA*, 17 (1969), 229–38.

11.48e Eagleton, Terry. "Joseph Conrad and *Under Western Eyes*." In 8.68, 21–32.

11.48f ———. "Form, Ideology and *The Secret Agent*." In 14.50, 55–63.

11.48g Williams, Raymond. "Joseph Conrad." In 8.22, 140–53.

11.48h Raskin, Jonah. "Conrad's Contradictions," "Season in Hell," "*Lord Jim:* White Skins," "The Darkness of the Gulf," and

"Russians and Revolutions." In 8.78, 126–48, 149–61, 162–69, 170–205, 206–21.

11.48i O'Flinn, Paul. "Capitalism, Racism and Joseph Conrad." In 8.13, 36–43.

11.48j Swingewood, Alan. "The Novel and the Problem of Social Order: Gissing and Conrad." (11.75f)

11.48k Jenkins, Gareth. "Conrad's *Nostromo* and History." *L&H*, No. 6 (Autumn 1977), 138–78.

11.48l Orr, John. "Conrad: The New Meaning of Tragic Irony." In 14.64, 99–114.

11.48m Laskowsky, Henry J. "Conrad's *Under Western Eyes*: A Marxian View." *MR*, No. 11 (Fall 1978), 90–104.

11.48n Zelnick, Stephen. "Conrad's *Lord Jim*: Meditations on the Other Hemispheres." *MR*, No. 11 (Fall 1978), 73–89.

11.48o Hawkins, Hunt. "Conrad's Critique of Imperialism: *Heart of Darkness.*" *PMLA*, 94 (March 1979), 286–99. (NM)
Conrad tends to take imperialism case by case and examine its effect, but "throughout his fiction Conrad condemned imperialism of all types."

Conroy, Jack

11.49a Larsen, Erling. "Jack Conroy's *The Disinherited* or, The Way It Was." In 9.54, 86–95. (NM)

Cooper, James Fenimore

11.50a Howard, David. "James Fenimore Cooper's *The Leatherstocking Tales*: 'without a cross'." In 8.52, 9–54.

11.50b Henderson, Harry B. "Cooper: The Range of the American Historical Novel." In 9.21, 50–90.

S.a. Zipes (9.30)

Cornford, John

11.51a Heinemann, Margot. "Poetry of the Thirties: Three Left-Wing Poets, Louis MacNeice, John Cornford, Clive Branson." (11.131a)

11.51b Holderness, Graham. "Freedom and Necessity: the Poetry of Marxism." *RL*, No. 6 (1977–78), 40–52.

S.a. Maxwell (14.61)

Crabbe, George

See Southall (8.17), Boyer (8.25)

Crane, Hart

11.52a Schappes, Morris U. "Robinson Jeffers and Hart Crane: A Study in Social Irony." (11.98a)

Crane, Stephen

11.53a Nye, Russell B. "Stephen Crane as Social Critic." *The Modern Quarterly*, 11 (Summer 1940), 48–54.

11.53b Geismar, Maxwell. "Stephen Crane: Halfway House." In 14.22, 69–136.

11.53c Solomon, Maynard. "Stephen Crane: A Critical Study." *Masses & Mainstream*, 9 (January 1956), 25–42; 9 (March 1956), 31–47.

Dahlberg, Edward

11.54a Chametzky, Jules. "Edward Dahlberg, Early and Late." In 9.54, 64–73. (NM)

Day-Lewis, Cecil

11.55a Harris, Henry. "The Symbols and Imagery of Hawk and Kestrel in the Poetry of Auden and Day-Lewis in the Thirties." (11.7i)

S.a. Brown (8.82), Maxwell (14.61)

Defoe, Daniel

11.56a Morton, A. L. "Mr. Crusoe and Mr. Gulliver." In 8.11, 33–40.

11.56b Kettle, Arnold. "Defoe and the Picaresque Tradition." In 8.6, 58–66.

11.56c ———. "In Defence of *Moll Flanders*." In *Of Books and Humankind: Poems and Essays for Bonamy Dobree*. Ed. John Butt. London: Routledge & Kegan Paul, 1964, 55–67.

11.56d Van Ghent, Dorothy. "On *Moll Flanders*." In 14.74, 33–43. Defoe desensualizes experience; life becomes a matter of accounting.

11.56e Rubinstein, Annette T. "Robinson Crusoe and His Socialist Successors." *Masses & Mainstream*, 9 (May 1956), 28–37.

11.56f Watt, Ian. "*Robinson Crusoe*, Individualism and the Novel," and "Defoe as Novelist: *Moll Flanders*." In 6.31, 62–96, 97–139. (NM)

11.56g West, Alick. "Daniel Defoe." In 8.20, 59–109; rpt. in 8.21, 178–228.

11.56h Pearlman, Elizabeth. "*Robinson Crusoe* and the Cannibals."

Mosaic, 1 (October 1967), 39–55.

Robinson Crusoe can be seen as an attempt to justify the neurotic bases of middle-class individualism and colonialism.

DeForest, John

11.57a Alsen, Eberhard. "Marx and DeForest: The Idea of Class Struggle in *Miss Ravenal's Conversion.*" *American Literature*, 48 (May 1976), 223–28. (NM)

Dickey, James

See Jameson (9.88)

Dickens, Charles

11.58a Jackson, T. A. *Charles Dickens: The Progress of a Radical.* New York: International Publishers, 1938.

11.58b Lindsay, Jack. *Charles Dickens: A Biographical and Critical Study.* London: Dakers, 1950.

11.58c ———. "Dickens' *Barnaby Rudge.*" In *Dickens and the Twentieth Century.* Ed. John Gross and Gabriel Pearson. London: Routledge & Kegan Paul, 1962, 91–106.

11.58d Mehring, Franz. "Charles Dickens." In 2.6, 438–42.

11.58e Orwell, George. "Charles Dickens." In *Inside the Whale.* London, 1940. Rpt. in *Decline of the English Murder and Other Essays.* Harmondsworth: Penguin, 1965, 80–141. (NM)

11.58f Kettle, Arnold. "Dickens' *Oliver Twist.*" In 8.6, 133–51.

11.58g ———. "Dickens and the Popular Tradition." *ZAA*, 9 (1961), 229–52. Rpt. in 2.3, 214–44.

11.58h ———. "Dickens' *Our Mutual Friend.*" In 11.58c (Gross and Pearson), 213–26.

11.58i ———. "Charles Dickens: The Novelist and the People." *MT*, February 1963, 48–54.

11.58j Van Ghent, Dorothy. "On *Great Expectations.*" In 14.74, 125–38.

11.58k Lucas, John. "Dickens and *Dombey and Son:* Past and Present Imperfect." In 8.57, 99–140. (NM)

11.58l Williams, Raymond. "Charles Dickens." In 8.22, 28–59.

11.58m ———. "Dickens and Social Ideas." In *Dickens 1970.* Ed. M. Slater. London: Chapman and Hall, 1970, 77–98. Rpt. in 14.8, 328–47.

Includes discussion of the ways in which the novel can communicate ideas.

11.58n Knight, Everett. "The Case of Dickens." In 6.15, 106–42.

11.58o Myers, William. "The Radicalism of *Little Dorritt.*" In 8.57, 77–104.

11.58p Smith, David. "*Mary Barton* and *Hard Times*: Their Social Insights." In 14.70, 97–112.

11.58q Craig, David. "*Hard Times* and the Condition of England." In 8.3, 109–31.

11.58r Easson, Angus. "The Mythic Sorrows of Charles Dickens." *L&H*, No. 1 (March 1975), 49–61.

11.58s O'Flinn, Paul. "Hands, Knees and a Book by Dickens." In 8.13, 60–66.

11.58t Stigant, Paul, and Peter Widdowson. "*Barnaby Rudge*: A Historical Novel?" *L&H*, No. 2 (October 1975), 2–44.

11.58u Filmer, Paul. "Dickens, Pickwick and Realism: On the Importance of Language to Socio-Literary Relations." In 14.50, 64–91.

A study of *Pickwick* shows the inadequacy of realism as critical or creative aesthetic. What we share with the work is not a common world, but a common language.

11.58v Green, Michael. "Notes on Fathers and Sons in *Dombey and Son.*" In 14.6, 256–64.

11.58w Feltes, N. N. "'The Greatest Plague of Life': Dickens, Masters and Servants." *L&H*, No. 8 (Autumn 1978), 197–213.

S.a. Craig (11.62d)

Donne, John

11.59a Southall, Raymond. "The Little World of John Donne." In 8.43, 86–94.

11.59b Aers, David, and Gunter Kress. "Darke Texts Need Notes: Versions of the Self in Donne's Verse Epistles." *L&H*, No. 8 (Autumn 1978), 138–58.

Dos Passos, John

11.60a Cowley, Malcolm. "Dos Passos: Poet Against the World." In 9.36, 134–46.

11.60b Whipple, T. K. "Dos Passos and the U.S.A." In 9.67, 85–92.

11.60c Sartre, Jean-Paul. "John Dos Passos and *1919.*" In 4.159, 94–103.

11.60d Geismar, Maxwell. "John Dos Passos: Conversion of a Hero." In 14.21, 89–139.

11.60e Finkelstein, Sidney. "Alienation and Rebellion to Nowhere: John Dos Passos and Henry Miller." In 9.6, 198–210.

11.60f Gurko, Leo. "John Dos Passos' *U.S.A.*: A 1930's Spectacular." In 9.54, 46–63. (NM)

11.60g Zasursky, Y. "Dos Passos' Experimental Novel." In 9.16, 331–50.

Dreiser, Theodore

11.61a Matthiessen, F. O. *Theodore Dreiser*. New York: William Sloane, 1951. (NM)

11.61b Whipple, T. K. "Theodore Dreiser." In 9.38, 70–93.

11.61c Burgum, Edwin Berry. "Theodore Dreiser and the Ethics of American Life." In 6.3, 292–301.

11.61d Geismar, Maxwell. "Theodore Dreiser: The Double Soul." In 14.22, 287–379.

11.61e Howe, Irving. "Dreiser: The Springs of Desire." In 14.37, 151–66.

11.61f Zasursky, Y. "Theodore Dreiser's *An American Tragedy*." In 9.16, 223–40.

Dryden, John

See Bronowski (7.4).

Eliot, George

11.62a Kettle, Arnold. "George Eliot: *Middlemarch*." In 8.6, 188–210.

11.62b Milner, Ian. "George Eliot and the Limits of Victorian Realism." *Philologica Pragensia* (Prague), 6 (1963), 48–59.

11.62c ———— . "George Eliot's Realist Art." *ZAA*, 12 (1964), 387–94.

11.62d Craig, David. "Fiction and the Rising Industrial Classes." *Essays in Criticism*, 17 (January 1967), 64–74.
On *Felix Holt*. Includes comments on *Bleak House, Women in Love*, Tom Mann, Ben Tillet.

11.62e Williams, Raymond. "George Eliot." In 8.22, 75–94.

11.62f Myers, William. "George Eliot: Politics and Personality." In 8.57, 105–30.

11.62g Southall, Raymond. "Fantasy and Reality in *Middlemarch*." In 8.17, 171–82.

11.62h Swann, Charles. "Evolution and Revolution: Politics and Form in *Felix Holt* and *The Revolution in Tanner's Lane*." In 14.5, 75–92.

11.62i Showalter, Elaine. "Feminine Heroes. Charlotte Brontë and George Eliot." (11.21k)

S.a. Levine (6.16)

Eliot, T. S.

11.63a Robbins, Russell Hope. *The T. S. Eliot Myth*. New York: Schuman, 1951.

11.63b Wilson, Edmund. "T. S. Eliot." In 9.68, 93–131.

11.63c Rahv, Philip. "T. S. Eliot." *Fantasy*, 2 (Winter 1932), 17–20. Eliot's development; evaluation of his poetry.

11.63d Schappes, Morris U. "T. S. Eliot Moves Right." *The Modern Monthly*, 7 (August 1933), 405–408.

11.63e West, Alick. "T. S. Eliot: *The Wasteland*," and "T. S. Eliot as Critic." In 8.19; rpt. in 8.21, 31–36, 37–46.

11.63f ———. "The Abuse of Poetry and the Abuse of Criticism of T. S. Eliot." *Marxist Quarterly* (London), January 1954, 22–32.

11.63g Ames, Russell. "Decadence in the Art of T. S. Eliot." *S&S*, 16 (Summer 1952), 193–221.

11.63h Williams, Raymond. "T. S. Eliot." In 4.194, 224–39.

11.63i ———. "Tragic Resignation and Sacrifice: Eliot and Pasternak." In 5.40, 156–73.

11.63j Morton, A. L. "T. S. Eliot: A Personal View." In 8.12, 155–66.

11.63k Harrison, John R. "T. S. Eliot." In 14.29, 145–62.

11.63l Lowenfels, Walter. "T. S. Eliot." *American Dialog*, 2, No. 1 (1965), 35–37.

11.63m Finkelstein, Sidney. "Alienation as a Literary Style: F. Scott Fitzgerald and T. S. Eliot." (11.68e)

11.63n Eagleton, Terry. "T. S. Eliot and the Uses of Myth." In 8.68, 138–78.

11.63o Craig, David. "The Defeatism of *The Waste Land*." In 8.3, 195–212.

11.63p Kramer, Jurgen. "T. S. Eliot's Concept of Tradition: A Revaluation." *NGC*, No. 6 (Fall 1975), 20–30.

S.a. Fekete (4.47), Rolfe (8.99)

Emerson, Ralph Waldo

11.64a Matthiessen, F. O. "Book One: From Emerson to Thoreau." In 9.25, 3–175. (NM)

11.64b Greenleaf, Richard. "Emerson and Wordsworth." *S&S,* 22 (Summer 1958), 218–30.

11.64c Rubinstein, Annette T. "Emerson, Thoreau and Jacksonian Democracy." *ZAA,* 24 (1976), 199–212.

S.a. Charvat (9.18)

Farrell, James T.

11.65a Salzman, Jack, and Dennis Flynn, eds. "James T. Farrell Issue." *Twentieth Century Literature,* 22 (February 1976). (M/NM)

Includes "An Interview with James T. Farrell," Alan Wald's "Farrell and Trotskyism," Jules Chametzky's "James T. Farrell's Literary Criticism," and other essays.

11.65b Wald, Alan M. *James T. Farrell: The Revolutionary Socialist Years.* New York: New York University Press, 1978.

Faulkner, William

11.66a Burgum, Edwin Berry. "William Faulkner's Pattern of American Decadence." In 6.3, 205–22.

11.66b Geismar, Maxwell. "William Faulkner: The Negro and the Female." In 14.21, 143–83.

11.66c Kroner, Jack. "William Faulkner." *New Foundations,* 2 (Fall 1948), 7–21.

See letters on article gathered in "Against White Supremacist Attitudes," 2 (Spring 1949), 154–57; Kroner's "Reply to Criticism," 2 (Summer 1949), 259–62.

11.66d Giles, Barbara. "The South of William Faulkner." *Masses & Mainstream,* 3 (February 1950), 26–40.

11.66e Sartre, Jean-Paul. "William Faulkner's *Sartoris,*" and "On *The Sound and the Fury*: Time in the Work of Faulkner." In 4.159, 78–83, 84–93.

11.66f Landor, M. "Faulkner in the Soviet Union." *Soviet Literature,* 1965, No. 12, 178–85.

11.66g ———. "Faulkner's Creative Method in the Making." In 9.16, 306–30.

11.66h Finkelstein, Sidney. "Conflict Between Humanization and Alienation: William Faulkner." In 9.6, 184–97.

11.66i Borden, Caroline. "Characterization in Faulkner's *Light in August.*" *L&I,* No. 13 (1972), 41–50.

11.66j Palievsky, P. V. "Faulkner's Road to Realism." In 9.98, 150–68.

11.66k Kent, George E. "The Black Women in Faulkner's Works, with the Exclusion of Dilsey." *Phylon,* 35 (December 1974), 430–41; 36 (March 1975), 55–67.

11.66l Harold, Brent. "The Value and Limitation of Faulkner's Fictional Method." *American Literature,* 47 (May 1975), 212–29.

11.66m Zlobin, G. "A Struggle Against Time." In 9.16, 285–305. On *The Sound and the Fury.*

Fielding, Henry

11.67a Watt, Ian. "Fielding and the Epic Theory of the Novel," and "Fielding as Novelist: *Tom Jones.*" In 6.31, 239–59, 260–89. (NM)

11.67b Sokolyansky, Mark G. "Genre Evolution in Fielding's Dramaturgy." *ZAA,* 20 (1972), 280–95.

11.67c ———. "Poetics of Fielding's Comic Epics." *ZAA,* 22 (1974), 251–65.

S.a. Loftis (14.54), Kettle (8.7)

Fitzgerald, F. Scott

11.68a Geismar, Maxwell. "F. Scott Fitzgerald: Orestes at the Ritz." In 14.20, 287–352.

11.68b Greenleaf, Richard. "The Social Thinking of F. Scott Fitzgerald." *S&S,* 16 (Spring 1952), 97–114.

11.68c Giles, Barbara. "The Dream of F. Scott Fitzgerald." *Mainstream,* 10 (March 1957), 1–12.

11.68d Way, Brian. "Scott Fitzgerald." *NLR,* No. 21 (October 1963), 36–51.

11.68e Finkelstein, Sidney. "Alienation as a Literary Style: F. Scott Fitzgerald and T. S. Eliot." In 9.6, 165–83.

11.68f Gusera, Elena. "F. Scott Fitzgerald in the Soviet Union." *Soviet Literature,* 1966, No. 6, 171–74.

11.68g Startsev, A. "Fitzgerald's Bitter Fate." In 9.98, 97–109.

11.68h Landor, M. "Gift of Hope." In 9.98, 111–15.
On *The Great Gatsby*.

11.68i Zelnick, Stephen. "The Incest Theme in *The Great Gatsby*: The False Poetry of Petty Bourgeois Consciousness." In 2.13, 327–40.

Forster, E. M.

11.69a Morton, A. L. "E. M. Forster and the Classless Society." In 8.10, 78–88.

11.69b ———. "An Englishman Discovers India." In 8.12, 150–54.

11.69c Kettle, Arnold. "E. M. Forster: *A Passage to India*." In 8.6, 158–72.

11.69d Raskin, Jonah. "Forster and Cary: Old and New," "Disconnections," "Trips East," and "School Lessons: History and Geometry." In 8.78, 222–41, 242–56, 257–85, 286–93.

11.69e O'Flinn, Paul. "Forster and Personal Relationships." In 8.13, 21–27.

Frost, Robert

11.70a Whipple, T. K. "Robert Frost." In 9.38, 94–114.

11.70b Howe, Irving. "Robert Frost: A Momentary Stay." In 14.36, 144–57.

11.70c Zverev, A. "A Lover's Quarrel with the World: Robert Frost." In 9.16, 241–60.

Frye, Northrop

11.71a Kogan, Pauline. *Northrop Frye: The High Priest of Clerical Obscurantism*. Montreal: Progressive Books and Periodicals, 1969.

11.71b Hanes, V. G. "Northrop Frye's Theory of Literature and Marxism." In 4.90, 17–33.

11.71c Fekete, John. "Northrop Frye: The Critical Theory of Capitulation." In 4.47, 107–31.

Fuchs, Daniel

11.72a Howe, Irving. "Daniel Fuchs' Williamsburg Trilogy: A Cigarette and a Window." In 9.54, 96–105. (NM)

Gaskell, Mrs.

11.73a Lucas, John. "Mrs. Gaskell and Brotherhood." In 8.57, 141–205. (NM)
Mrs. Gaskell examined in the context of the social problem novels of

the 1840s and 1850s. Her achievement is to see the 'masses' as human.

11.73b Smith, David. "*Mary Barton* and *Hard Times*: Their Social Insights." In 14.70, 97–112.

11.73c ———. "Mrs. Gaskell and the Nature of Social Change." *L&H*, No. 1 (March 1975), 3–27.

11.73d Beer, Gillian. "Carlyle and *Mary Barton*: Problems of Utterance." (11.35c)

S.a. Kettle (8.54)

Gibbon, Lewis Grassic

11.74a Burke, James. "Lewis Grassic Gibbon." *Left Review*, 2 (February 1936), 220–25.

A thoughtful assessment of the trilogy *A Scot's Quair.*

11.74b Nelson, Marion. "The Kailyard Comes to Life: Lewis Grassic Gibbon." *New Frontier*, 1 (January 1937), 21–23.

11.74c Lindsay, Jack. "Lewis Grassic Gibbon: A Great Scots Novelist—The Cycle of Industrialization." In 4.103, 167–72.

11.74d Carter, Ian. "Lewis Grassic Gibbon, *A Scot's Quair* and the Peasantry." *History Workshop*, No. 6 (Autumn 1978), 169–85.

11.74e Johnson, Roy. "Lewis Grassic Gibbon and *A Scot's Quair*: Politics in the Novel." In 8.97, 42–58.

Gissing, George

11.75a Poole, Adrian D. B. *Gissing in Context*. London: Macmillan, 1975.

11.75b Goode, John. "Gissing, Morris, and English Socialism." *Victorian Studies*, 12 (December 1968), 201–26.

11.75c ———. "George Gissing's *The Nether World*." In 8.57, 207–41.

11.75d ———. Introd. to *The Nether World*. By George Gissing. Brighton: Harvester Press, 1974, v–xiv.

11.75e Howe, Irving. "George Gissing: Poet of Fatigue." In 14.36, 169–91.

11.75f Swingewood, Alan. "The Novel and the Problem of Social Order: Gissing and Conrad." In 6.29, 122–41.

11.75g Edmonds, Rod. "The Conservatism of Gissing's Early Novels." *L&H*, No. 7 (Spring 1978), 48–69.

Glasgow, Ellen

11.76a Geismar, Maxwell. "Ellen Glasgow: The Armor of the Legend." In 14.22, 219–83.

11.76b Giles, Barbara. "Character and Fate: The Novels of Ellen Glasgow." *Mainstream*, 9 (September 1956), 20–31.

Godwin, William

11.77a Farouk, Marion Omar. "*Mandeville*: A Tale of the Seventeenth Century—Historical Novel or Psychological Study?" In 8.9, 111–17.

11.77b Kuczynski, Ingrid. "Pastoral Romance and Political Justice." In 8.9, 101–10.

Ideas developed in *Imogen* are consistent with those explored in *Political Justice*.

S.a. Kettle (8.54)

Golding, William

11.78a Mitchell, Juliet. "Concepts and Techniques in William Golding." *NLR*, No. 15 (1962), 63–71.

11.78b Southall, Raymond. "*Lord of the Flies*." *MT*, February 1974, 51–54.

Golding's island as a negative utopia.

11.78c O'Flinn, Paul. "William Golding and Original Sin." In 8.13, 7–13.

Goldsmith, Oliver

See Boyer (8.25), Southall (8.17)

Gray, Thomas

11.79a Rudich, Norman. "The Dialectics of Poesis: Literature as a Mode of Cognition." *Boston University Studies in the Philosophy of Science*, 2 (1965), 343–400.

A study of Gray's "Elegy" as the vehicle for a refutation of New Criticism, which leads to a discussion of the content and modes of literary communication.

S.a. Southall (8.17)

Greene, Graham

11.80a Kettle, Arnold. "Graham Greene: *The Heart of the Matter*." In 8.6, 179–85.

11.80b Eagleton, Terry. "Reluctant Heroes: The Novels of Graham Greene." In 8.68, 108–37.

Griffiths, Trevor

11.81a Wolff, Janet. *"Bill Brand,* Trevor Griffiths, and the Debate about Political Theatre." *RL,* No. 8 (1978), 56–61.

11.81b Wolff, Janet, et al. "Problems of Radical Drama: The Plays and Productions of Trevor Griffiths." In 14.5, 133–53.

Grove, Frederick Philip

11.82a Penner, Roland. "Two Novels of F. P. Grove." *New Frontiers,* 1 (Winter 1953), 32–35.

Analysis of *Our Daily Bread* and *Master of the Mill.*

11.82b Mathews, Robin. "Frederick P. Grove: The Tragic Vision." In 10.8, 63–74.

Hamilton, Patrick

11.83a Widdowson, P. J. "The Saloon Bar Society: Patrick Hamilton's Fiction in the 1930s." In 8.97, 117–37.

Hamilton "at his best, does for pre-war England what Isherwood's 'Berlin' novels do for Germany.... reveal[s] the meaning of ostensibly trivial lives."

Hammett, Dashiell

11.84a Hulley, Kathleen. "From the Crystal Sphere to Edge City: Ideology in the Novels of Dashiell Hammett." In 9.4, 111–28. (NM)

Hardy, Thomas

11.85a Hicks, Granville. "The Pessimism of Thomas Hardy." In 8.51, 109–44.

11.85b Kettle, Arnold. "Thomas Hardy: *Tess of the D'Urbervilles.*" In 8.6, 50–64.

11.85c Williams, Raymond. "Thomas Hardy." In 8.22, 95–118.

11.85d Eagleton, Terry. Introd. to *Jude the Obscure.* By Thomas Hardy. London: Macmillan, 1974, 9–20.

11.85e Brooker, Peter. "Thomas Hardy's 'Wistlessness': An Exercise in the Social Reading of Poetry." *L&H,* No. 1 (March 1975), 79–92.

11.85f O'Flinn, Paul. "The Sinking of the Titanic: Is Britain Going Under With It?" In 8.13, 44–51.

11.85g Bromley, Roger. "The Boundaries of Hegemony: Thomas Hardy and *The Mayor of Casterbridge.*" In 14.5, 30–40.

11.85h Howard, Jeanne. "Thomas Hardy's 'Mellstock' and the Registrar General's Stinsford." *L&H,* No. 6 (Autumn 1977), 179–202.

Hawthorne, Nathaniel

11.86a Matthiessen, F. O. "Book Two: Hawthorne." In 9.25, 179–368. (NM)

11.86b Howard, David. "*The Blithedale Romance* and a Sense of Revolution." In 8.52, 55–97.

S.a. Barnett (9.17), Henderson (9.21), Zipes (9.30)

Heller, Joseph

11.87a Oglesby, Carl. "The Deserters: The Contemporary Defeat of Fiction." In 2.2, 33–52.

On Camus and *Catch-22*.

Hemingway, Ernest

11.88a Kashkeen, I. "Ernest Hemingway: A Tragedy of Craftsmanship." *International Literature*, 1935, No. 5, 72–90. Rpt. in 9.72, 29–40.

11.88b _____ . "Alive in the Midst of Death: Ernest Hemingway." In *Hemingway and His Critics*. Ed. Carlos Baker. New York: Hill and Wang, 1961, 162–79.

11.88c Burgum, Edwin Berry. "Ernest Hemingway and the Psychology of the Lost Generation." In 6.3, 184–204.

11.88d Geismar, Maxwell. "Ernest Hemingway: You Could Always Come Back." In 14.21, 37–85.

11.88e Howard, Milton. "Hemingway and Heroism." *Masses & Mainstream*, 5 (October 1952), 1–8.

11.88f Barnes, Lois L. "The Helpless Hero of Ernest Hemingway." *S&S*, 17 (Winter 1953), 1–25.

11.88g Rubinstein, Annette T. "Brave and Baffled Hunter." *Mainstream*, 13 (January 1960), 1–23.

11.88h Knapp, Daniel. "Hemingway: The Naming of the Hero." *SOL*, 2, No. 2 (1961), 30–41.

11.88i Orlova, R. "For Whom the Bell Tolls." In 9.98, 117–48.

11.88j Solovyov, E. "The Color of Tragedy." In 9.16, 351–83.

11.88k Lennox, Sara. " 'We Could Have Had Such a Damned Good Time Together': Individual and Society in *The Sun Also Rises* and *Mutmassunger uber Jakob*." *Modern Language Studies*, 7 (1977), 227–32.

Henryson, Robert

11.89a Siegmund-Schultze, Dorothea. "Henryson's Departure from the Medieval Norm." In 8.9, 81–91.

Hines, Barry

11.90a Gray, Nigel. "School Days Are the Happiest Days of Your Life: *Kes*, Barry Hines (1968)." In 8.70, 25–45. (NM)

Hobbes, Thomas

11.91a Southall, Raymond. "Thomas Hobbes and the Art of Political Theory." In 8.43, 105–12.

Holcroft, Thomas

See Ter-Abramova (8.45)

Hopkins, Gerard Manley

11.92a Eagleton, Terry. "Nature and Fall in Hopkins: A Reading of 'God's Grandeur'." *Essays in Criticism*, 23 (January 1973), 68–75.

Housman, A. E.

11.93a Spender, Stephen. "A. E. Housman." *Daily Worker* (London), October 29, 1936, 4.

Class analysis of Housman's values; includes comments on T. E. Lawrence, Kipling.

11.93b Morton, A. L. "The Land of Lost Content." In 8.10, 67–71.

11.93c Story, Patrick. "Housman's Cherry Trees: Toward the Practice of Marxist Explication." In 2.10, 81–88.

S.a. Bronowski (7.4)

Howells, William Dean

11.94a Smith, Bernard. "Howells: The Genteel Radical." *The Saturday Review of Literature*, August 11, 1934, 41–42.

11.94b Arvin, Newton. "The Usableness of Howells." *The New Republic*, 91 (June 30, 1937), 227–28. Rpt. in *The American Pantheon*. Ed. Daniel Aaron and Sylvan Schendler. New York: Dell, 1966, 128–34.

11.94c Getzels, Jacob Warren. "William Dean Howells and Socialism." *S&S*, 2 (Summer 1938), 376–86.

See the responses by Conrad Wright, 2 (Fall 1938), 514–17, and George Warren Arms, 2 (Spring 1939), 245–48.

Hughes, Ted

11.95a Smith, Stan. "Wolf Masks: The Early Poetry of Ted Hughes." *New Blackfriars*, 56 (September 1975), 414–26.

Huxley, Aldous

11.96a Burgum, Edwin Berry. "Aldous Huxley and His Dying
Swan." In 6.3, 140–56.

11.96b Adorno, Theodor. "Aldous Huxley and Utopia." In 4.1,
97–11

S.a. Kettle (8.6), Morton (8.11)

James, Henry

11.97a Geismar, Maxwell. *Henry James and the Jacobites*. Boston:
Houghton Mifflin, 1963. (NM)

11.97b Arvin, Newton. "Henry James and the Almighty Dollar."
The Hound and Horn, 7 (April–June 1934), 434–43. Rpt. in *The
American Pantheon*. Ed. Daniel Aaron and Sylvan Schendler.
New York: Dell, 1966, 153–63.

11.97c Cantwell, Robert. "The Return of Henry James." *The New
Republic*, 81 (December 12, 1934), 119–21.

11.97d Howe, Irving. "Henry James: The Political Vocation." In
14.35, 139–58.
On *The Princess Casamassima*. See also "Henry James: Politics
and Character" (on *The Bostonians*), 182–99.

11.97e _____. "Henry James and the American Scene." In 14.37,
112–21.

11.97f Goode, John. "The Art of Fiction: Walter Besant and Henry
James." In 8.52, 243–81.

11.97g _____. "Character and the Novel." *NLR*, No. 40
(November–December 1966), 55–75.
Focused on James, but raises issues of much wider significance.

11.97h Rubinstein, Annette T. "Henry James, American Novelist,
or: Isabel Archer, Emerson's Grand-daughter." In 2.13, 311–26.

S.a. Durand (9.4)

Jeffers, Robinson

11.98a Schappes, Morris U. "Robinson Jeffers and Hart Crane: A
Study in Social Irony." *Dynamo*, 1 (March–April 1934), 15–22.

11.98b Humphries, Rolfe. "Robinson Jeffers." *The Modern
Monthly*, 8 (January 1935), 680–89; 8 (February 1935), 748–53.

Johnson, Samuel

11.99a Brown, Stuart. "Dr. Johnson and the Old Order." *Marxist
Quarterly* (New York), 1 (October–December 1937), 418–30.

11.99b Southall, Raymond. "Johnson: Shakespeare and the Prince of Abyssinia." In 8.43, 144–62.

Jones, Ebenezer

11.100a Lindsay, Jack. "Ebenezer Jones: An English Symbolist." In 8.2, 151–76.

Jonson, Ben

11.101a Knights, L. C. "Tradition and Ben Jonson," and "Jonson and the Anti-Acquisitive Attitude." In 14.45, 179–99, 200–27.

11.101b Southall, Raymond. "Ben Jonson and the Art of Living." In 8.43, 95–104.

Joyce, James

11.102a Mirsky, Dimitri. "James Joyce." *International Literature*, 1934, No. 1, 92–102.

11.102b West, Alick. "James Joyce: *Ulysses*." In 8.19; rpt. in 8.21, 104–27.

11.102c Schlauch, Margaret. "The Language of James Joyce." *S&S*, 3 (Fall 1939), 482–97.

11.102d Niebyl, Karl H. "An Economist Considers James Joyce." *The University of Kansas City Review*, 8 (October 1941), 47–58.

11.102e Burgum, Edwin Berry. "*Ulysses* and the Impasse of Individualism," and "The Paradox of Skepticism in *Finnegan's Wake*." In 6.3, 95–108, 109–19.

11.102f Kettle, Arnold. "The Consistency of James Joyce." In *The Modern Age*. Vol. 7. The Penguin Guide to English Literature. Ed. Boris Ford. Harmondsworth: Penguin, 1961, 301–14.

11.102g Delany, Paul. "Joyce's Political Development and the Aesthetic of *Dubliners*." In 2.11, 256–66.
Joyce had an active interest in socialism from 1903 to 1907; *Dubliners* comes out of the crisis of his political beliefs. (Comment on article by Gaylord C. LeRoy, 266–68.)

11.102h Zhantiera, B. C. "Joyce's *Ulysses*." In 2.7, 138–72.

11.102i Lindsay, Jack. "Time in Modern Literature: Proust and Joyce." In 4.103, 53–69.

S.a. Pascal (6.23)

Keats, John

11.103a Wesling, Donald. "The Dialectical Criticism of Poetry: An Instance from Keats." In 14.70, 81–96.

Kempe, Margery

11.104a Delany, Sheila. "Sexual Economics, Chaucer's Wife of Bath, and *The Book of Margery Kempe*." (11.40c)

Kerouac, Jack

11.105a Sigal, Clancy. "Nihilism's Organization Man." *Universities and Left Review*, 4 (Summer 1958), 59–65.

*S.a.*Breslow (9.74)

Kingsley, Charles

11.106a Morton, A.L. "Parson Lot." In 8.12, 137–43.

S.a. Kettle (8.54)

Kipling, Rudyard

11.107a Dunham, Jack. "Rudyard Kipling Re-Estimated." *MT*, August 1965, 242–48.

11.107b Raskin, Jonah. "Chaos: The Culture of Imperialism," "Kipling's Contrasts," "Portrait of the Artist as Imperialist," "Terror," "Imperia Romana," and "*Kim*: The Middle Way." In 8.78, 14–36, 37–45, 46–71, 72–88, 89–98, 99–125.

S.a. Orwell (8.14), Spender (11.93a)

Klein, A. M.

11.108a Duran, Gillian. "A.M. Klein and Working-Class Poetry." *L&I*, No. 17 (1974), 25–30.

Koestler, Arthur

11.109a Harrington, Michael. "The Unpolitical Political: Koestler Suspended in Mid-Air." *Anvil*, 7 (Winter 1956), 6–8.

11.109b Siegel, Paul. "Arthur Koestler's *Darkness at Noon*: A Marxist Retrospective." *International Socialist Review*, 35 (January 1974), 18–30.

S.a. Garaudy (4.56), Swingewood (6.29), Orwell (8.14), Howe (14.35)

Langland, William

11.110a Aers, David. "Imagination and Ideology in *Piers Plowman*." *L&H*, No. 7 (Spring 1978), 2–19.

S.a. Cantarow (8.26)

Lardner, Ring

11.111a Geismar, Maxwell. "Ring Lardner: Like Something Was Going to Happen." In 14.21, 3–36.

Laurence, Margaret

11.112a Lever, Bernice. "Literature and Canadian Culture: An

Interview with Margaret Laurence," and "Nature Imagery in the Canadian Fiction of Margaret Laurence." *Alive,* No. 41 (1975), 18-19, 20-22.

Lawrence, D. H.

11.113a Sanders, Scott. *D. H. Lawrence: The World of the Major Novels.* New York: Viking Press, 1973.

For a critique, see Efron (11.113o).

11.113b Delany, Paul. *D. H. Lawrence's Nightmare: The Writer and His Circle in the Years of the Great War.* New York: Basic Books, 1978. (NM)

11.113c Caudwell, Christopher. "D. H. Lawrence: A Study of the Bourgeois Artist." In 4.26, 44-72.

11.113d Williams, Raymond. "D. H. Lawrence." In 8.22, 199-215.

11.113e ———. "Social and Personal Tragedy: Tolstoy and Lawrence." In 5.40, 121-38.

11.113f Hall, Stuart. "*Lady Chatterley's Lover*: The Novel and Its Relationship to Lawrence's Work." *NLR,* No. 6 (November-December 1960), 32-35.

11.113g Way, Brian. "Sex and Language: Obscene Words in D. H. Lawrence and Henry Miller." *NLR,* No. 27 (September-October 1964), 66-80.

11.113h Harrison, John R. "D. H. Lawrence." In 14.29, 163-89.

11.113i Eagleton, Terry. "D. H. Lawrence." In 8.68, 191-218.

11.113j Goode, John. "D. H. Lawrence." In *The Twentieth Century.* Ed. Bernard Bergonzi. London: Sphere Books, 1970, 106-52.

11.113k Wasserman, Jerry. "*St. Mawr* and the Search for Community." In 14.70, 113-24.

11.113l Craig, David. "Lawrence and Democracy." In 8.3, 143-67.

11.113m West, Alick. "D. H. Lawrence." In 8.21, 258-83.

11.113n Morris, Tom. "On *Etruscan Places*." *Paunch,* No. 40-41 (April 1975), 8-39.

11.113o Efron, Arthur. "Towards a Dialectic of Sensuality and Work." *Paunch,* No. 44-45 (May 1976), 152-70.

Hints about this dialectic in Marx are taken up by Wilhelm Reich and Lawrence in *The Rainbow.* But Marxists like Scott Sanders (11.113a) cannot cope with Lawrence's emphasis on the involuntary.

11.113p Lindsay, Jack. "D. H. Lawrence and *Women and Love.*" In 4.103, 99–123.

S.a. Pascal (6.23), Craig (11.62d), Ohmann (13.37)

Lawrence, T. E.

11.114a Caudwell, Christopher. "T. E. Lawrence: A Study in Heroism." In 4.26, 20–43.

11.114b Howe, Irving. "T. E. Lawrence: The Problem of Heroism." In 14.37, 294–326.

S.a. Spender (11.93a)

Layton, Irving

11.115a Harvey, John. "Mankind: The Conscience of Poets." *The Marxist Quarterly* (Toronto), No. 9 (Spring 1964), 4–15.

Layton's vision of the artist's role compares unfavorably with A. Y. Jackson's and Evgenii Yevtushenko's.

Comment: N.E. Story, 71–86; reply, Harvey, No. 10 (Summer 1964), 70–79.

11.115b Sommer, Richard. "The Civilised Killer." *Canadian Dimension*, 5 (June–July 1968), 33–35.

Not "furious posturings" on political and sexual matters, but rather the contemplation of life's delights gives Layton's poems what political insight they have to offer.

Leavis, F. R.

11.116a Mulhern, Francis. *The Moment of 'Scrutiny'.* London: New Left Books, 1979.

Analysis of the journal *Scrutiny*, of which Leavis was chief editor for twenty years, until it closed in 1953.

11.116b Morton, A. L. "Culture and Leisure." *Scrutiny*, 1 (March 1933), 324–26.

Reply to Leavis's "Under Which King, Bezonian?"

11.116c Williams, Raymond. "Two Literary Critics: ii. F. R. Leavis." In 4.194, 252–63.

11.116d Anderson, Perry. "Components of the National Culture." In *Student Power.* Ed. Alexander Cockburn and Robin Blackburn. Harmondsworth: Penguin, 1969, 214–84.

The "Literary Criticism" section (268–76) is essentially a respectful but critical analysis of Leavis and *Scrutiny*.

11.116e Milner, Andrew. "Leavis and English Literary Criticism." *Praxis*, No. 2 (Winter 1976), 91–106.

11.116f Lawford, Paul. "Conservative Empiricism in Literary Theory: A Scrutiny of the Work of F. R. Leavis." *RL*, No. 1 (Spring 1976), 12–15; "F. R. Leavis: A Scrutiny: Part II." *RL*, No. 2 (Summer 1976), 9–11.

Lessing, Doris

11.117a Raskin, Jonah. "Doris Lessing at Stony Brook: An Interview." *New American Review*, No. 8 (1970), 166–79.

11.117b Howe, Florence. "A Conversation with Doris Lessing." *Contemporary Literature*, 14 (Autumn 1973), 418–36.

11.117c Swingewood, Alan. "Structure and Ideology in the Novels of Doris Lessing." In 14.50, 38–54.

Lewis, Sinclair

11.118a Whipple, T. K. "Sinclair Lewis." In 9.38, 208–29.

11.118b Cantwell, Robert. "Sinclair Lewis." In 9.36, 92–102.

11.118c Geismar, Maxwell. "Sinclair Lewis: The Cosmic Bourjoyce." In 14.20, 69–150.

11.118d Wharton, Fred. "Sinclair Lewis." *Masses & Mainstream*, 4 (April 1951), 84–94.

11.118e Motylyova, T. "Sinclair Lewis and His Best Novels." In 9.16, 261–84.

Lewis, Wyndham

11.119a Jameson, Fredric. *Fables of Aggression: Wyndham Lewis, the Modernist as Fascist*. Berkeley: University of California Press, 1979.

11.119b Rickword, Edgell. "Wyndham Lewis." In *Scrutinies*, ed. Edgell Rickword. Vol. II. London: Wishart, 1931, 139–61.

11.119c Harrison, John R. "Wyndham Lewis." In 14.29, 77–108.

Lindsay, Jack

11.120a West, Alick. "Jack Lindsay." In 8.20, 185–208.

*11.120b Lindsay, Jack. "Autobiographical Notes." *ZAA*, 3 (1955), 72–74.

11.120c Valentina, Jacques. "Jack Lindsay and Russian Readers." *Soviet Literature*, 1966 No. 2, 170–73.

Lindsay, Vachel

11.121a Whipple, T. K. "Vachel Lindsay." In 9.38, 184–207.

Livesay, Dorothy

11.122a Resnick, Philip. "Ontario Story." *Canadian Dimension*, 6 (July 1969), 38.

Livesay's radical social commentary flows out of real-life experience, unlike Canadian anti-Vietnam poetry. (Review of *Documentaries*.)

11.122b Kreisel, Henry. "The Poet as Radical: Dorothy Livesay in the Thirties." *CV II*, 4 (Winter 1979), 19–21. (NM)

Essay-review of *Right Hand, Left Hand*.

S.a. McKenzie (10.52)

London, Jack

*11.123a Labor, Earl, ed. "Jack London Number." *Modern Fiction Studies*, 22 (Spring 1976).

See especially: Nathaniel Teich on "Marxist Dialectics in Content, Form, Point of View in Jack London's *The Iron Heel*," 85–100, and Howard Lachtman's selected checklist of London criticism, 107–25.

11.123b Barltrop, Robert. *Jack London: The Man, the Writer, the Rebel*. London: Pluto Press, 1976.

11.123c Whipple, T. K. "Jack London—Wonder Boy." In 9.67, 93–104.

11.123d Foner, Philip S. "Jack London: American Rebel." Introd. to *Jack London: American Rebel*. New York: The Citadel Press, 1947, 3–130.

11.123e Geismar, Maxwell. "Jack London: The Short Cut." In 14.22, 137–216.

11.123f Siegel, Paul. "Jack London's *Iron Heel*: Its Significance for Today." *International Socialist Review*, 35 (July–August 1974), 18–29.

11.123g Shields, A. "Why We Honor Jack London." *Political Affairs*, 55 (April 1976), 44–57.

11.123h Beauchamp, Gorman. "*The Iron Heel* and *Looking Backward*: Two Paths to Utopia." *American Literary Realism*, 9 (Autumn 1976), 307–14. (NM)

Lovecraft, Howard Phillips

11.124a Buhle, Paul. "Dystopia as Utopia: Howard Phillips Lovecraft and the Unknown Content of American Horror Literature." In 2.9, 118–31.

McClung, Nellie
11.125a Fairley, Margaret. "Nellie McClung." *New Frontiers*, 5 (Summer 1956), 19-23.

MacDiarmid, Hugh
11.126a Niven, Barbara. "Hugh MacDiarmid's Poetry." *MT*, August 1962, 239-44.

11.126b Arundel, Honor. "MacDiarmid and the Scottish Tradition." In 8.9, 193-98.

11.126c Craig, David. "MacDiarmid the Marxist Poet." In 8.3, 230-53.

11.126d _____ . "A Great Radical: Hugh MacDiarmid, 1892-1978." *MT*, February 1979, 55-60.

S.a. Kocmanová (8.75)

McLachlan, Alexander
11.127a Hopwood, V. G. "A Burns of the Backwoods." *New Frontiers*, 1 (Fall 1952), 31-38.
Compilers misrepresent McLachlan by emphasizing his weak landscape poetry at the expense of his more realistic work.

11.127b Hughes, Ken. "Poet Laureate of Labour." *Canadian Dimension*, 11 (March 1976), 33-40.

MacLeish, Archibald
11.128a Van Ghent, Dorothy. "The Poetry of Archibald MacLeish." *S&S*, 2 (Fall 1938), 500-11.

MacLennan, Hugh
11.129a Lynn, S. "A Canadian Writer and the Modern World." *The Marxist Quarterly* (Toronto), 1 (Spring 1962), 36-43.
MacLennan's *The Watch That Ends the Night* makes the search for truth an inward rather than an outward quest.

11.129b Roberts, Ann. "The Dilemma of Hugh MacLennan." *The Marxist Quarterly* (Toronto), 3 (Autumn 1962), 58-65.
MacLennan's pessimism is contrasted with Gabrielle Roy's optimism.

11.129c Clark, J. Wilson. "Hugh MacLennan's Comprador Outlook." *L&I*, No. 12 (1972), 1-8.

11.129d Duran, Gillian. "Terrorism, Human Nature and Hugh MacLennan's *Return of the Sphinx*." *L&I*, No. 15 (1973), 51-58.

11.129e Mathews, Robin. "Hugh MacLennan: The Nationalist Dilemma." In 10.8, 75–90.

McLuhan, Marshall,

11.130a Finkelstein, Sidney. *Sense and Nonsense of McLuhan.* New York: International Publishers, 1968.

11.130b Baker, Bert. "McLuhanism: The Reply of a Technological Idiot." *MT*, June 1971, 171–75.

11.130c Fekete, John. "Marshall McLuhan: The Critical Theory of Counterrevolution." In 4.47, 135–89.

S.a. Lang (15.113)

MacNeice, Louis

11.131a Heinemann, Margot. "Poetry of the Thirties: Three Left-Wing Poets, Louis MacNeice, John Cornford, Clive Branson." *MT*, November 1976, 343–54.

S.a. Paulin (11.71)

MacQueen, Thomas

11.132a Fairley, Margaret. "Socialist Poet of Upper Canada." *New Frontiers*, 4 (Spring 1955), 34–38.

Mailer, Norman

11.133a Finkelstein, Sidney. "The Existential Trap: Norman Mailer and Edward Albee." *American Dialog*, 2 (February–March 1965), 23–28.

11.133b Nikolyukin, A. N. "Realism and Modernism in the Works of Norman Mailer." In 9.98, 72–87.

S.a. Lukács (4.105), Finkelstein (9.6), Jameson (9.88)

Malamud, Bernard

11.134a Finkelstein, Sidney. "The Anti-Hero of Updike, Bellow, and Malamud." (11.218a)

Marlowe, Christopher

11.135a Henderson, Philip. *Christopher Marlowe.* 1966; Brighton: Harvester Press, 1974.

11.135b Green, Clarence. "Doctor Faustus: Tragedy of Individualism." *S&S*, 10 (Summer 1946), 275–83.

11.135c Greenblatt, Stephen. "Marlowe, Marx and Anti-Semitism." *Critical Inquiry*, 5 (Winter 1978), 291–307.

S.a. Kettle (8.7)

Marvell, Andrew

11.136a Hill, Christopher. "Society and Andrew Marvell." In 8.35, 337-66.

Massinger, Philip

11.137a Knights, L. C. "The Significance of Massinger's Social Comedies." In 14.45, 270-300.

Maugham, W. Somerset

11.138a Jeffrey-Jones, Rhodri. "W. Somerset Maugham: Anglo-American Agent in Revolutionary Russia." *American Quarterly,* 28 (Spring 1976), 90-106. (NM)
Criticizes Maugham's anti-Bolshevik activities in the weeks prior to the Bolshevik revolution of 1917.

Melville, Herman

11.139a James, C. L. R. *Mariners, Renegades and Castaways: The Story of Herman Melville and the World We Live In.* New York: C. L. R. James, 1953.

11.139b _____. *The Old World and the New: Shakespeare, Melville, and Others.* Detroit: Facing Reality Publications, 1971.

11.139c Matthiessen, F. O. "Book Three: Melville." In 9.25, 371-514. (NM)

11.139d Fuentes, Carlos. "Prometheus Unbound." In 2.2, 142-58.

11.139e Oglesby, Carl. "Melville, or Water Consciousness & Its Madness." In 2.8, 123-41.

11.139f Adler, Joyce. "Melville on the White Man's War Against the Indian." *S&S,* 36 (Winter 1972), 417-42.

11.139g _____. "Melville's *Benito Cereno*: Slavery and Violence in the Americas." *S&S,* 38 (Spring 1974), 19-48.

11.139h _____. "*Billy Budd* and Melville's Philosophy of War." *PMLA,* 91 (March 1976), 266-78.

11.139i _____. "Melville's *Typee* and *Omoo*: Of 'Civilized' War on 'Savage' Peace." *MR,* No. 10 (Spring 1978), 85-102.

11.139j Henderson, Harry B. "Melville: Rebellion, Tragedy and Historical Judgment." In 9.21, 127-74.

11.139k Barnett, Louise K. "Bartleby as Alienated Worker." *Studies in Short Fiction,* 11 (Fall 1974), 379-85.

11.139l Franklin, H. Bruce. "Herman Melville: Artist of the Worker's World." In 2.13, 287-309.

A longer version of this article appears as Chapter 2, "The Worker as Criminal and Artist: Herman Melville," in 9.7, 31–70.

11.139m Kaye, Jackie. *"Moby Dick*: Capitalism as Epic." *RL*, No. 1 (Spring 1976), 9–11.

11.139n Ujházy, Maria. "Herman Melville: Social Critic." *ZAA*, 25 (1977), 209–12.

S.a. Barnett (9.17), Zipes (9.30)

Mencken, H. L.

11.140a Geismar, Maxwell. "H. L. Mencken: On the Dock." In 14.20, 3–66.

Meredith, George

11.141a Lindsay, Jack. *George Meredith: His Life and Work.* London: Bodley Head, 1956.

11.141b Goode, John. *"The Egoist*: Anatomy or Striptease." In *Meredith Now.* Ed. Ian Fletcher. New York: Barnes and Noble, 1971, 205–21. Rpt. in George Meredith, *The Egoist.* Ed. Robert M. Adams. New York: Norton, 1979, 502–18.

11.141c Howard, David. "George Meredith: 'Delicate' and 'Epical' Fiction." In 8.52, 131–72.

Middleton, Thomas

11.142a Knights, L. C. "Middleton and the New Social Classes." In 14.45, 256–69.

Mill, John Stuart

11.143a Williams, Raymond. "Mill on Bentham and Coleridge." In 4.194, 65–84.

11.143b Southall, Raymond. "Mill and *Laissez-Faire.*" In 8.17, 159–70.

Miller, Arthur

11.144a Burgum, Edwin Berry. "Playwriting and Arthur Miller." *The Contemporary Reader*, 1 (August 1953), 24–32.

11.144b Baxandall, Lee. "The Theatre of Arthur Miller." *Encore* (London), May–June 1964, 16–19; March–April 1965, 19–23.

S.a. Williams (5.40), Finkelstein (9.6)

Miller, Henry

11.145a Orwell, George. "Inside the Whale." In *The Collected Essays, Journalism and Letters of George Orwell.* Vol. 1. Ed. Sonia Orwell and Ian Angus. 1968; Harmondsworth: Penguin, 1970, 540–78.

Originally published in 1940, this is an excellent essay on Miller's antipolitical stance and its significance.

11.145b Way, Brian. "Sex and Language: Obscene Words in D. H. Lawrence and Henry Miller." (11.113g)

11.145c Finkelstein, Sidney. "Alienation and Rebellion to Nowhere: John Dos Passos and Henry Miller." (11.60e)

Milton, John

11.146a Hill, Christopher. *Milton and the English Revolution.* 1977; Harmondsworth: Penguin, 1979.

11.146b Illo, John. "The Misreading of Milton." *Columbia University Forum*, 8 (Summer 1965), 38–42. Rpt. in 2.2, 178–92.
Areopagitica is a tract for revolution, not toleration.

11.146c Tisch, J. H. "Irregular Genius: Some Aspects of Milton and Shakespeare on the Continent at the End of the Eighteenth Century." In 8.9, 301–24.

11.146d Grossman, Allen. "Milton's Sonnet 'On the Late Massacre in Piedmont': A Note on the Vulnerability of Persons in a Revolutionary Situation." In 2.8, 283–301.
Superb study of historical context and poetics.

11.146e Southall, Raymond. "Paradise Lost and the Puritan Debacle." In 8.43, 113–32.

11.146f Goldstein, Leonard. "The Good Old Cause and Milton's Blank Verse." *ZAA*, 23 (1975), 133–42.

11.146g Wilding, Michael. "Regaining the Radical Milton." In 2.5, 119–44.

11.146h Hodge, Robert. "Satan and the Revolution of the Saints." *L&H*, No. 7 (Spring 1978), 20–33.

Mitchell, W. O.

11.147a Mathews, Robin. "W. O. Mitchell: Epic Comedy." In 10.8, 109–18.

Moodie, Susanna

11.148a Mathews, Robin. "Susanna Moodie: Pink Toryism." In 10.8, 27–44.

More, Thomas

11.149a Kautsky, Karl. *Thomas More and His Utopia.* 1927; New York: Russell and Russell, 1959.

11.149b Ames, Russell. *Citizen Thomas More and His Utopia.* Princeton, N. J.: Princeton University Press, 1949.

11.149c Morton, A. L. "The Island of Saints." In 8.11, 46–77.

11.149d Southall, Raymond. "More's Utopia: The Case for a Palace Revolution." In 8.43, 11–20.

Morris, William.

11.150a Thompson, E. P. *William Morris: Romantic to Revolutionary.* 1955; rev. ed. London: Merlin Press, 1977. Reviewed by Reamy Jansen, *MR*, No. 10 (Spring 1978), 120–26; Michael Scrivener, *Telos*, No. 35 (Spring 1978), 231–37.

11.150b ———— . "Romanticism, Moralism and Utopianism: The Case of William Morris." *NLR*, No. 99 (September–October 1976), 83–111. Rpt. as "Postscript: 1976" in rev. ed. of 11.150a, 763–816.

Review of twenty-one years of Morris scholarship; argument that Marxism has much to learn from Morris's brand of socialism. See Willard Wolfe's "On William Morris," *NLR*, No. 103 (May–June 1977), 94–95, for a critique of Thompson; reply by Thompson, 95–96.

11.150c Lindsay, Jack. *William Morris: Writer.* London: William Morris Society, 1961.

11.150d ———— . *William Morris: His Life and Work.* London: Constable, 1975.

A 400-page version of the earlier pamphlet.

11.150e Henderson, Philip. *William Morris: His Life, Work and Friends.* New York: McGraw-Hill, 1967.

11.150f Meier, Paul. *William Morris: The Marxist Dreamer.* 2 vols. 1972; New York: Humanities Press, 1978. Reviewed by A. L. Morton, *MT*, May 1973, 148–52.

11.150g Hicks, Granville. "Socialism and William Morris." In 8.51, 69–108.

11.150h Morton, A. L. "The Dream of William Morris." In 8.11, 149–82.

11.150i Munby, L. M. "William Morris's Romances and the Society of the Future." *ZAA*, 10 (1962), 56–69.

11.150j Kocmanová, Jessie. "The Socialist Poems of William Morris." *MT*, August 1966, 240–50.

11.150k Goode, John. "Gissing, Morris and English Socialism." (11.75b)

11.150l _____. "William Morris and the Dream of Revolution." In 8.57, 221–80.

Argues that Morris's fiction and poetry constitute a truly revolutionary literature that takes a creatively different direction from the work of Hardy, Gissing, and James.

Murdoch, Iris

11.151a Pearson, Gabriel. "Iris Murdoch and the Romantic Novel." *NLR,* Nos. 13–14 (January–April 1962), 137–45.

Naipaul, V. S.

11.152a McClure, John A. "V. S. Naipaul and the Politics of Despair." *Marxist Perspectives,* No. 1 (Fall 1978), 6–19.

Nashe, Thomas

11.153a Weimann, Robert. "Thomas Nashe and Elizabethan Humanism." *Filologiai Kozlony* (Budapest), 7 (1961), 40–44.

Naughton, Bill

11.154a Gray, Nigel. "A Bit of What You Fancy Does You Good: *Alfie,* Bill Naughton (1966)." In 8.70, 161–94. (NM)

Nelson, Truman

11.155a Nelson, Truman. "On Creating Revolutionary Art and Going Out of Print." In 2.8, 92–110.

11.155b Schafer, William J. "Truman Nelson: Heeding the Voices of Revolution." *MR,* No. 7 (Fall 1976), 66–82.

Newlove, John

11.156a Gervais, C. H. "Alienation in John Newlove's Poetry." *Alive,* No. 41 (1975), 28.

Norris, Frank

11.157a Geismar, Maxwell. "Frank Norris: And the Brute." In 14.22, 3–66.

11.157b Fried, Lewis. "The Golden Brotherhood of *McTeague.*" *ZAA,* 23 (1975), 36–40.

O'Casey, Sean

11.158a Howard, Milton. "Orwell or O'Casey?" (11.162d)

11.158b Ayling, Ronald. "O'Casey's Words Live On." *New World Review,* 34 (November 1966), 52–59.

Sympathetic discussion of O'Casey's allegiance to Russian Communism.

11.158c Lindsay, Jack. "Sean O'Casey as a Socialist Artist." In
4.103, 124–38.

11.158d Mitchell, Jack. "Theatre of Sean O'Casey." *ZAA*, 26
(1978), 28–47.

Odets, Clifford

11.159a Weales, Gerald. *Clifford Odets, Playwright*. New York:
Pegasus, 1971. (NM)

S.a. Siegel (9.101)

O'Hara, Frank

See Boone (13.8)

Olsen, Tillie

11.160a Stimpson, Catherine R. "Tillie Olsen: Witness as Servant."
Polit, 1 (Fall 1977), 1–12.

O'Neill, Eugene

11.161a Whipple, T. K. "Eugene O'Neill." In 9.38, 230–53.

11.161b Lawson, John Howard. "The Tragedy of Eugene O'Neill."
Masses & Mainstream, 7 (March 1954), 7–18.

11.161c Finkelstein, Sidney. "Sociological and Literary Depiction of
Alienation: Marx, Balzac and Eugene O'Neill." In 9.6, 136–64.

11.161d Williams, Raymond. "Private Tragedy: Strindberg, O'Neill,
Tennessee Williams." In 5.40, 106–20.

11.161e Koreneva, M. "Eugene O'Neill and the Traditions of
American Drama." In 9.16, 143–59.

Orwell, George

11.162a Williams, Raymond. *George Orwell*. New York: Viking
Press, 1971.

Extends chapter on Orwell in 4.194.

11.162b Zwerdling, Alex. *Orwell and the Left*. New Haven, Conn.:
Yale University Press, 1974. (NM)

11.162c Deutscher, Isaac. "*1984*: The Mysticism of Cruelty." In
Heretics and Renegades and Other Essays. London: H.
Hamilton, 1955, 35–50.

11.162d Howard, Milton. "Orwell or O'Casey?" *Masses &
Mainstream*, 8 (January 1955), 20–26.

11.162e Howe, Irving. "Orwell: History as Nightmare." In
14.35, 235–51.

11.162f Eagleton, Terry. "George Orwell and the Lower Middle Class Novel." In 8.68, 71–107.

11.162g O'Flinn, J. P. "Orwell on Literature and Society." In 2.12, 603–12.

Orwell's literary criticism constitutes a pioneering attempt to combine social and cultural analysis; it belongs to the heritage of the Left, not the Right.

11.162h _____. "*Animal Farm, 1984* and Socialist Revolution." In 8.13, 14–20.

11.162i Siegel, Paul N. "The Cold War: *1984* Twenty-Five Years After." *Confrontation*, No. 8 (Spring 1974), 148–56. Rpt. as "Rereading Orwell's *1984*" in *International Socialist Review*, 35 (February 1975), 24–27.

11.162j Orr, John. "George Orwell: The Nightmare of the Real." In 14.64, 160–71.

S.a. Morton (8.11)

Osborne, John

11.163a Milne, Tom. "*Luther* and *The Devils*." *NLR*, No. 12 (November–December 1961), 55–58.

11.163b West, Alick. "John Osborne." *Filologiai Kozlony* (Budapest), 9 (1963), 25–28.

Paine, Tom

11.164a Thde, Horst. "The Heirs to Paine's Democratic Tradition." In 8.9, 92–100.

Content and form in Paine; his continuing influence.

Parrington, V. L.

11.165a Smith, Bernard. "Parrington's 'Main Currents'." *The New Republic*, 98 (February 15, 1939), 40–43. Rpt. in *Books That Changed Our Minds*. Ed. Malcolm Cowley and Bernard Smith. New York: Doubleday, Doran & Co., 1939, 179–91.

11.165b Hicks, Granville. "The Critical Principles of V. L. Parrington." *S&S*, 3 (Fall 1939), 443–60.

11.165c Lawson, John Howard. "Parrington and the Search for Tradition." *Mainstream*, 1 (Winter 1947), 23–43.

Pater, Walter

11.166a West, Alick. "Walter Pater." In 8.19, 11–23; rpt. in 8.21, 229–41.

11.166b Oakley, John. "The Boundaries of Hegemony: Pater." In 14.5, 18–29.

Pearse, Padraic

11.167a Clausen, Christopher. "Padraic Pearse: The Revolutionary as Artist." *Shaw Review*, 19 (May 1976), 83–92. (NM)

Plath, Sylvia

11.168a Zollman, Sol. "Sylvia Plath and Imperialist Culture." *L&I*, No. 2 (Summer 1969), 11–22.

11.168b Howe, Irving. "The Plath Celebration: A Partial Dissent." In 14.38, 158–69.

Poe, Edgar Allen

11.169a Harap, Louis. "Edgar Allen Poe and Journalism." *ZAA*, 19 (1971), 160–81.

11.169b ———. "Poe and Dostoevsky: A Case of Affinity." In 2.13, 271–85.

11.169c ———. "The Pre-Established Affinities of Poe and Baudelaire." *Praxis*, No. 2 (Winter 1976), 119–28.

S.a. Zipes (9.30)

Pope, Alexander

11.170a Delany, Sheila. "Sex and Politics in Pope's 'Rape of the Lock'." In 2.13, 173–90.

Pound, Ezra

11.171a Schlauch, Margaret. "The Anti-Humanism of Ezra Pound." *S&S*, 13 (Summer 1949), 258–69.

11.171b Harrison, John R. "Ezra Pound." In 14.29, 111–42.

11.171c Howe, Irving. "The Case of Ezra Pound." In 14.38, 109–20.

11.171d Rabate, Jean-Michel. "'Sounds Pound': History and Ideology in the China Cantos." In 9.4, 21–42.

Priestley, J. B.

11.172a West, Alick. "J. B. Priestley." In 8.20, 155–83.

Pynchon, Thomas

See: Levine (6.16)

Ransom, John Crowe

11.173a Fekete, John. "John Crowe Ransom: The Critical Theory of Defensive Reaction." In 4.47, 43–103.

Read, Herbert

11.174a West, Alick. "Herbert Read: Surrealism." In 8.19; rpt. in 8.21, 47–53.

Richards, I. A.

11.175a West, Alick. "I. A. Richards." In 8.19; rpt. in 8.21, 54–65.

11.175b Williams, Raymond. "Two Literary Critics: i. I. A. Richards." In 4.194, 239–46.

Richardson, John

11.176a Mathews, Robin. "John Richardson: The Wacousta Factor." In 10.8, 13–25.

Richardson, Samuel

11.177a Van Ghent, Dorothy. "On *Clarissa Harlowe* [*sic.*]." In 14.74, 45–63.

Clarissa embodies the dream of her class and the myths of a Puritan-capitalistic culture.

11.177b Watt, Ian. "Love and the Novelist: *Pamela*," and "Richardson as Novelist: *Clarissa*." In 6.31, 140–79, 216–48. (NM)

11.177c Hill, Christopher. "Clarissa Harlowe and Her Times." In 8.35, 367–94.

Roberts, Charles G. D.

11.178a Mathews, Robin. "Charles G. D. Roberts: Father of Canadian Poetry." In 10.8, 45–62.

Robinson, Edwin Arlington

11.179a Whipple, T. K. "Edwin Arlington Robinson." In 9.38, 45–69.

11.179b Howe, Irving. "A Grave and Solitary Voice: An Appreciation of Edwin Arlington Robinson." In 14.38, 96–108.

Roethke, Theodore

11.180a Lecourt, Jean-Philippe. "Theodore Roethke: The Inner Wilderness and the Barrier of Ideology." In 9.4, 43–64. (NM)

Rossetti, Dante Gabriel

11.181a LeRoy, Gaylord. "Dante Gabriel Rossetti." In 8.56, 121–47.

Roth, Philip

11.182a Segal, Alan. "*Portnoy's Complaint* and the Sociology of Literature." *British Journal of Sociology*, 22 (September 1971), 257–68. (NM)

11.182b Howe, Irving. "Philip Roth Reconsidered." In 14.38, 137–57.

Ruskin, John

11.183a Hicks, Granville. "The Social Criticism of John Ruskin." *International Literature*, 1938, No. 2, 78–80.

11.183b LeRoy, Gaylord. "John Ruskin." In 8.56, 86–103.

11.183c Morton, A. L. "The Conscience of John Ruskin." In 8.12, 144–49.

11.183d Lindsay, Jack. "John Ruskin." In 2.5, 91–118.

S.a. Williams (4.194)

Rutherford, Mark

11.184a Morton, A. L. "The Last Puritan." In 8.10, 49–57.

11.184b Swann, Charles. "Evolution and Revolution: Politics and Form in *Felix Holt* and *The Revolution in Tanner's Lane.*" (11.62h)

Salinger, J. D.

11.185a Geismar, Maxwell. "J. D. Salinger: The Wise Child and the *New Yorker* School of Fiction." In 14.23, 195–209.

11.185b Giles, Barbara. "The Lonely War of J. D. Salinger." *Mainstream*, 12 (February 1959), 1–13.

11.185c Way, Brian. "*Franny and Zooey* and J. D. Salinger." *NLR*, No. 15 (May–June 1962), 72–82.

11.185d Larner, Jeremy. "Salinger's Audience: An Explanation." *Partisan Review*, 29 (Fall 1962), 294–98.

11.185e Finkelstein, Sidney. "Cold War, Religious Revival and Family Alienation: William Styron, J. D. Salinger and Edward Albee." (11.206b)

11.185f Panova, Vera. "On J. D. Salinger's Novel." In 9.98, 4–10.

11.185g Ohmann, Carol, and Richard Ohmann. "Reviewers, Critics, and *The Catcher in the Rye.*" *Critical Inquiry*, 3 (Autumn 1976), 15–37.

S.a. Breslow (9.74)

Sandburg, Carl

11.186a Whipple, T. K. "Carl Sandburg." In 9.38, 161–83.

11.186b Arvin, Newton. "Carl Sandburg." In 9.36, 67–73.

Saroyan, William

11.187a Burgum, Edwin Berry. "The Lonesome Young Man on the Flying Trapeze." In 6.3, 260–71.

Scott, Walter

11.188a Lukács, Georg. "The Classic Form of the Historical Novel: 2. Sir Walter Scott." In 6.19, 30–63.

11.188b Kettle, Arnold. "Scott: *The Heart of the Midlothian.*" In 8.6, 114–32.

11.188c Diakonova, Nina. "The Aesthetics of Sir Walter Scott." *ZAA*, 24 (1976), 5–21.

11.188d Swann, Charles. "Past Into Present: Scott, Galt, and the Historical Novel." *L&H*, No. 3 (March 1976), 65–82.

S.a. Levine (6.16)

Shakespeare, William

*11.189a Folsom, Michael B. *Shakespeare: A Marxist Bibliography.* 1965; 2nd rev. ed. New York: The American Institute for Marxist Studies, 1971.

11.189b *Shakespeare Jahrbuch* (Weimar, 1865–). Annual collection of essays, some in English.

*11.189c "Marxist Interpretations of Shakespeare." *The Shakespeare Newsletter*, 24 (September–November 1974).

Special issue includes brief articles by Paul N. Siegel, Louis Marder, Robert Weimann; compendium of extracts from Marxist analyses of individual plays; brief bibliography.

11.189d "Towards a Marxist Understanding of Shakespeare: A Symposium." *S&S*, 41 (Spring 1977), 1–68.

Selected papers from the 1976 International Shakespeare Association Conference: Robert Weimann, Introduction, "Shakespeare and Marxist Methodology," 2–6; Margot Heinemann, "Shakespearean Contradictions and Social Change," 7–16; Thomas Metscher, "Shakespeare in the Context of Renaissance Europe," 17–24; Annette T. Rubinstein, "Bourgeois Equality in Shakespeare," 25–35; Michael P. Hamburger, "*Gestus* and the Popular Theatre," 36–42; Bruce Ehrlich, "Shakespeare's Colonial Metaphor: On the Social Function of Theatre in *The Tempest*," 43–65.

11.189e Finkelstein, Sidney. *Who Needs Shakespeare?* New York: International Publishers, 1973.

Analyses of the major plays.

11.189f Shanker, Sidney. *Shakespeare and the Uses of Ideology.* The Hague: Mouton, 1975. (NM)

11.189g Levin, Harry. *Shakespeare and the Revolution of the Times.* New York: Oxford University Press, 1976. (NM)

11.189h Weimann, Robert. *Shakespeare and the Popular Tradition in the Theater: Studies in the Social Dimension of Dramatic Form and Function.* Ed. Robert Schwartz. Baltimore: Johns Hopkins University Press, 1978. Includes discussion of ritual and mimesis; folk plays, mystery plays, moralities, and interludes; Elizabethan society, theater, and language; Shakespeare's drama.

11.189i Barber, Charles. "Prince Hal, *Henry V,* and the Tudor Monarchy." In *The Morality of Art: Essays Presented to G. Wilson Knight.* Ed. D. W. Jefferson. New York: Barnes & Noble, 1969, 67–75.

11.189j Stone, William B. "Literature and Class Ideology: *Henry IV Part One.*" *CE,* 33 (May 1972), 891–900.

11.189k Siegel, Paul N. "Falstaff and His Social Milieu." *Shakespeare Jahrbuch,* No. 110 (1974), 139–45.

11.189l _____ . "Marx, Engels and the Historical Criticism of Shakespeare." *Shakespeare Jahrbuch,* No. 113 (1977), 124–34.

11.189m _____ . "Richard III as Businessman." *Shakespeare Jahrbuch,* No. 114 (1978), 101–106.

11.189n _____ . "Monarchy, Aristocracy and Bourgeoisie in Shakespeare's History Plays." *S&S,* 42 (Winter 1978–79), 478–82.

11.189o Stribrny, Zdenek. "The Idea and Image of Time in Shakespeare's Early Histories." *Shakespeare Jahrbuch,* No. 110 (1974), 129–38.

11.189p _____ . "The Idea and Image of Time in Shakespeare's Second Historical Tetralogy." *Shakespeare Jahrbuch,* No. 111 (1975), 51–66.

11.189q Schlosser, Anselm. "Dialectic in *The Merchant of Venice.*" *ZAA,* 23 (1975), 5–11.

11.189r O'Flinn, Paul. "William Shakespeare and More Original Sin," and "Capitalism, Competition and *King Lear.*" In 8.13, 67–72, 73–79.

11.189s Krieger, Elliott. "The Dialectics of Shakespeare's Comedies." *MR,* No. 7 (Fall 1976), 83–89.

11.189t _____ . "The Quality of Persons and the Time: *Twelfth Night.*" *ZAA,* 25 (1977), 317–33.

11.189u Delany, Paul. "*King Lear* and the Decline of Feudalism." *PMLA*, 92 (May 1977), 429–40.

11.189v Barker, Clive. "Marxist Interpretations of Shakespeare: A Director's Comments." *Shakespeare Jahrbuch*, No. 114 (1978), 115–22.

S.a. Kettle (8.7), Lewis (8.96), Goldstein (11.39b), Southall (11.99b), James (11.139b), Tisch (11.146c), Davis (12.8), Kogan (12.19)

Shaw, George Bernard

11.190a West, Alick. *George Bernard Shaw: A Good Man Fallen Among Fabians*. New York: International Publishers, 1950.

11.190b Caudwell, Christopher. "George Bernard Shaw: A Study of the Bourgeois Superman." In 4.26, 1–19.

11.190c Hobshawn, Eric J. "Bernard Shaw's Socialism." *S&S*, 11 (Fall 1947), 305–26.

11.190d Kettle, Arnold. "Bernard Shaw and the New Spirit." In 8.2, 209–28.

11.190e Britain, I. M. "Bernard Shaw, Ibsen, and the Ethics of English Socialism." *Victorian Studies*, 21 (Spring 1978), 381–401.

Shelley, Percy Bysshe

11.191a Aveling, Eleanor, and Edward Aveling. *Shelley's Socialism*. 1888; London: Journeyman Press, 1978.

11.191b Cameron, Kenneth Neill. *The Young Shelley: Genesis of a Radical*. 1940; New York: Collier, 1962.

11.191c ———. *Shelley and His Circles, 1773–1822*. Cambridge, Mass.: Harvard University Press, 1961.

11.191d ———. *Shelley: The Golden Years*. Cambridge, Mass.: Harvard University Press, 1974.

11.191e Mathews, G. M. *Shelley*. Harlow, Essex: Longman, 1970.

11.191f Wojcik, Manfred. "In Defense of Shelley." *ZAA*, 11 (1963), 143–88.

S.a. Bronowski (7.4)

Sidney, Philip

11.192a Danby, John E. "Sidney's Arcadia: The Great House Romance," and "Sidney and Late-Shakespearian Romance." In 8.29, 46–73, 74–107.

S.a. Bronowski (7.4), Siegel (7.23), Jakobson (13.23)

Sillitoe, Alan

11.193a Prince, Rod. "Saturday Night and Sunday Morning." *NLR*, No. 6 (November–December 1960), 14–17.

11.193b Klotz, Gunther. "Alan Sillitoe's Heroes." In 8.9, 259–63.

11.193c Craig, David. "Sillitoe and the Roots of Anger." In 8.3, 270–85.

11.193d Gray, Nigel. "Life Is What You Make It: *Saturday Night and Sunday Morning*, Alan Sillitoe (1958)." In 8.70, 103–32. (NM)

11.193e Sabine, Nathan. "The Proper Subject of *Saturday Night and Sunday Morning*," *ZAA,* 24 (1976), 57–70.

Sinclair, Upton

11.194a Dell, Floyd. *Upton Sinclair: A Study in Social Protest.* 1927; New York: AMS Press, 1973.

11.194b Cantwell, Robert. "Upton Sinclair." In 9.36, 37–47.

11.194c Gilenson, B. "A Socialist of the Emotions: Upton Sinclair." In 9.16, 199–222.

Sitwell, Edith

11.195a Lindsay, Jack. "Edith Sitwell." *American Dialog*, 2, No. 1 (1965), 33–34.

Smith, Herbert

11.196a Crepon, Carl-Thomas. "Artistic Techniques in Herbert Smith's Novels." In 8.9, 254–58.
Assessment of the strengths and weaknesses of this contemporary proletarian writer.

Smollett, Tobias

11.197a Punter, David. "Smollett and the Logic of Domination." *L&H*, No. 2 (October 1975), 60–83.

11.197b Southall, Raymond. "The Politics of Sensibility." In 8.17, 36–51.

Snow, C. P.

11.198a Willetts, Ron. "A World Without a Hero: A Preliminary Comment on the Writings of C. P. Snow." *MT*, March 1961, 80–86.

Spender, Stephen
See Brown (8.82)

Spenser, Edmund

11.199a Siegel, Paul. "Spenser and the Calvinist View of Life." *Studies in Philology*, 41 (April 1944), 201–22.

11.199b Green, P. "Spenser and the Masses: Social Commentary in *The Faerie Queene.*" *Journal of the History of Ideas*, 35 (September 1974), 389–406.

S.a. Siegel (7.23), Cantarow (8.26)

Stein, Gertrude

11.200a Wilson, Edmund. "Gertrude Stein." In 9.68, 237–56.

11.200b Burgum, Edwin Berry. "The Genius of Miss Gertrude Stein." In 6.3, 157–83.

S.a. McCaffery (13.33)

Steinbeck, John

11.201a Whipple, T. K. "Steinbeck: Through a Glass Darkly." In 9.67, 105–11.

11.201b Burgum, Edwin Berry. "The Fickle Sensibility of John Steinbeck." In 6.3, 272–91.

11.201c Geismar, Maxwell. "John Steinbeck: Of Wrath or Joy." In 14.21, 237–70.

11.201d Mendelson, M. "From *The Grapes of Wrath* to *The Winter of Our Discontent.*" In 9.16, 411–26.

Stephanson, Stephan G.

11.202a Milnes, H. "Stephen G. Stephanson." *New Frontiers*, 2 (Fall 1953), 1–7.

Appreciation of this unknown late nineteenth-century (1853–1927) Canadian poet.

Stevens, Wallace.

11.203a Howe, Irving. "Wallace Stevens: Another Way of Looking at the Blackbird." In 14.36, 158–67.

Stevenson, Philip

*11.204a Maltz, Albert. "In Memoriam Philip Stevenson (Lars Lawrence) 1896–1965." *ZAA*, 14 (1966), 377–80.

A Stevenson bibliography by Eberhard Bruning follows.

Storey, David.

11.205a Gray, Nigel. "Show Them You Can Take It: *This Sporting Life*, David Storey (1960)." In 8.70, 135–59. (NM)

Styron, William

11.206a Geismar, Maxwell. "William Styron: The End of Innocence." In 14.23, 239–50.

11.206b Finkelstein, Sidney. "Cold War, Religious Revival and Family Alienation: William Styron, J. D. Salinger and Edward

Albee." In 9.6, 211–42.

11.206c Landor, M. "Centaur-Novels." (11.16c)

Swift, Jonathan

11.207a Morton, A. L. "The Madness of Swift," and "Mr. Crusoe and Mr. Gulliver." In 8.11, 21–32, 33–40.

11.207b Magennis, John. "Jonathan Swift." *Irish Review*, October 1945, 3–4.

11.207c Kott, Jan. "*Gulliver's Travels*: The Philosophical Journey." *Arena* (London), 2 (February–March 1951), 28–35.
Swift's realism foreshadows socialist realism.

11.207d West, Alick. "Jonathan Swift: Satire and Revolution." In 8.21, 242–58.

11.207e Southall, Raymond. "*Gulliver's Travels*: Swift and the Enormities of Commonsense." In 8.17, 18–35.

Swinburne, A. C.

See Bronowski (7.4)

Tennyson, Alfred

11.208a Garman, Douglas. "Tennyson and His Age." *Left Review* (London), 2 (August 1936), 570–79.
A thorough and useful assessment.

11.208b Eagleton, Terry. "Politics and Sexuality in 'The Princess' and 'In Memoriam'." In 14.6, 97–106.

Thackeray, William Makepeace

11.209a Kettle, Arnold. "Thackeray: *Vanity Fair*." In 8.6, 171–87.

11.209b Adam, Ian W. "Society as Novelist." (11.29a)

Thomas, Edward

11.210a Smith, Stan. "A Language Not To Be Betrayed: Language, Class and History in the Work of Edward Thomas." *L&H*, No. 4 (Autumn 1976), 56–80.

Thomson, James

11.211a LeRoy, Gaylord. "James Thomson." In 8.56, 104–20.

Thoreau, Henry David

11.212a Matthiessen, F. O. "Book One: From Emerson to Thoreau." (11.64a)

11.212b Sillen, Samuel. "Thoreau in Today's America." *Masses & Mainstream*, 7 (December 1954), 1–9. Rpt. in *Looking Forward*. New York: International Publishers, 1954, 153–63.

11.212c Smith, Edwin S. "A Thoreau for Today." *Mainstream*, 13

(April 1960), 1-24; 13 (May 1960), 42-55.
11.212d Lynd, Staughton. "Henry Thoreau: The Admirable Radical." *Liberation*, 7 (February 1963), 21-26.
See also Truman Nelson's response, 8 (April 1963), 23-25.
11.212e Rubinstein, Annette T. "Emerson, Thoreau and Jacksonian Democracy." (11.64c)
Traven, B.
11.213a Baumann, Michael L. *B. Traven: An Introduction.* Albuquerque: University of New Mexico Press, 1976. (NM) Challenges Miller's view (11.213d) and calls Traven a "humanistic or Christian anarchist"; analysis of *The Death Ship* is central.
11.213b Stone, Judy. *The Mystery of B. Traven.* Los Altos, Cal.: William Kaufmann, 1977.
Mostly biography, but some analysis of Traven's work, plus a twenty-page sampler from the novels.
11.213c Powell, Lawrence Clark. "Who Is B. Traven?" *New Masses*, 28 (August 2, 1938), 22-23. Rpt. in 9.58, 301-306.
11.213d Miller, Charles H. "B. Traven, Pure Proletarian Writer." In 9.54, 114-33. (NM)
11.213e Raskin, Jonah. "Labor, Mystery and Rebellion: The Story of B. Traven." *Liberation*, 20 (July-August 1977), 18-20, 30.
Part of a forthcoming book on Traven.
Tressell, Robert
11.214a Ball, F. C. *Tressell of Mugsborough.* London: Lawrence and Wishart, 1951.
11.214b ———— . *One of the Damned: Life and Times of Robert Tressell.* London: Weidenfeld and Nicolson, 1973.
Deals with Tressell's life in greater detail than the earlier work and uses correspondence hitherto unavailable.
11.214c Beeching, Jack. "The Uncensoring of *The Ragged Trouser'd Philanthropists.*" *Marxist Quarterly* (London), 2 (October 1955), 217-29.
11.214d Mitchell, John B. "*The Ragged Trouser'd Philanthropists*: Cornerstone of a Proletarian Literary Culture and of Socialist Realism in English Literature." *ZAA*, 10 (1962), 33-55.
11.214e Webb, Igor. "'What Culture Is Appropriate to the Worker?': Two English Working-Class Novelists: Robert

Tressell and Jack Common." *RT*, No. 1 (Winter 1975–76), 10–15.

Trilling, Lionel

11.215a Landor, M. "Centaur-Novels." (11.16c)

Trumbo, Dalton

11.216a Kriegel, Leonard. "Dalton Trumbo's *Johnny Got His Gun*." In 9.54, 106–13. (NM)

Twain, Mark

11.217a Foner, Philip S. *Mark Twain: Social Critic*. New York: International Publishers, 1958.

A "detailed examination of Mark Twain's thinking on a wide variety of social, political and economic issues."

11.217b Neider, Charles. *Mark Twain and the Russians: An Exchange*. New York: American Century, 1960.

Debate on Twain between Neider and Soviet critic Y. Bereznitsky.

11.217c Egan, Michael. *Mark Twain's Huckleberry Finn: Race, Class and Society*. London: Sussex University Press, 1977.

11.217d Arvin, Newton. "Mark Twain: 1835–1935." *The New Republic*, 83 (June 13, 1935), 125–27.

11.217e Dinamov, Sergei. "The Satire and Humor of Mark Twain: A Soviet View of an American Classic." *International Literature*, 1935, No. 5, 91–95.

11.217f Remes, Carol. "The Heart of Huckleberry Finn." *Masses & Mainstream*, 8 (November 1955), 8–16.

S.a. Henderson (9.21)

Updike, John

11.218a Finkelstein, Sidney. "The Anti-Hero of Updike, Bellow and Malamud." *American Dialog*, 7 (Spring 1972), 12–14, 30.

11.218b Landor, M. "Centaur-Novels." (11.16c)

11.218c Mendelson, M. O. "Social Criticism in the Works of Updike, Styron and Trilling." In 9.98, 62–70.

Almost exclusively on Updike's *Couples*.

Voynich, E. L.

11.219a Kettle, Arnold. "E. L. Voynich: A Forgotten English Novelist." *Essays in Criticism*, 7 (April 1957), 163–74.

Waterhouse, Keith

11.220a Gray, Nigel. "Laugh and the World Laughs With You: *Billy*

Liar, Keith Waterhouse (1959)." In 8.70, 49–72. (NM)
Waugh, Evelyn
11.221a Eagleton, Terry. "Evelyn Waugh and the Upper-Class Novel." In 8.68, 33–70.
S.a. Lucas (8.97)
Wells, H. G.
11.222a Kagarlitsky, J. *The Life and Thought of H. G. Wells.* London: Sidgwick and Jackson, 1966.
11.222b Caudwell, Christopher. "H. G. Wells: A Study in Utopianism." In 4.26, 73–95.
11.222c Arnot, R. Page. "Retrospect on H. G. Wells." *Modern Quarterly*, 2 (Summer 1947), 196–207.
S.a. Morton (8.11)
Wesker, Arnold
11.223a Hoffman, Ursula. "What Does Arnold Wesker Mean?" In 8.9, 237–47.
West, Nathanael
11.224a Ujházy, Maria. "The Satire of Nathanael West." *ZAA*, 26 (1978), 221–31.
Wharton, Edith
11.225a Howe, Irving. "Edith Wharton: Convention and the Demons of Modernism." In 14.38, 122–36.
Wheeler, T. M.
11.226a Seehase, George. "*Sunshine and Shadow* and the Structure of Chartist Fiction." *ZAA*, 21/2 (1973), 126–36.
S.a. Mitchell (8.59)
Whiting, John
11.227a Milne, Tom. "*Luther* and *The Devils*." (11.163a)
Whitman, Walt
11.228a Arvin, Newton. *Whitman.* 1938; New York: Russell and Russell, 1969.
11.228b Sillen, Samuel. Introd. to *Walt Whitman: Poet of American Democracy.* 1944; New York: International Publishers, 1955, 11–46.
11.228c Spier, Leonard. "Walt Whitman." *International Literature*, 1935, No. 9, 72–89.
11.228d Stevenson, Philip. "Walt Whitman's Democracy." *New Masses*, 27 (June 14, 1938), 129–33.

11.228e Matthiessen, F. O. "Book Four: Whitman." In 9.25, 517–656. (NM)

11.228f Mirsky, Dimitri. "Whitman: Poet of American Democracy." In *Walt Whitman Abroad*. Ed. Gay Wilson Allen. Syracuse, N.Y.: Syracuse University Press, 1955, 169–85.

11.228g "Walt Whitman, 1819–1969." *American Dialog*, 5 (Spring–Summer 1969).
Special issue includes articles and poetry by Abe Capek, Langston Hughes, Walter Lowenfels, and other American and European writers.

Wiebe, Rudy

11.229a Tefs, Wayne. "Where Is Your Voice Coming From, Rudy Wiebe?" *Canadian Dimension*, 13, No. 2 (1978), 51–52.
Considers Wiebe's significance on the occasion of the publication of *The Scorched Wood People*.

Wilde, Oscar

11.230a Hicks, Granville. "Oscar Wilde and the Cult of Art." In 8.51, 217–60.

11.230b LeRoy, Gaylord. "Oscar Wilde." In 8.56, 148–67.

11.230c West, Alick. "Oscar Wilde." In 8.20, 123–53.

Williams, Tennessee

11.231a Williams, Raymond. "Private Tragedy: Strindberg, O'Neill, Tennessee Williams." (11.161d)

Williams, William Carlos

11.232a Newman, Charles Henry. "How Objective is Objectivism?" *Dynamo*, 1 (Summer 1934), 26–29.

Wolfe, Thomas

11.233a Burgum, Edwin Berry. "Thomas Wolfe's Discovery of America." In 6.3, 302–21.

11.233b Geismar, Maxwell. "Thomas Wolfe: The Unfound Door." In 14.21, 187–235.

11.233c Stevens, Virginia. "Thomas Wolfe's America." *Mainstream*, 11 (January 1958), 11–24.

11.233d Capek, Abe. "The Development of Thomas Wolfe in the Light of His Letters." *ZAA*, 10 (1962), 162–78.

Wollstonecraft, Mary

11.234a James, R. "On the Reception of Mary Wollstonecraft's *A Vindication of the Rights of Women*." *Journal of the History of*

Ideas, 39 (April–June 1978), 293–302. (NM)

Woolf, Virginia

11.235a Hawthorn, Jeremy. *Virginia Woolf's Mrs. Dalloway: A Study In Alienation*. London: Chatto and Windus, 1975.

11.235b Burgum, Edwin Berry. "Virginia Woolf and the Empty Room." In 6.3, 120–39.

11.235c Blanchard, Margaret. "Socialization in *Mrs. Dalloway*." In 2.11, 287–305.
Comment on the article by Elaine Reuben, 305–307.

11.235d Bell, Barbara Currier, and Carol Ohmann. "Virginia Woolf's Criticism: A Polemical Preface." In *Feminist Literary Criticism: Explorations in Theory*. Ed. Josephine Donovan. Lexington: University of Kentucky Press, 1975, 48–60.

11.235e Showalter, Elaine. "Virginia Woolf and the Flight Into Androgyny." In 14.69, 263–97.

11.235f Zwerdling, Alex. "Mrs. Dalloway and the Social System." *PMLA*, 92 (January 1977), 69–82. (NM)

11.235g Barrett, Michele. "Towards a Sociology of Virginia Woolf Criticism." In 14.50, 145–60.
Finds a consistent political feminism in Woolf, although one somewhat impaired by elements of mysticism.

11.235h Marcus, Jane. "Tintinnabulations." *Marxist Perspectives*, No. 5 (Spring 1979), 144–67.
A review-essay of recent studies of Woolf, from a radical-feminist perspective.

Wordsworth, William

11.236a Danby, John E. *The Simple Wordsworth: Studies in the Poems 1797–1907*. New York: Barnes & Noble, 1961.

11.236b ———. *William Wordsworth: The Prelude and Other Poems*. London: Edward Arnold, 1963.

11.236c Douglas, Wallace C. "The Problem of Wordsworth's Conservatism." *S&S*, 12 (Fall 1948), 387–99.

11.236d Kiernan, V. G. "Wordsworth and the People." In *Democracy and the Labour Movement*. Ed. John Saville. London: Lawrence and Wishart, 1956. Rpt. in 2.3, 161–206.

11.236e Greenleaf, Richard. "Emerson and Wordsworth." (11.64b)

11.236f Glen, Heather. "The Poet in Society: Blake and Wordsworth on London." (11.19h)

11.236g Friedman, Michael H. "Wordsworth's Grasmere: A Rentier's Vision." *Polit*, No. 1 (Fall 1977), 35–59.

11.236h Southall, Raymond. "The Natural World of Wordsworth." In 8.17, 76–104.

S.a. Bronowski (7.4)

Wright, Richard

11.237a Burgum, Edwin Berry. "The Promise of Democracy in Richard Wright's *Native Son*," and "The Art of Richard Wright's Short Stories." In 6.3, 223–40, 241–59.

11.237b Kennedy, James G. "The Content and Form of *Native Son*." In 2.11, 269–83.
Comment on article by Annette Conn, 284–86.

11.237c Siegel, Paul N. "The Conclusion of Richard Wright's *Native Son*." *PMLA*, 89 (May 1974), 517–23.

11.237d Orlova, R. "Richard Wright: Writer and Prophet." In 9.16, 384–410.

11.237e Robinson, Cedric. "The Emergent Marxism of Richard Wright's Ideology." *Race and Class*, 19 (Winter 1978), 221–37.

S.a. Green (9.86), Howe (14.36)

Wyatt, Thomas

11.238a Southall, Raymond. *The Courtly Maker*. Oxford: Basil Blackwell, 1964.
An extensive and detailed study of Wyatt and the courtly love convention.

Yeats, W. B.

11.239a Kahn, Derek. "W. B. Yeats." *Left Review* (London), 2 (March 1936), 252–58.

11.239b O'Brien, Conor Cruise. "Passion and Cunning: An Essay on the Politics of W. B. Yeats." In *In Excited Reverie*. Ed. A. Norman Jeffares and K. G. W. Cross. London: Macmillan, 1965, 207–78. (NM)
A detailed and convincing refutation of the myth of the apolitical Yeats.

11.239c ———. "Yeats and Irish Politics." In 14.39, 303–17.

11.239d Harrison, John R. "W. B. Yeats." In 14.29, 39–73.

S.a. Barrell (8.1), Orwell (8.14)

-12-

Teaching English

12.1 Berland J., and D. McGill. "Literacy: The Atrophy of Confidence—Part One." *Working Teacher*, 1 (Summer 1977), 18–26; "Part Two," 1 (Fall 1977), 29–34. Rpt., abridged, as "The Literacy Crisis: Beyond Banality and 'Basics' and Down to Business." *This Magazine*, 12 (March 1978), 12–14.

12.2 Bowles, Samuel, and Herbert Gintis. *Schooling in Capitalist America: Educational Reform and the Contradictions of Economic Life.* New York: Basic Books, 1976. Reviewed by Louis Kampf and Wayne O'Neil, *RT*, No. 5 (July 1977), 43–48.

12.3 Cannon, Ellen, and Carey Kaplan. "An Experiment with Innovative Teaching in a Small Conservative Liberal Arts College." *RT*, No. 4 (March 1977), 17–20.

12.4 Cantarow, Ellen. "The Social Uses of Literature: Reclaiming Our Roots." *RT*, No. 3 (November 1976), 34–38.

12.5 Castles, Stephen, and Wiebke Wurtenberg. *The Education of the Future: An Introduction to the Theory and Practice of Socialist Education.* London: Pluto Press, 1979.

12.6 Craig, David, and Margot Heinemann, eds. *Experiments in English Teaching: New Work in Higher and Further Education.* London: Edward Arnold, 1976. (M/NM)
See especially: Kettle and Martin on the open university, Hawthorn on communication studies, Green on cultural studies at Birmingham, and Gray on teaching creative writing.

12.7 Davies, Tony. "Education, Ideology and Literature." *RL*, No. 7 (1978), 4–15.
"Literature" as an area of study is an ideological category,

deriving from Arnold and others.

12.8 Davis, Lennard, et al. "A Guide to Marxist Teaching in Traditional Courses." *RT*, No. 7 (March 1978), 1-17; No. 8 (May 1978), 31-34; No. 9 (September 1978), 26-29.

Davis, Brent Harold, Richard Ohmann, Barry Phillips, and Jack Weston discuss the period course (eighteenth-century British), the major author course (Shakespeare), courses in myth (romance and comedy), genre, film and the western, and freshman composition.

*12.9 Dieterich, Daniel, ed. *Teaching About Doublespeak*. Urbana, Ill.: NCTE, 1976.

See especially: Richard Ohmann, "Doublespeak and Ideology in Advertisements: A Kit for Teachers," and the useful general guide to classroom resources.

12.10 Dixon, Bob. *Catching Them Young*. Vol. 1: *Sex, Race and Class in Children's Fiction*. Vol. 2: *Political Ideas in Children's Fiction*. London: Pluto Press, 1977.

Companion volumes designed for the rank-and-file teacher and concerned parent struggling against right-wing bias in children's literature.

12.11 Elshtain, Jean Bethke. "The Social Relations of the Classroom: A Moral and Political Perspective." *Telos*, No. 27 (Spring 1976), 97-110.

Argues that Marxists should avoid pedagogies influenced by popular psychology.

12.12 Franklin, H. Bruce. "The Teaching of Literature in the Highest Academies of the Empire." In 2.12, 548-57. Rpt. in 12.18, 101-29.

Reprint includes Franklin's rebuttal to responses to original article in *CE*.

12.13 Harold, Brent. "Beyond Student-Centered Teaching: The Dialectical Materialist Form of a Literature Course." In 2.11, 200-12.

Comment on article by Harold Brent, 212-14.

12.14 Jelinek, Estelle. "Teaching Women's Autobiographies." *CE*, 38 (September 1976), 32-45.

12.15 Kampf, Louis. "The Scandal of Literary Scholarship." In *The*

Dissenting Academy. Ed. Theodore Roszak. New York: Vintage, 1968, 43–61.

12.16 ———. " 'It's Alright, Ma (I'm Only Bleeding)': Literature and Language in the Academy." *PMLA*, 87 (May 1972), 377–83.

12.17 ———. "Teaching Technology and Culture." *RT*, No. 1 (December 1975), 16–18.

12.18 Kampf, Louis, and Paul Lauter, eds. *The Politics of Literature: Dissenting Essays on the Teaching of English.* New York· Pantheon Books, 1972.
Essays on teaching literature and language. Three (by Franklin, Ellis, and Kessel) from 2.12; others by Cantarow, Ohmann, Labov, O'Neil, Howe, Delany, Vicinus, and Robinson.

12.19 Kogan, Pauline. "Two Lines in the Teaching of *Macbeth.*" *L&I*, No. 3 (Fall 1969), 5–13.

12.20 Lapides, Robert. "Teaching Basic Skills: Working with Contradictions." *RT*, No. 8 (May 1978), 8–9.

12.21 Lauter, Paul. "Retrenchment: What the Managers Are Doing." *RT*, No. 1 (December 1975), 27–35.

12.22 Leeson, Robert. *Children's Books and Class Society.* London: Writers and Readers Publishing Cooperative, 1978.
Discusses who writes for children, how printing and distribution affect contents, and related questions.

12.23 LeRoy, Gaylord C. "The Radical Teacher in Our Discipline." *CE*, 33 (April 1972), 756–64.

12.24 ———. "Literary Study and Political Activism: How to Heal the Split." In 2.13, 75–104.

12.25 Mathews, Robin. "Literature, the Universities and Liberal Ideology," "Research, Curriculum, Scholarship and Endowment in the Study of Canadian Literature," and "Canadian Culture and the Liberal Ideology." In 10.8, 167–80, 181–90, 191–208.

*12.26 Norton, Theodore Mills, and Bertell Ollman. *Studies in Socialist Pedagogy.* New York: Monthly Review Press, 1979.
Mostly North American contributors; includes a bibliography on socialist teaching.

12.27 Ohmann, Richard. *English in America: A Radical View of the Profession.* New York: Oxford University Press, 1976.

Ohmann examines English departments, freshman composition, textbooks, the MLA, the Advanced Placement system, and related topics. Reviewed by Reamy Jansen, *RT*, No. 3 (November 1976), 12–15; Patrick Story, *MR*, No. 7 (Fall 1976), 106–10.

12.28 ———. "Teaching a Large Course on Contemporary Fiction." *RT*, No. 3 (November 1976), 28–30.

12.29 Parmalee, Patty. "Teaching Nazi Culture." *RT*, No. 8 (May 1978), 35–38.

*12.30 Pateman, Trevor, ed. *Counter-Course: A Handbook for Course Criticism.* Harmondsworth: Penguin, 1972.

See the badly organized but interesting bibliography, and Joe Spriggs's equally sloppy, less interesting, "Doing Eng. Lit."

12.31 Shor, Ira. "Writing About Work: A Project in Literacy and Labor Studies." *RT*, No. 4 (March 1977), 21–24.

Excellent practical suggestions result from this description of a remedial writing course.

12.32 Voight, Leonard. "The Literature of Work." *RT*, No. 9 (September 1978), 38–42.

Description of an introductory literature course focusing on work.

Others: Ohmann (13.38) and others on teaching literacy in section 13; Crews (4.32), *This Magazine* (10.37), *Working Teacher* (10.44), Bisseret (13.7), Ohmann (13.38), Murdock (15.62, 15.63)

-13-

Language, Linguistics, and Literacy

*13.1 Lawford, Paul. "Supplement on Russian Formalism, Structuralism, Semiotics." In 1.5, 35–43.
A fairly useful bibliographical source, especially for the non-Marxist items (Lévi-Strauss, the Prague School) excluded from this *Guide*.

13.2 Bann, Stephen. "Structuralism and the Revival of Rhetoric " In 14.66, 68–84.

13.3 Barthes, Roland. *Writing Degree Zero*. 1953; New York: Hill and Wang, 1968.
Marxist defense of modernism against socialist realism. Barthes's work after *Mythologies* (15.31) could not be considered Marxist; see Paul Delany, *Partisan Review*, 45 (1978), 466–70, for a brief but useful account of Barthes's movement away from Marxism. Also 13.4a & b.

13.4a Jayne, Edward. "Zero Degree Form: The Anti-Dialectics of Roland Barthes." *MR*, No. 9 (Fall 1977), 52–70.

13.4b Thody, Philip. "Roland Barthes and the English Tradition." In 14.66, 57–67.

13.5 Bennett, Tony. *Formalism and Marxism*. London: Methuen, 1979.
A Marxist treatment of Althusser, Russian Formalism, etc.

13.6 Bernstein, Basil. *Class, Codes and Control: Theoretical Studies Towards a Sociology of Language*. 3 vols. 1971; New York: Schocken Books, 1975 (NM)
Includes Bernstein's controversial arguments about the limits

that positioning within the working class places upon language and experience. See Rosen (13.42), Sinha (13.53).

13.7 Bisseret, Noelle. *Education, Class Language and Ideology.* London: Routledge & Kegan Paul, 1979.

13.8 Boone, Bruce. "Gay Language as Political Praxis: The Poetry of Frank O'Hara." *Social Text*, No 1 (Winter 1979), 59–92.

13.9 Brown, Cynthia Stokes. "Literacy as Power." *RT*, No. 8 (May 1978), 10–14.

13.10 Cohen, Marcel. "Social and Linguistic Structure." *Diogenes*, 15 (Fall 1956), 38–47.

13.11 Colman, Morris. *On Consciousness, Language, and Cognition: Three Studies in Materialism.* New York: The American Institute for Marxist Studies, 1978.

13.12 Coward, Rosemary, and John Ellis. *Language and Materialism: Developments in Semiology and the Theory of the Subject.* London: Routledge & Kegan Paul, 1977.
An introduction to influential currents in the development of Marxist approaches to language, linguistics, and semiotics. Deals in detail with Saussure, Lévi-Strauss, Barthes, Lacan, Kristeva. Reviewed by Diana Adlam and Angie Salfeld, *Ideology and Consciousness*, No. 3 (Spring 1978), 95–111; Terry Eagleton, *Oxford Literary Review*, 3 (Spring 1979), 99–103.

13.13 Culler, Jonathan. *Structuralist Poetics: Structuralism, Linguistics and the Study of Literature.* Ithaca, N.Y.: Cornell University Press, 1975. (NM)
A key contemporary text on structuralism and language.

13.14 DeGeorge, Richard, and Fernande DeGeorge, eds. *The Structuralists: From Marx to Lévi-Strauss.* New York: Anchor Books, 1972. (M/NM)
Includes selections from Marx (Preface to *A Contribution to the Critique of Political Economy*, prefaces to the first and second editions plus chapter 32 of *Capital*), Althusser (from *Reading Capital*), Freud, Jakobson, Foucault, Lacan, Barthes, Saussure.

13.15 Delany, Sheila. "Political Style/Political Stylistics." *Style*, 8 (Fall 1974), 437–51.

*13.16 Dittmar, Norbert. *Sociolinguistics: A Critical Survey of*

Theory and Application. London: Edward Arnold, 1976.
Includes an excellent annotated bibliography.

13.17 Ehrmann, Jacques, ed. *Literature and Revolution*. Boston: Beacon Press, 1967. (M/NM)
Essays on European and Chinese subjects, from a linguistic orientation for the most part, by Barthes, Serge, Gombrowicz, Blanchot, and others; all originally appeared in *Yale French Studies*, No. 39 (1967).

13.18 Ehrlich, Victor. *Russian Formalism: History and Doctrine*. 1955; The Hague: Mouton, 1969.

13.19 ———. "Some Pitfalls of Literary Structuralism." *Modern Occasions*, 1 (Fall 1971), 518–26.

13.20 Hawkes, Terence. *Structuralism and Semiotics*. Berkeley: University of California Press, 1977. (NM)
A useful introduction to the subject; but see the unfavorable review by Roger Woods, *Ideology and Consciousness*, No. 5 (Spring 1979), 137–41.

13.21 Hoyles, Martin, ed. *The Politics of Literacy*. London: Writers and Readers Publishing Cooperative, 1977.

13.22 Hymes, Dell H., ed. *Studies in the History of Linguistics: Traditions and Paradigms*. Bloomington: Indiana University Press, 1974. (NM)

13.23 Jakobson, Roman. "The Grammatical Texture of a Sonnet from Sir Philip Sidney's *Arcadia*." In 8.42a.

13.24a Liehm, A. J. "Roman Jakobson at Eighty." *RL*, No. 6 (1977–78), 3–15.
An interview.

*13.25 Jameson, Fredric. *The Prison-House of Language: A Critical Account of Structuralism and Russian Formalism*. Princeton, N.J.: Princeton University Press, 1972.
A central text for Marxist studies of language; good bibliography.

13.26 ———. "Metacommentary." *PMLA*, 86 (January 1971), 9–18.

13.27 ———. "The Ideology of the Text." *Salmagundi*, Nos. 31–32 (Fall 1975–Winter 1976), 204–46.
On viewing the object of study as a text to decipher and interpret

rather than an empirically existing reality to know; *Tel Quel*, Barthes, Gombrich, others.

13.28 Kress, Gunther, and Robert Hodge. *Language as Ideology*. London: Routledge & Kegan Paul, 1979.

13.29 Labov, William. *Sociolinguistic Patterns*. Philadelphia: University of Pennsylvania Press, 1972.

13.30 Lawton, D. *Social Class, Language, and Education*. London: Routledge & Kegan Paul, 1968.

13.31 Lazere, Donald. "Literacy and Political Consciousness: A Critique of Left Critiques." *RT*, No. 8 (May 1978), 15-19.

In part, a reply to O'Neil (13.39); see O'Neil's "Lazere and Me: A Response," No. 8 (May 1978), 20. Both articles are from a cluster in this issue of *RT* on "The Politics of Literacy." (Also: 12.20, 13.9, 13.54.)

13.32 Lewis, Thomas E. "Notes Toward a Theory of the Referent." *PMLA*, 94 (May 1979), 459-75. (NM)

13.33 McCaffery, Steve, ed. "The Politics of the Referent." *Open Letter*, 3rd series, 7 (Summer 1977), 60-107.

McCaffery, Bruce Andrews, Ray DePalma, Ron Silliman, and Ellsworth Snyder write on Gertrude Stein, John Cage, and general topics involving the relations of linguistic and capitalistic structures.

13.34 Mace, Jane. *Working with Words: Literacy Beyond School*. London: Writers and Readers Publishing Cooperative, 1976.

13.35 Macksey, Richard, and Eugenio Donato, eds. *The Structuralist Controversy: The Languages of Criticism and the Sciences of Man*. Baltimore: The Johns Hopkins University Press, 1970. (M/NM)

Includes Goldmann's "Structure: Human Reality and Methodological Concept," plus essays by Poulet, Todorov, Barthes, Derrida, and others.

*13.36 Mueller, Claus. *The Politics of Communication: A Study in the Political Sociology of Language, Socialization, and Legitimation*. New York: Oxford University Press, 1973.

13.37 Ohmann, Richard. "Generative Grammars and the Concept of Literary Style." *Word*, 20 (December 1964), 423-39. Rpt. in *Contemporary Essays on Style*. Ed. Glenn A. Love and Michael

Payne. Glenview, Ill.: Scott, Foresman, 1969, 133–57.
Theory of style based on Chomsky is used to explicate Conrad, James, Lawrence, Dylan Thomas, others.

13.38 ———. "Language, Power, and the Teaching of English." *College English Association Forum*, October 1975, 1, 7–9.

13.39 O'Neil, Wayne. "Why *Newsweek* Can't Explain Things." *RT*, No. 2 (June 1976), 11–15.
A commentary on *Newsweek's* "Why Johnny Can't Write" and the literacy debate.

13.40 Orwell, George. "Politics and the English Language." In *Shooting an Elephant and Other Essays*. London: Secker and Warburg, 1950, 85–102.
This frequently reprinted attack on jargon and cliché from both right and left is only the best-known example of a continuous preoccupation in Orwell's work.

*13.41 Rank, Hugh. *Language and Public Policy*. Urbana, Ill.: NCTE, 1974. (NM)
Includes guide to classroom resources.

13.42 Rosen, Harold. *Language and Class*. Bristol: Falling Wall Press, 1972.
Reply to Basil Bernstein's argument about the limits of working-class language (13.6).

13.43 Rossi-Landi, Ferruccio. *Ideologies of Linguistic Reality*. The Hague: Mouton, 1973.

*13.44 ———. *Linguistics and Economics*. The Hague: Mouton, 1975.

13.45 Rutherford, John. "Structuralism." In 14.66, 54–55.

13.46 Schaff, Adam. *Langauge and Cognition*. 1964; New York: McGraw-Hill, 1973.

13.47 ———. *Structuralism and Marxism*. 1974; Oxford: Pergamon Press, 1978.

13.48 Schlauch, Margaret. *The Gift of Language*. 1942; New York: Dover, 1955.

13.49 ———. *The English Language in Modern Times*. London: Oxford University Press, 1954.
English language since 1400.

13.50 ———. *Language and the Study of Languages Today*.

Warsaw: Polish Scientific Publishers, 1967.

13.51 ———. "Semantics as Social Evasion." *S&S*, 6 (Fall 1942), 315–30.

13.52 ———. "Early Tudor Colloquial English." *Philologica Pragensia*, 1 (1958), 97–104.

13.53 Sinha, Chris. "Class, Language and Education." *Ideology and Consciousness*, No. 1 (May 1977), 77–92.
A review of the whole Bernstein school.

13.54 Sporn, Paul. "The Politics of Literacy and the Radical Teacher." *RT*, No. 8 (May 1978), 5–7.

13.55 Stalin, Joseph. *Marxism and Linguistics*. New York: International Publishers, 1951.

13.56 Thomson, George. "Speech and Thought." In *The First Philosophers*. London: Lawrence and Wishart, 1955. Rpt. in 2.3, 25–46.

13.57 ———. "Marxism and Classical Philology." In *Geras: Studies Presented to George Thomson*. Prague: Charles University, 1963.

13.58 Wesker, Arnold. *Words as Definition of Experience*. London: Writers and Readers Publishing Cooperative, 1978.
On the problems of cultural literacy, self-expression, language teaching.

13.59 West, Alick. "Language and Rhythm," and "Idiom." In 8.19; rpt. in 8.21, 75–80, 81–84.

Others: "Socio-Criticism" (2.14), Fokkema and Kunne-Ibsch (4.55), Sartre (4.163), Williams (4.196), Schlauch (11.102c), Bigsby (15.14)

–14–

Literature and Society; The Sociology of Literature

Unless otherwise noted, works here are non-Marxist.

*14.1 Angenot, Marc. "A Select Bibliography of the Sociology of Literature." *Science-Fiction Studies*, 4 (November 1977), 295–308.

14.2 Albrecht, M. C., J. H. Barnett, and M. Griff, eds. *The Sociology of Art and Literature: A Reader.* New York: Praeger, 1970. Mainly non-Marxist articles on the visual and performing arts; includes Goldmann's "The Sociology of Literature: Status and Problems of Method" (4.63).

14.3 Altick, R. D. *The English Common Reader: A Social History of the Mass Reading Public, 1800-1900.* Chicago: University of Chicago Press, 1957.

14.4 Auerbach, Erich. *Mimesis: The Representation of Reality in Western Literature.* 1946; Princeton, N.J.: Princeton University Press, 1953.

14.5 Barker, Francis, et al., eds. *Literature, Society and the Sociology of Literature: Proceedings of the Conference Held at the University of Essex, July 1976.* [Colchester]: University of Essex, 1977. Predominantly Marxist collection includes articles on individual authors, film, little magazines, Marxist theory, and Russian formalism. Also: Stuart Hall, "A Critical Survey of the Theoretical and Practical Achievements of the Last Ten Years"; David Musslewhite, "Towards a Political Aesthetics."

14.6 _____. *1848: The Sociology of Literature.* Colchester: University of Essex, 1978. Predominantly Marxist collection from the July 1977 Essex

Conference. Individual nineteenth-century authors; 1848 and Marxist aesthetics; David Musselwhite's "Novel as Narcotic."

14.7 Bradbury, Malcolm. *The Social Context of Modern English Literature.* New York: Schocken Books, 1971.

A rather unmemorable study of the organization of literary culture in England from 1870 to the present. Reviewed anon., *TLS*, October 8, 1971, 1205–1206.

14.8 Burns, Elizabeth, and Tom Burns, eds. *Sociology of Literature and Drama: Selected Readings.* Harmondsworth: Penguin, 1973.

A comprehensive though mainly non-Marxist collection. Includes essays by Zeraffa, Goldmann, Girard, Frye, Barthes, Lévi-Strauss, Watt, Lukács, Simmel, Raymond Williams, and others.

14.9 Cole, G. D. H. *Politics and Literature.* London: Hogarth Press, 1929.

On Hooker, Bacon, Hobbes, Locke, DeFoe, Swift, Burke, Paine, Godwin, Shelley, Cobbett, Bentham, Coleridge, others.

14.10 Daiches, David. *Literature and Society.* London: Victor Gollancz, 1938.

14.11 ———. "Literature and Social Mobility." In *Aspects of History and Class Consciousness.* Ed. Istvan Meszaros. London: Routledge & Kegan Paul, 1971, 152–72.

*14.12 Duncan, Hugh D. *Language and Literature in Society: A Sociological Essay on Theory and Method in the Interpretation of Linguistic Symbols.* Chicago: University of Chicago Press, 1953.

"Chiefly a development of Kenneth Burke's ideas" (1.4); contains a "Bibliographical Guide to the Sociology of Literature," 146–216.

14.13 Egbert, Donald Drew. *Social Radicalism and the Arts, Western Europe: A Cultural History from the French Revolution to 1968.* New York: Knopf, 1970.

14.14 Empson, William. *Some Versions of Pastoral.* 1935; London: Chatto and Windus, 1968.

Begins with section on "Proletarian Literature."

14.15 Enzer, Hyman. "Sociology and the Beaux Arts." *Arts in Society*, 3, No. 3 (1965), 412–24.

14.16 Escarpit, Robert. *Sociology of Literature.* 1958; London: Frank Cass, 1971.

A seminal text on the production, distribution, and consumption of literature.

14.17 Febvre, Lucien, and Henri Martin. *The Coming of the Book: The Impact of Printing, 1450–1800.* 1971; Atlantic Highlands, N.J.: Humanities Press, 1976.

14.18 Filmer, P. "The Literary Imagination and the Explanation of Socio-Cultural Change in Modern Britain." *European Journal of Sociology,* 10 (1969), 271–91.

14.19 Foulkes, A. P., ed. *The Uses of Criticism.* Bern: Herbert Lang, 1976. (M/NM)

Includes both American and European critics on "the institutional and social use of literary criticism and interpretation."

14.20 Geismar, Maxwell. *The Last of the Provincials: The American Novel, 1915–1925.* 1947; Boston: Houghton Mifflin, 1959.

On Mencken, S. Lewis, Cather, Anderson, Fitzgerald.

14.21 _____. *Writers in Crisis: The American Novel, 1925–1940.* 1947; New York: Dutton, 1971.

Lardner, Hemingway, Dos Passos, Faulkner, Wolfe, and Steinbeck.

14.22 _____. *Rebels and Ancestors: The American Novel, 1890–1915.* 1953; New York: Hill and Wang, 1963.

Norris, Crane, London, Glasgow, Dreiser.

14.23 _____. *American Moderns: From Rebellion to Conformity.* New York: Hill and Wang, 1958.

Essays and reviews on Dreiser, Hemingway, Dos Passos, Faulkner, Lewis, Wolfe, as well as more recent American novelists (Styron, Bellow, Salinger); also, articles on American literature in mid-century.

14.24 Girard, René. *Deceit, Desire and the Novel: Self and Other in Literary Structure.* 1961; Baltimore: The Johns Hopkins University Press, 1966.

A study of European authors by a critic who has been an important influence on Goldmann.

14.25 _____. *'To Double Business Bound': Essays on Literature, Mimesis and Structural Anthropology.* Baltimore: The Johns

Hopkins University Press, 1978.

14.26 ———. "From the Divine Comedy to the Sociology of the Novel." In 14.8, 101–108.

Sums up argument of *Deceit, Desire and the Novel* (14.24) and comments on the relationship between Christianity and Marxism as he sees it.

14.27 Graña, César. *Fact and Symbol: Essays in the Sociology of Art and Literature.* New York: Oxford University Press, 1971.

*14.28 Guérard, Albert Leon. *Literature and Society.* Boston: Lothrop, Lee and Shepard, 1935.

Contains an extensive bibliography, which, though dated, is more useful than the text itself.

14.29 Harrison, John R. *The Reactionaries: A Study of the Anti-Democratic Intelligentsia.* New York: Schocken Books, 1967.

An account of the politics of the major British and Anglo-American modernists (Yeats, Eliot, Pound, Lawrence, Wyndham Lewis).

14.30 Hauser, Arnold. *The Social History of Art.* 4 vols. London: Routledge & Kegan Paul, 1951.

Wide-ranging Marxist study; particularly useful on the relations between literature and the visual arts.

14.31 Hoggart, Richard. *Speaking to Each Other.* Vol. I: *About Society.* Vol. II: *About Literature.* New York: Oxford University Press, 1970.

Hoggart helped found the Institute for Contemporary Cultural Studies at Birmingham University after writing *The Uses of Literacy* (15.47), still his best-known work.

14.32 ———. *Only Connect: On Culture and Communication.* London: Chatto and Windus, 1971.

14.33 ———. "Contemporary Cultural Studies: An Approach to the Study of Literature and Society." In *Contemporary Criticism.* Ed. Malcolm Bradbury and David Palmer. London, Edward Arnold, 1970, 155–70.

14.34 ———. The Literary Imagination and the Sociological Imagination." *Les Langues Modernes,* 64 (November–December 1970), 78–86.

14.35 Howe, Irving. *Politics and the Novel.* New York: Horizon Press, 1957.

Study of the relations between politics and the novel form in Stendhal, Dostoevsky, Conrad, Turgenev, James and other Americans, Malraux, Silone, Koestler, Orwell.

14.36 _____ . *A World More Attractive: A View of Modern Literature and Politics.* New York: Horizon Press, 1963.

Essays on T. E. Lawrence, Wharton, Baldwin and Wright, Mailer, Whitman, Frost, Stevens, Gissing, Celine, Aleichem, other writers and topics.

14.37 _____ . *Decline of the New.* New York: Harcourt, Brace & World, 1970.

Seven essays from 14.36, plus new ones on "The Culture of Modernism," I. B. Singer, James, Dreiser, Orwell, "The New York Intellectuals," other writers and topics.

14.38 _____ . *The Critical Point: On Literature and Culture.* New York: Horizon Press, 1973.

On "The City in Literature," Zola, Dostoevsky, Solzhenitsyn and Lukács, E. A. Robinson, Pound, Bellow, Roth, Plath, Kate Millett, other writers and topics.

14.39 _____ , ed. *The Idea of the Modern in Literature and the Arts.* New York: Horizon Press, 1967.

Useful and wide-ranging collection from contributors of varying perspectives, including Adorno on Surrealism, Hauser on film, Sartre on Baudelaire (all reprints).

14.40 Hynes, Samuel. *The Auden Generation: Literature and Politics in England in the 1930s.* London: The Bodley Head, 1976.

Year by year account of the political and artistic events in the 1930s. Reviewed by Jane Marcus, *MR*, No. 10 (Spring 1978), 117–20.

14.41 Ingle, Stephen. *Socialist Thought in Imaginative Literature.* Totowa, N.J.: Rowman and Littlefield, 1979.

"It is concerned with the contribution to the development of socialist thought made by imaginative writers" like Morris, Shaw, Wells, Huxley, and Orwell, between the 1880s and the 1940s.

14.42 Inglis, Fred, ed. *Literature and Environment: Essays in Reading and Social Studies.* London: Chatto and Windus, 1971.

14.43 James, Louis. *Fiction for the Working Man 1830-1850: A Study of the Literature Produced for the Working Classes in Early Victorian England.* London: Oxford University Press, 1963.

14.44 Kahn, Lisa M. "The Industrial Proletariat as Portrayed in Literature and Art from 1844-1923." *Faculty Research Journal: Texas Southern University,* 1, No. 1 (1976), 74-84.

14.45 Knights, L. C. *Drama and Society in the Age of Jonson.* London: Chatto and Windus, 1937.

Knights rejects the Marxist version of social history for one closer to the *Scrutiny* model, and his historical and literary-critical analyses are not closely meshed. Nevertheless, a pioneering work in literary sociology, which includes "The Background" (economic life and social theory), studies in individual dramatists, "Drama and Society," and "Dekker, Heywood and Citizen Morality."

14.46 Kostelanetz, Richard. *The End of Intelligent Writing: Literary Politics in America.* London: Sheed and Ward, 1974.

14.47 Kovačević, Ivanka. *Fact Into Fiction: English Literature and the Industrial Scene, 1750-1850.* Leicester: Leicester University Press, 1975.

An introduction to writings on the industrial scene, together with a selection of pieces by lesser-known authors of the time.

14.48 Laqueur, Walter, and George L. Mosse, eds. *Literature and Politics in the Twentieth Century.* New York: Harper & Row, 1967.

Predominantly non-Marxist essays on writers and literary movements in the U.S., Europe, and Japan.

14.49 Larkin, Maurice. *Man and Society in Nineteenth-Century Realism: Determinism and Literature.* Totowa, N.J.: Rowman and Littlefield, 1977.

Surveys social and intellectual changes in Europe and how Balzac, Flaubert, Mrs. Gaskell, George Eliot, and others responded to them.

14.50 Laurenson, Diana, ed. *The Sociology of Literature: Applied Studies.* Keele: University of Keele, 1978.

Mainly non-Marxist essays on English authors, English fiction and criticism, film, European topics.

14.51 Laurenson, Diana, and Alan Swingewood. *The Sociology of Literature.* London: MacGibbon and Kee, 1972.
Sections on "Theory," "The Writer and Society," and "The Sociology of the Novel." Influence of Goldmann; discussions of Fielding, Sartre, N. West, Orwell.

14.52 "Literature and Revolution." *Perspectives on Contemporary Literature,* 2 (May, November 1976).
Special issue contains mainstream essays on European and American writers.

*14.53 "Literature and Society." *WPCS,* No. 4 (Spring 1973).
Special issue has articles on individual authors and critics, genres; bibliography on textual analysis.

14.54 Loftis, John. *Comedy and Satire from Congreve to Fielding.* Stanford, Cal.: Stanford University Press, 1959.
Changes in social orientation of comedy as power shifts from landed to merchant classes.

14.55 _____. *The Politics of Drama in Augustan England.* Oxford: Oxford University Press, 1963.

14.56 Lowenthal, Leo. *Literature and the Image of Man: Sociological Studies of the European Drama and Novel, 1600-1900.* Boston: Beacon Press, 1957.

14.57 _____. *Literature, Popular Culture, and Society.* Englewood Cliffs, N.J.: Prentice-Hall, 1961.
See especially "Literature and Society," 141–61.

14.58 _____. "Literature and Sociology." In *Relations of Literary Study: Essays on Interdisciplinary Contributions.* Ed. James Thorpe. New York: MLA, 1967, 89–110.

14.59 McRobbie, Kenneth, ed. *Chaos and Form: History and Literature: Ideas and Relationships.* Winnipeg: University of Manitoba Press, 1972. (M/NM)
Essays on literature, history, and philosophy from medieval times to the present.

14.60 Maglin, Nan Bauer. "Visions of Defiance: Work, Political Commitment, and Sisterhood in 21 Works of Fiction, 1898–1925." *Praxis,* No. 3 (1976), 98–112.

*14.61 Maxwell, D. E. S. *Poets of the Thirties.* London: Routledge & Kegan Paul, 1969.
Non-Marxist but sympathetic studies of Caudwell, Cornford,

Day-Lewis, and Auden. Also, "Marx and the Muse" and useful bibliography.

14.62 Meakin, David. *Man and Work: Literature and Culture in Industrial Society.* London: Methuen, 1976.
The importance of work in the writings of mainly modern authors. Reviewed by Bernard Bergonzi, *L&H*, No. 7 (Spring 1978), 107–108.

14.63 Moers, Ellen. *Literary Women.* Garden City, N.Y.: Doubleday, 1976.
"Dictionary Catalogue of Literary Women," 272–320, includes valuable and extensive notes on the writings of authors covered. Reviewed by Annette T. Rubinstein, *S&S*, 42 (Fall 1978), 356–61.

14.64 Orr, John. *Tragic Realism and Modern Society: Studies in the Sociology of the Modern Novel.* London: Macmillan, 1977.

14.65 Routh, Harold Victor. *God, Man and Epic Poetry: A Study in Comparative Literature.* 2 vols. Cambridge: Cambridge University Press, 1927.

14.66 Routh, Jane, and Janet Wolff, eds. *The Sociology of Literature: Theoretical Approaches.* Keele: University of Keele, 1977.
David Coward on "The Sociology of Literary Response," Wolff on hermeneutics, Joan Rockwell on "A Theory of Literature and Society," other essays on language and Marxist theory.

*14.67 Sammons, Jeffrey L. *Literary Sociology and Practical Criticism: An Inquiry.* Bloomington: Indiana University Press, 1977.
In part a dialogue with contemporary Marxist theory: Jay, Jameson, Goldmann, Morawski, etc. Chapters on "Value," "Elitism," related topics.

14.68 Scott, Wilbur, ed. "The Sociological Approach: Literature and Social Ideas." In *Five Approaches to Literary Criticism.* New York: Collier, 1962, 123–76.
Includes introduction, essays by Joseph Wood Krutch, Orwell, Caudwell.

14.69 Showalter, Elaine. *A Literature of Their Own: British Women Novelists from Brontë to Lessing.* Princeton, N.J.: Princeton University Press, 1977. Reviewed by Jane Marcus, *MR*, No. 9 (Fall 1977), 146–49; Annette T. Rubinstein, *S&S*, 42 (Fall 1978), 356–61.

14.70 "Sociological Perspectives on Literature." *Mosaic*, 5 (Winter 1971-72). Rpt. as *Sociological Perspectives on Literature*. Ed. R. G. Collins and Kenneth McRobbie. Winnipeg: University of Manitoba Press, 1972. (M/NM)

Essays on individual authors, critics, periods, and theoretical topics.

14.71 "Sociology of Literary Creativity." *International Social Science Journal*, 19 (1967). (M/NM)

Special issue includes Goldmann (4.63), Leenhardt, and Pospelov on sociology of literature; also Eco, Lukács, Mouillard, and Waltz on European topics.

14.72 Taine, Hippolyte. *History of English Literature*. 1872; New York: Unger, 1965.

The classic, pioneering attempt to treat literature as the product of simple environmental determinations.

14.73a Birchall, Ian. "Ambition and Modesty: Literature and Social Sciences in the Work of Hippolyte Taine." In 14.70, 31-46.

14.74 Van Ghent, Dorothy. *The English Novel: Form and Function*. 1953; New York: Harper, 1961.

Particularly useful are the chapters on *Moll Flanders, Clarissa, Pride and Prejudice,* and *Great Expectations.*

Others: "Socio-Criticism" (2.14), Bisztray (4.21), Craig and Egan (4.30), Goldmann (4.63), McGuigan (4.166e), Gurvitch (5.18), Lukács (5.25), Goldmann (6.11, 6.12), Watt (6.31), Calverton (9.34), Burke (9.40), Craib (11.18a), Segal (11.182a), Barrett (11.235g), Bigsby (15.14), "The Sociology of Popular Culture" (15.24), Jarvie (15.107), Lang (15.113), Mayer (15.120)

-15-

Appendix:

A Reading List on Mass Culture

The study of mass culture has generated a great number of works in recent years, and this Appendix is only a sampling of the growing field. Readers wishing to explore it further should consult the journals and bibliographies listed below.

A. GENERAL
i. Journals

15.1 *Cineaste* (New York)

15.2 *Cine Tracts* (Montreal)

15.3 *Cultural Correspondence* (Providence, R.I.)

15.4 *Culture & Context* (Montreal)

15.5 *The Cultural Worker* (Amherst, Mass.)

15.6 *Discourse* (Berkeley, Cal.)

15.7 *Jump Cut* (Berkeley, Cal.)

15.8 *Media Ecology Review* (New York)

15.9 *Open Secret* (London)

15.10 *Screen* (London)

15.11 *Toward Revolutionary Art* (San Francisco)

15.12 *Wedge* (London)

Others: *Social Text* (3.18), *Working Papers in Cultural Studies* (3.21)

ii. Bibliographies and Collections

15.13 Abbs, Peter, ed. *The Black Rainbow: Essays on the Present Breakdown of Culture.* London: Heinemann, 1975.
Radical perspective represented by Charles Parker on popular song, Fred Inglis on architecture.

15.14 Bigsby, C. W. E., ed. *Approaches to Popular Culture.* London: Edward Arnold, 1973. (M/NM)

The "Perspectives" section contains essays on political (Bigsby), scientific (Raymond Williams), Marxist (David Craig), sociological, structural, and linguistic approaches. An excellent compilation, spoilt only by a failure to make any distinction between mass and popular culture.

15.15 Casty, Alan, ed. *Mass Media and Mass Man.* New York: Holt, Rinehart, 1968.

Most mass culture anthologies have too little Marxist representation to include in this Appendix, but Casty includes selections by Mills and Adorno, plus critical articles on the coverage of political events and labor issues.

*15.16 de Camargo, Marina. "Ideological Analysis of the Message: A Bibliography." *WPCS,* No. 3 (Autumn 1972), 123–41.

A brief and clear introduction to three types of communications analysis—structural, ideological, and content—with a useful bibliography for each.

*15.17 Friedman, L. *Sex Role Stereotyping in the Mass Media: An Annotated Bibliography.* New York: Garland, 1977. (NM)

*15.18 International Mass Media Research Centre. *Marxism and the Mass Media: Towards a Basic Bibliography.* No. 1. New York: International General, 1972. No. 2, 1973. No. 3, 1974. Nos. 4–5, 1976.

(Nos. 1 and 2 are collected in No. 3.) More for specialists than for readers new to the subject.

*15.19 "Mass Culture, Political Consciousness and English Studies." Ed. Donald Lazere. *CE,* 38 (April 1977).

Includes introduction, articles by Stanley Aronowitz, Kate Ellis, Todd Gritlin, Robert Cirino, Louis Kampf, Fredric Jameson, and others, on soap opera, racism, alternative communications systems, advertising, sports, theoretical subjects. Lazere's "Selected Bibliography" is unannotated but comprehensive on American items.

15.20 Mattelart, Armand, and Seth Siegelaub, eds. *Communication and Class Struggle.* Vol. 1. *Capitalism and Imperialism.* New York: International General, 1978.

Sixty-four selections on the formation of capitalist communication apparatus, ideology, mass culture. Vol. 2, *Liberation, Socialism*, is forthcoming.

15.21 "Radicalism and Culture." *Radical America*, 2 (November–December 1968).

Special issue includes David Gross, "Towards a Radical Theory of Culture," Jeremy Shapiro, "Notes on a Radical Theory of Culture."

15.22 Rosenberg, Bernard, and David Manning White, eds. *Mass Culture: The Popular Arts in America*. Glenview, Ill.: The Free Press, 1957.

The pioneering mass culture anthology and its successor (15.23) are serious compilations and reprint some left, or leftish, essays. Sections: mass literature, film, TV, music, advertising, perspectives, overview.

15.23 _____ . *Mass Culture Revisited*. New York: Van Nostrand Reinhold, 1971.

Sections: overview, TV, film, magazines/newspapers, spy fiction, advertising, alternatives (including rock, comics).

*15.24 "The Sociology of Popular Culture." Ed. George H. Lewis. *Current Sociology*, 26 (Winter 1978).

The first part of this special issue (1–70) summarizes sociological approaches and lists research centers; the second (71–154) is an annotated bibliography. Both parts include radical items on mass culture.

15.25 "Special Section on Mass Culture." *Social Text*, No. 1 (Winter 1979), 94–180.

John Brenkman, Stanley Aronowitz, Fredric Jameson, Sylvia Winter, and Michael E. Brown in advanced theoretical articles on mass media, film, reification and utopia, "Sambos and Minstrels," anti-theater, and the new right and media.

15.26 Thompson, Denys, ed. *Discrimination and Popular Culture*. 1964; London: Heinemann, 1973.

This anthology follows in the tradition of F. R. Leavis and Thompson's own *Culture and Environment*, which—together with 15.190—inaugurated a significant line of mass culture criticism in Britain that is often dismissed by socialists as conservative and elitist. *Discrimination* has essays on town-scape, advertising, press, TV and radio, pop music, magazines, and film.

iii. Individual Studies

15.27 Adorno, Theodor W. *The Jargon of Authenticity.* 1964; London: Routledge & Kegan Paul, 1973.

15.28 _____ . "The Culture Industry Reconsidered." *NGC*, No. 6 (Fall 1975), 12–19.

Further comments on thesis developed in Horkheimer and Adorno, *Dialectic of the Enlightenment* (15.49), and attacked by Waldman (15.79a).

15.29 Aronowitz, Stanley. "Colonized Leisure, Trivialized Work." In *False Promises: The Shaping of American Working-Class Consciousness.* New York: McGraw-Hill, 1974, 51–134.

Useful in showing how microcosmic analysis of working-class leisure activities can be combined with a macrocosmic analysis of contemporary capitalism.

15.30 Baran, Paul A., and Paul M. Sweezy. *Monopoly Capital.* New York: Monthly Review Press, 1966.

Comment on the structure and functions of the media, especially advertising, under U.S. capitalism.

15.31 Barthes, Roland. *Mythologies.* 1957; New York: Hill and Wang, 1972.

Although Barthes later moved away from Marxism (see 13.3), this early work provides valuable suggestions for analyzing in a radical fashion such phenomena of daily life as wrestling and steak and chips. Provides an analysis of the way signs function in everyday objects and events to legitimate an oppressive order, plus a long essay on "Myth Today." Reviewed by John Berger, *New Society*, February 24, 1972, 407–408.

15.32 Benjamin, Walter. "The Work of Art in the Age of Mechanical Reproduction." In 4.13, 217–51.

Benjamin's argument—that the removal of the 'aura' of high art by technical reproducibility opened possibilities both for liber-ation and enslavement—has been very influential in radical criticism of the mass media; examples: Enzenberger (15.39), Berger (15.154).

15.33 Brantlinger, Patrick. "Mass Communications and Teachers of English." *CE*, 37 (January 1976), 490–509.

A critical and radical survey of readers available for mass communications English courses, examining their political implications.

15.34 ———. "Giving the Public What it Wants." *Public Doublespeak Newsletter* (Urbana: NCTE), 3, No. 2 (1976), 1–2.

15.35 Briginshaw, Richard. "Capitalism's Mass Media." *Labour Monthly* (London), 59 (September 1977), 411–14.

15.36 Chadwick, Jon. "Alternative Culture." *MT*, March 1976, 78–84.

Developments in film, TV, drama, etc. in Britain.

15.37 Debord, Guy. *Society of the Spectacle*. Detroit: Black and Red, 1970.

A seminal but difficult text. In his 211 *pensées*, Debord sees the spectacle—the image consumed passively—as the result of modern commodity production.

15.38 Domhoff, G. William. *Who Rules America?* Englewood Cliffs, N.J.: Prentice-Hall, 1967.

Includes comments on ruling-class control of the mass media.

15.39 Enzenberger, Hans Magnus. *The Consciousness Industry: On Literature, Politics and the Media*. New York: The Seabury Press, 1974.

Collection of essays by a contemporary German Marxist influenced by Benjamin (15.32); includes proposals for regaining popular control of the media. Enzenberger stands at the opposite pole from Adorno and Horkheimer in Marxist criticism of mass culture; he is hopeful that the media can be used for the left. See especially "The Industrialization of the Mind" (1962) and "Constituents of a Theory of the Media" (1970), both also reprinted in *Raids and Reconstructions: Essays in Politics, Crime and Culture* (London: Pluto Press, 1976).

15.40a Aronowitz, Stanley. "Enzenberger on Mass Culture/ A Review Essay." *MR*, No. 7 (Fall 1976), 90–99.

Locates Enzenberger in relation to contemporary critical Marxism, and compares European and American left on mass culture.

15.41 Fruchter, Norman. "Movement Propaganda and the Culture of the Spectacle." *Liberation*, 16 (May 1971), 4–17. Argues that the New Left in the U.S. became assimilated into the culture of the spectacle. Followed by dissenting commentaries by Todd Gitlin and Lee Baxandall (18–22).

15.42 Gans, Herbert. *Popular Culture and High Culture*. New York: Basic Books, 1974. (NM)

15.43 Goldmann, Lucien. "Possibilities of Cultural Action Through the Mass Media." In 4.61, 40–50.

15.44 Gouldner, Alvin. *The Dialectic of Ideology and Technology*. New York: The Seabury Press, 1975.

*15.45 Hall, Stuart, and Paddy Whannel. *The Popular Arts: A Critical Guide to the Mass Media*. London: Hutchinson, 1964. An educationally oriented introduction to the evaluation of popular fiction, film, television, etc.

15.46 Halloran, J., P. Elliot, and G. Murdock. *Demonstrations and Communication: A Case Study*. Harmondsworth: Penguin, 1970. (M/NM) This exhaustive critical analysis of media coverage of the anti-Vietnam demonstration in London (October 1968) provides a good model for detailed explication of media bias.

15.47 Hoggart, Richard. *The Uses of Literacy: Aspects of Working-class Life with Special Reference to Publications and Entertainment*. 1957; Harmondsworth: Penguin, 1958. (NM) The strength of this pioneering text on British working-class culture lies in its densely remembered detail. Part Two, "Yielding Place to New" (169–346), is on mass culture.

15.48 Horkheimer, Max. "Art and Mass Culture." In *Critical Theory*. New York: Herder and Herder, 1972, 273–90.

15.49 Horkheimer, Max, and Theodor Adorno. "The Culture Industry: Enlightenment as Mass Deception." In *Dialectic of the Enlightenment*. 1947; New York: Herder and Herder, 1972.

15.50 Imrie, Malcolm. "'Red Letters': The Academy in Peril." *Wedge*, 1 (Summer 1977), 43–46. Critique of 15.12 that argues that Marxist criticism cannot avoid centering on mass culture at this time.

15.51 Jones, Bryn. "The Politics of Popular Culture." *WPCS*, No. 6 (Autumn 1974), 25–30.

15.52 Kayer, Hans Cristoph. "The Sadist and the Clown: The Changing Nazi Image in the American Media." *Journal of Popular Culture*, 10 (Spring 1977), 848–51. (NM)

15.53 Khezwana, Naison. "The British Mass Media and Zimbabwe." *Labour Monthly* (London), 60 (November–December 1978), 467–76.

15.54 Lumer, Robert. "Mass Culture Under Capitalism." *Political Affairs*, 54 (October 1975), 28–39.

15.55 Macdonald, Dwight. *Against the American Grain: Essays on the Effects of Mass Culture*. New York: Random House, 1962. (NM)
A pessimistic vision of the effects of mass culture on high culture, especially literature.

15.56 ———. "A Theory of Mass Culture." *Diogenes*, No. 3 (Summer 1953), 1–17. (NM)
Reprinted in numerous collections.

15.57 McQuail, Dennis. *Towards a Sociology of Mass Communications*. 1969; Harmondsworth: Penguin, 1972. (NM)
The best British sociological introduction to the subject; a lucid overview that includes references to radical scholarship.

15.58 Marcuse, Herbert. *One-Dimensional Man*. Boston: Beacon Press, 1964.
Influential though controversial Marxist argument that mass culture and mass society erase individuality, critical capacity, and libidinal expression.

15.59 ———. "Repressive Tolerance." In *A Critique of Pure Tolerance*. By Paul Wolff, Barrington Moore, and Herbert Marcuse. Boston: Beacon Press, 1969, 81–118.

15.60 Mattelart, Armand. *Multinational Corporations and the Control of Culture: The Ideological Apparatuses of Imperialism*. Atlantic Highlands, N.J.: Humanities Press, 1979.

15.61 Mills, C. Wright. "Mass Media and Public Opinion." In *Power, Politics and People: Collected Essays of C. Wright Mills*. Ed. I. L. Horowitz. New York: Oxford University Press, 1963, 577–98.

15.62 Murdock, Graham. "Education, Culture and the Myth of Classlessness." In *Work and Leisure.* Ed. J. T. Haworth and M. A. Smith. London: Lepus Books, 1975, 119–32.

15.63 Murdock, Graham, and Guy Phelps. *Mass Media and the Secondary School.* London: Macmillan, 1973.
A study of the effects of media consumption at high-school level.

15.64 Murdock, Graham, and Peter Golding. "For a Political Economy of Mass Communications." In *The Socialist Register 1973.* Ed. Ralph Miliband and John Saville. London: The Merlin Press, 1973, 205–34.
The structure of ownership and control in British mass media; the effect of emerging economic structures on the production of culture.

15.65 Negt, Oskar. "Mass Media: Tools of Domination or Instruments of Liberation? Aspects of the Frankfurt School's Communications Analysis." *NGC*, No. 14 (Summer 1978), 61–82.
A good introduction to many of the major figures in Marxist communications analysis; discussion of the Frankfurt School (Adorno, Horkheimer, Marcuse), Balázs (15.83), Benjamin, Brecht, Enzenberger.

15.66 Real, Michael. *Mass-Mediated Culture.* Englewood Cliffs, N.J.: Prentice-Hall, 1977. (NM)
Introduction and conclusion survey contemporary theories of mass culture, including the Marxist perspective.

15.67 Robinson, Lillian S. "The Critical Task," "Criticism: Who Needs It?" and "On Reading Trash." In 4.150, 47–52, 69–94, 200–22.
On mass culture directed at a working-class audience.

15.68 Sallach, David L. "Class Domination and Ideological Hegemony." *The Sociological Quarterly,* 15 (Winter 1974), 38–50.
Gramsci's model of hegemony is applied in a discussion of the mass media as instruments of domination.

15.69 Sandman, Peter M., David M. Rubin, and David B. Sachman. *Media: An Introductory Analysis of American Mass Communications.* Englewood Cliffs, N.J.: Prentice-Hall, 1972. (NM)
One of the best critical sociological introductions to the study of the media.

15.70 Schiller, Herbert. *Mass Communications and the American Empire*. Boston: Beacon Press, 1971.
Scholarly and factual Marxist critique of the economics and politics of the mass media.

15.71 _____ . *The Mind Managers*. Boston: Beacon Press, 1973.

15.72 _____ . *Communication and Cultural Domination*. White Plains, N.Y.: International Arts and Sciences Press, 1976.
Mass-cultural commerce between imperialist and imperialized countries.

15.73 Swingewood, Alan. *The Myth of Mass Culture*. London: Macmillan, 1977.
An introduction to the theories of mass culture and proletarian culture that argues that Marxist, Leavisite, and pluralist perspectives are all "profoundly conservative" because they see culture in *passive* terms.

15.74 White, Hayden. "Structuralism in Popular Culture." *Journal of Popular Culture*, 7 (Spring 1974), 759–75. (NM)

15.75 Williams, Raymond. *Communications*. 1962; rev. ed. London: Chatto and Windus, 1966.
Williams is a pioneer in the socialist study of mass culture in Britain. His work assumes a continuity between mass culture and literary culture in its content and method of study. *Communications* is divided into definitions, history, content, controversy, proposals, and further reading.

15.76 _____ . "Communications," "Advertising." In *The May Day Manifesto 1968*. Ed. Raymond Williams. Harmondsworth: Penguin, 1968, 39–41, 41–44.

15.77 Williams, Raymond, et al. "The Role of the Mass Media: A Discussion." *Wedge*, 1 (Summer 1977), 33–38.
General consensus that the 'indoctrination' model is too simple to account for the works of the press, broadcasting, etc.

Others: Aronowitz (4.4), Gross (4.69), Hall (4.73), Williams (4.194, 4.195, 4.196), Finkelstein (11.130a), Baker (11.130b), Fekete (11.130c)

B. FILM, RADIO, TELEVISION

15.78 Adorno, T. W. "How to Look at Television." *Quarterly of Film, Radio and Television*, 8 (1954), 229–35.
Various reprints.

15.79a Waldman, Diane. "Critical Theory and Film: Adorno and 'The Culture Industry' Revisited." *NGC*, No. 12 (Fall 1977), 39–60.
A thoughtful critique of the kind of 'literary' dismissals of film that Waldman finds in 15.28 and 15.49.

15.80 Baker, Bert. *The T.V. Tie-up.* London: Communist Party of Great Britain [1961].

15.81 ———. "What Is Television?" *MT*, January 1964, 343–47.

15.82 ———. "The Future of Television." *Comment* (London), 10 (April 1972), 138–41.
The Communist Party of Great Britain needs to understand the contradictions of TV and the media in order to work out a policy of change.

15.83 Balázs, Béla. *Theory of the Film: Character and Growth of a New Art.* 1945/1952; New York: British Book Center, 1971.
Despite its date, this Hungarian work remains one of the best introductions to film theory for students new to the subject. Balázs's approach is materialist, lucid, and undogmatic.

15.84 Barnouw, Erik. *Tube of Plenty: The Evolution of American Television.* New York: Oxford University Press, 1975.
This is liberal rather than radical scholarship, but it is a standard work with a critical edge to it.

15.85 Ben-Horin, Daniel. "Television Without Tears: An Outline of a Socialist Approach to Popular Television." *Socialist Revolution*, No. 35 (September–October 1977) 7–35.
Review of left critiques and actual work in TV; a socialist approach must take account of viewer psychology and needs, production technique, integration with a political movement. Useful notes.

15.86 Caughie, John. "The Television Festive." *Screen*, 18 (Winter 1977), 91–107.
Since a Marxist takeover some years back, *Screen* has specialized in semiologically influenced Marxist analyses of film and British TV.

15.87 Cawelti, John G. *The Six-Gun Mystique.* Bowling Green, Ohio: Bowling Green University Popular Press, 1971. (NM)

15.88 Chambers, Iain, et al. "Marxism and Culture." *Screen,* 18 (Winter 1977), 109–19.

15.89 Citron, Michelle, et al. "Women and Film: A Discussion of Feminist Aesthetics." *NGC,* No. 13 (Winter 1978), 83–107.
Interview concerning both mass culture and 'art' films relevant to women.

15.90 Communist Party of Great Britain. "The Future of Broadcasting: Evidence Submitted by the Communist Party to the Committee on Broadcasting." *MT,* March 1961, 86–94.
CPGB proposals for changes in the structure and policies of British state radio and TV.

15.91 Coward, Rosalind. "Class, 'Culture,' and the Social Formation." *Screen,* 18 (Spring 1977), 75–105.

15.92 Denkin, Harvey. "Linguistic Models in Early Soviet Cinema." *Cinema Journal,* 17 (Fall 1977), 1–13.
Film speech and construction in Eikhenbaum, Eisenstein, and Vertov, in whose work the montage principle expressed the essence of Marxism.

15.93 Eaton, Mick. "Television Situation Comedy." *Screen,* 19 (Winter 1978/79), 61–89.

15.94 Eisenstein, Sergei. *Film Form and Film Sense.* New York: Meridian, 1957.
Compilation completed just before Eisenstein's death in 1948.

15.95 Fiske, John, and John Hartley. *Reading Television.* London: Methuen, 1978. (NM)

15.96 Furhammer, Leif, and Folke Isaksson. *Politics and Film.* 1968; New York: Praeger, 1971. (NM)

15.97 Gitlin, Todd. "Sixteen Notes on Television and the Movement." In 2.8, 335–66.
Gitlin offers useful comments on the way TV can both spawn and incorporate opposition, and on the ways around incorporation.

15.98 Greene, Naomi. "Brecht, Godard, and Epic Cinema." *Praxis,* No. 1 (Spring 1975), 19–24.

15.99 Grimshaw, Mark, and Carl Gardner. " 'Free Radio' in Italy." *Wedge*, No. 1 (Summer 1977), 14–17.

A discussion of the independent radio stations that have sprung up in Italy offers a concrete vision of what socialist democratization of the media might mean.

15.100 Groombridge, Brian. *Television and the People: A Program for Democratic Participation.* Harmondsworth: Penguin, 1972. (NM)

Useful descriptions of participatory experiments with TV in a number of countries.

15.101 Guback, Thomas H. "American Interests in the British Film Industry." *The Quarterly Review of Economics and Business*, 8 (Summer 1967), 7–21.

15.102 Hall, Stuart. "Television and Culture." *Sight and Sound*, 45 (Autumn 1976), 246–52.

Provides a useful, readable introduction to TV as a *form* that transforms items from other media.

15.103 Hauser, Arnold. "The Film Age." In 14.30, Vol. 4, 226–59.

15.104 Heath, Stephen. "Television: A World in Action." *Screen*, 18 (Summer 1977), 7–59.

15.105 Henny, Leonard. "The Role of Filmmakers in Revolutionary Social Change." *Praxis,* No. 2 (Winter 1976), 157–75.

15.106 Hogenkamp, Bert. "Film and the Workers' Movement in Britain, 1929–1939." *Sight and Sound*, 45 (Spring 1976), 68–76.

15.107 Jarvie, Ian C. *Movies and Society*. New York: Basic Books, 1970. (NM)

Published in England as *Toward a Sociology of the Cinema*, this is a comprehensive study. See especially "Part 4. The Sociology of Evaluation."

15.108 Kaplan, E. Ann. "Lina Wertmuller's Sexual Politics." *Marxist Perspectives*, No. 2 (Summer 1978), 94–105.

15.109 Kellner, Douglas. "TV, Ideology, and Emancipatory Popular Culture." *Socialist Review*, No. 45 (May–June 1979), 13–53.

15.110 Kleinhans, Chuck, and Julia Lesage. "Marxism and Film Criticism: The Current Situation." *MR*, No. 8 (Spring 1977), 146–49.

Survey of European and Anglo-American Marxist film criticism.

15.111 Knutsen, Peter. "Dragnet: The Perfect Crime?" *Liberation*, 18 (May 1974), 28–31.

15.112 Kracauer, Siegfried. *Theory of Film: The Redemption of Physical Reality*. 1960; New York: Oxford University Press, 1974. (NM)

15.113 Lang, Kurt, and Gladys E. Lang. *Politics and Television*. Chicago: Quadrangle, 1968. (NM)
Sociological studies of the way TV covered particular political events. Critique of McLuhanism.

15.114 Lawson, John Howard. *Film: The Creative Process: The Search for an Audio-Visual Language and Structure*. New York: Hill and Wang, 1964.

15.115 Liehm, Antonin. "The Contemporary Social Film: Its Contents and Authentic Characteristics." *Praxis*, No. 1 (Spring 1975), 111–14.

15.116 Lopate, Carol. "Daytime Television: You'll Never Want to Leave Home." *Radical America*, 11 (January–February 1977), 33–51.

15.117 Lukács, Georg. "The Poetry of the Film." *New Hungarian Quarterly*, 15 (Summer 1974), 62–67.
An early (1913) comparison of film and theater.

15.118 Macbean, James Roy. *Film and Revolution*. Bloomington: Indiana University Press, 1975.
See especially "Post-Bazin Aesthetics: The Theory and Practice of Marxist Film Criticism" (285–326). Rest of book is on revolutionary films by Godard and others.

15.119 Mander, Jerry. *Four Arguments for the Elimination of Television*. New York: William Morrow, 1978. (NM)

15.120 Mayer, J. P. *Sociology of Film: Studies and Documents*. London: Faber and Faber, 1946. (NM)

15.121 Mayne, Judith. "Eisenstein, Vertov, and the Montage Principle." In 2.10, 116–24.

15.122 Montagu, Ivor. *Film World: A Guide to Cinema*. Harmondsworth: Penguin, 1964. (NM)

15.123 Morin, Edgar. *The Stars*. New York: Evergreen, 1960. (NM)
Psycho-social study.

15.124 Neale, Steve. "Propaganda." *Screen*, 18 (Autumn 1977), 9–40.

15.125 Newcomb, Horace, ed. *Television: The Critical View*. New York: Oxford University Press, 1976.
Contains radical essays by Adorno, Schroeder.

15.126 Nowell-Smith, Geoffrey. "Television–Football–the World." *Screen*, 19 (Winter 1978-9), 45–59.

15.127 Pearce, Frank. "Art and Reality: Gangsters in Film and Society." In 14.50, 245–70.

15.128 Potamkin, Harry A. *The Compound Cinema: The Film Writings*. Ed. L. Jacobs. New York: Teacher's College Press of Columbia University, 1977.
Important radical American film writer of the thirties.

15.129 Quart, Leonard. "On Altman: Image as Essence." *Marxist Perspectives*, No. 1 (Spring 1978), 118–25.

15.130 Renault, Gregory. "Over the Rainbow: Dialectic and Ideology in *The Wizard of Oz*." *Praxis*, No. 4 (1978), 169–80.
On the 1939 film.

15.131 Rustin, Michael. "The Semiology of 'La Chinoise'." In 14.50, 221–44.
A practical analysis that shows how semiology could be united with a radical political perspective.

15.132 SCAN. *TV Handbook*. London: SCAN, 1974.
On bias, content, unions, and ownership in British TV. Suggestions for fighting media monopoly.

15.133 Sharits, Paul. "Words Per Page,"and "A Cinematic Model for Film Studies in Higher Education." *Film Culture*, Nos. 65–66 (1978), 29–43, 43–68.

15.134 Skornia, Harry. *Television and Society: An Inquest and Agenda for Improvement*. New York: McGraw-Hill, 1965.
Liberal rather than radical, but solid criticism by one with substantial experience in the medium.

15.135 ———. *Television and the News*. Palo Alto, Cal.: Pacific Books, 1968.

15.136 Slutski, Boris. "The Writer and Television: Contact with Poetry." *Soviet Studies in Literature*, 13 (Summer 1977), 52–56.

15.137 Smith, Robert Rutherford. *Beyond the Wasteland: The Criticism of Broadcasting*. Urbana, Ill.: NCTE, 1976. (NM)
Discusses techniques of, and issues in, broadcast criticism.

15.138 "Television Supplement." *NLR*, No. 7 (January–February

1961), 30–48.

NLR's presentation to the Pilkington Committee, a British government body inquiring into broadcasting.

15.139 Tracey, Michael. *The Production of Political Television.* London: Routledge & Kegan Paul, 1977. (NM)

15.140 Tuchman, Gaye, ed. *The TV Establishment.* Englewood Cliffs, N.J.: Prentice-Hall, 1974.

A collection that aims to show the way television "maintains hegemony and legitimates the *status quo*." Sections on making news, audience, hegemony.

*15.141 Williams, Raymond. *Television: Technology and Cultural Form.* 1974; New York: Schocken Books, 1975.

Much technological detail, somewhat at the expense of Williams's socialist perspective.

15.142 _____ . "A Lecture on Realism." *Screen*, 18 (Spring 1977), 61–74.

15.143 Winston, Brian, et al. *Television Coverage of Industrial Relations: Evidence Presented to the Committee on the Future of Broadcasting.* Glasgow: SSRC, 1975. (NM)

15.144 Woddis, Jack. "Television: The Wednesday Explosion." *Labour Monthly* (London), 49 (March 1967), 135–36.

15.145 Wollen, Peter. *Signs and Meaning in the Cinema.* 1969; rev. ed. London: Secker and Warburg, 1972.

Useful as a readable introduction to cinema semiology and auteur theory.

15.146 Wright, Will. *Sixguns and Society: A Structural Study of the Western.* Berkeley: University of California Press, 1975. (NM)

An analysis of the Western that connects the genre to political changes in the U.S.

Others: Davis (12.8), Barker (14.5), Laurenson (14.50)

C. OTHER MEDIA

15.147 Adorno, Theodor W. "On Popular Music." *Studies in Philosophy and Social Science*, 9, No. 1 (1941), 17–48.

Adorno discusses content, presentation, and audience in terms of concepts like standardization and glamor.

15.148 _____ . "A Social Critique of Radio Music." *Kenyon Review*, 7 (Spring 1945), 208–17.

15.149 Angell, Norman. *The Press and the Organization of Society.* London: Labour Publishing Company, 1922.
A pioneering socialist analysis of the press and a proposal for worker control.

15.150 Aronson, James. *The Press and the Cold War.* Indianapolis: Bobbs-Merrill, 1970.
A radical journalist's account of the press's anticommunism.

15.151 _____ . *Packaging the News.* New York: International Publishers, 1971.

15.152 _____ . *Deadline for the Media.* Indianapolis: Bobbs-Merrill, 1972.

15.153 Bagdikian, Ben. "The Media Monopolies." *The Progressive*, June 1978, 31–34.

15.154 Berger, John. *Ways of Seeing.* London: Penguin, 1972.
Provocative work of British art critic on perception, images in advertising, and how to analyze visual material (much of it based on Benjamin); originally a four-part BBC film series.

15.155 Brohm, Jean-Marie. *Sport: A Prison of Measured Time.* 1976; London: Ink Links, 1978.
Essays ranging from the sociology to the imagery of sport, written for those who oppose "the dominant institutionalized form of bodily development."

15.156 Buhle, Paul. "The New Comics and American Culture." In 2.8, 367–411.
A valuable if uncritical survey of information about American comics.

15.157 Burchill, Julie, and Tony Parsons. *'The Boy Looked at Johnny': The Obituary of Rock and Roll.* London: Pluto Press, 1979. (NM)

15.158 Bushell, Terry. "Thoughts on Leisure and Sport. I. Leisure." *MT*, December 1975, 366–75; "II. Sport." *MT*, February 1976, 64–70.

15.159 Cawelti, John G. *Adventure, Mystery and Romance: Formula Stories as Art and Popular Culture.* Chicago:

University of Chicago Press, 1976. (NM)

15.160 Chapple, Steve, and Reebee Garofalo. *Rock 'n Roll Is Here to Pay: The History and Politics of the Music Industry*. Chicago: Nelson-Hall, 1977. (NM)

15.161 Chester, Andrew. "For a Rock Aesthetic." *NLR*, 59 (January–February 1970), 83–87.

See also the "Comment" on Chester by Richard Merton, 88–96.

15.162 Chomsky, Noam. "The U.S. Media and the Tet Offensive." *Race and Class*, 20 (Summer 1978), 21–40. (NM)

A case study in news as propaganda.

15.163 Cirino, Robert. *Don't Blame the People*. New York: Random House, 1971.

Systematic and critical study of bias in news reporting.

15.164 _____ . *Power to Persuade: Mass Media and the News*. New York: Bantam, 1974.

15.165 Clarke, John, and Tony Jefferson. "Working-Class Youth Cultures." In *Working Class Youth Cultures*. Ed. G. Mungham and G. Pearson. London: Routledge & Kegan Paul, 1976, 138–58.

Summary of work done at the Centre for Contemporary Cultural Studies at Birmingham University. Useful section on "Reading Youth Cultural Styles." See also 15.198.

15.166 Cohen, Stanley, and Jock Young, eds. *The Manufacture of News: A Reader*. Beverly Hills, Cal.: Sage Publications, 1973. (M/NM)

15.167 Cohen, Stanley. "Breaking Out, Smashing Up and the Social Context of Aspiration." *WPCS*, 5 (Spring 1974), 37–64. On youth culture.

15.168 Cole, Harvey R. *Socialism and the Press*. London: Gollancz, 1952.

Attitudes toward socialism in the British Press.

15.169 Critcher, Charles, and Paul Willis. "Women in Sport." *WPCS*, 5 (Spring 1974), 3–36.

15.170 Denisoff, Serge. "Massification and Popular Music." *Journal of Popular Culture*, 9 (Summer 1975), 886–94. (NM)

15.171 Denisoff, Serge, and Mark H. Levine. "Generations & Counter-Culture: A Study in the Ideology of Music." *Youth and*

Society, 2 (September 1970), 33–58. (NM)

15.172 Dorfman, Ariel. "Salvation and Wisdom of the Common Man: The Theology of *Reader's Digest*." *Praxis*, No. 3 (1976), 41–56.

15.173 Ewen, Stuart. *Captains of Consciousness: Advertising and the Social Roots of Consumer Culture*. New York: McGraw-Hill, 1976.
By all accounts, one of the major radical texts on mass culture.

*15.174 Flood-Page, M., and Pete Fowler. "Writing About Rock." *WPCS*, 2 (Spring 1972), 139–60.

15.175 Frith, Simon. *The Sociology of Rock*. London: Constable, 1978.
Sections on the production, consumption, and ideology of rock, understood as "a mass medium which is *general* to contemporary capitalist culture."

15.176 _____. "Rock and Popular Culture." *Socialist Revolution*, No. 31 (January–February 1977), 97–112.

15.177 Hadwin, Arnold. "Fighting Radicalism: The Role of the Press." *Socialist Commentary*, September 1976, 8–9.

15.178 Hall, Stuart. "The Social Eye of *Picture Post*." *WPCS*, No. 2 (Spring 1972), 71–120.

15.179 Harrison, S. *Poor Men's Guardians: A Record of the Struggles for a Democratic Newspaper Press, 1763-1973*. London: Lawrence and Wishart, 1974.

15.180 Hart, James D. *The Popular Book: A History of America's Literary Taste*. 1950; Berkeley: University of California Press, 1963. (NM)
Useful academic account of social background and ideology of readers, nature of the popular book, similar topics.

15.181 Hoch, Paul. *Rip Off the Big Game: The Exploitation of Sports by the Power Elite*. Garden City, N.Y.: Doubleday, 1972.
A Marxist attack on the sports establishment in the U.S.

15.182 Inglis, Fred. *The Imagery of Power: A Critique of Advertising*. London: Heinemann, 1972.
The result of Inglis's commission to update Denys Thompson's pioneering critique of advertising, *Voice of Civilization* (1944).

15.183 _____. *The Name of the Game: Sport and Society*. London:

Heinemann Educational, 1977.

*15.184 Jones, Bryn. "A Bibliography of Rock." *WPCS*, No. 2 (Spring 1972), 129–38.

15.185 Jones, Jennifer. "A Woman's Place." *Wedge*, No. 1 (Summer 1977), 47–53.

On sexism in architecture.

15.186 Kaplan, Frederick I. "Intimacy and Conformity in American Soap Opera." *Journal of Popular Culture*, 9 (Winter 1975), 622–25. (NM)

15.187 Koenig, René. *A La Mode: The Social Psychology of Fashion.* New York: The Seabury Press, 1973. (NM)

15.188 Kofsky, Frank. *Lenny Bruce: The Comedian as Social Critic and Secular Moralist.* New York: Monad Press, 1974.

15.189 Laing, Dave. *The Sound of Our Time.* London: Sheed and Ward, 1969.

Brief comments on the transformation from folk to pop music, and on a theoretical framework for studying popular music. Draws on Adorno, Ian Birchall, others.

15.190 Leavis, Q. D. *Fiction and the Reading Public.* 1932; London: Chatto and Windus, 1968. (NM)

See annotation to 15.26.

15.191 McCann, Eamonn. *The British Press and Northern Ireland.* London: Northern Ireland Socialist Research Centre, 1971.

15.192 McDonnell, Kevin. "Football: Whose Divisions?" *Wedge*, No. 2 (Spring 1978), 14–20.

An excellent Marxist account of the history and present functions of British soccer.

15.193 Molotch, Harvey, and Marilyn Lester. "Accidents, Scandals and Routines: Resources for Insurgent Methodology." *The Insurgent Sociologist*, 3, No. 4 (1973), 1–11.

15.194 Murdock, Graham. "Political Deviance: The Press Presentation of a Militant Mass Demonstration." In 15.166, 156–75.

15.195 Norwood, Graham. "The Press and the Perks." *Labour Monthly* (London), 60 (September 1978), 363–65.

15.196 Patterson, Tim. "Notes on the Historical Application of Marxist Cultural Theory." *S&S*, 39 (Fall 1975), 275–91.

Includes analysis of white country music in the U.S.

15.197 Piccone, Paul. "From Youth Culture to Political Praxis." *Radical America*, 3 (November 1969), 15–21.

15.198 "Resistance Through Rituals." *WPCS*, Nos. 7 & 8 (Summer 1975). Rptd. as *Resistance Through Rituals: Youth Subcultures in Post-war Britain.* Ed. Stuart Hall and Tony Jefferson. London: Hutchinson, 1976.

Includes articles on law and order campaigns, "teds," "mods," "skinheads," drug culture, communes, reggae, and other topics; comments on theory, method, ethnography.

15.199 Roediger, David. "Racism, Reconstruction, and the Labour Press: The Rise and Fall of the *St. Louis Daily Press*, 1864–1866." *S&S*, 42 (Summer 1978), 156–77.

15.200 Rossi, Lee D. "The Whore Vs. the Girl-Next-Door: Stereotypes of Women in *Playboy, Penthouse,* and *Oui.*" *Journal of Popular Culture,* 9 (Summer 1975), 90–94. (NM)

15.201 Sedgwick, Peter. "The Reader's Digest." *NLR*, Nos. 13–14 (January–April 1962), 129–36.

A literary, social, and psychological critique.

15.202 Smith, Michael A., et al. *Leisure and Society in Britain.* London: Allen Lane, 1973. (M/NM)

Reprints excerpts from Williams (4.194, 4.195) and Hoggart (14.31); also theoretical articles and articles on miners and pigeon racing, holidays and class, other topics.

15.203 Sullivan, John. "The New *Maclean's*: Import Substitution in the Ideology Market." *This Magazine*, 11 (January–February 1977), 5–9.

15.204 Talbot, Colin Maxwell. *Colin Talbot's Greatest Hits.* Sydney: Wild & Woolley, 1977. (NM)

On sport, rock and roll, other topics in Australia.

15.205 Tankard, James W. "The Effect of Advertising on Language: Making the Sacred Profane." *Journal of Popular Culture,* 9 (Fall 1975), 325–30. (NM)

15.206 Taylor, Ian. "Soccer Consciousness and Soccer Hooliganism. In *Images of Deviance.* Ed. Stanley Cohen. Harmondsworth: Penguin, 1971, 134–64.

One of the best examples of the new radical sociology of deviance (15.166 is another example) in Britain. Taylor discusses a number of issues relevant to a 'reading' of soccer.

15.207 Todd, Judith. *The Big Sell: The Structure and Strategy of the Mass Media.* London: Lawrence and Wishart, 1961.
Mainly on the ideology and economics of the British press in the earlier part of this century.

15.208 Tuchman, Gaye. "Objectivity as Strategic Ritual: An Examination of Newsmen's Notions of Objectivity." *American Journal of Sociology,* 77 (January 1972), 660–79.

15.209 Tunstall, Jeremy. *The Media Are American: Anglo-American Media in the World.* New York: Columbia University Press, 1977.

15.210 Visnevskaya, I. "The Detective Story as an Ideological Weapon." *Current Digest of the Soviet Press,* July 22, 1964, 13–16.

Others: "Change" (6.6), Fitting (6.9), Lawford (13.1)

INDEX

A. CRITIC INDEX

This is an index to critics who have at least three separate items in different sections of the Guide. *Under each critic listed, numbers alone indicate works by that critic; numbers followed by names (in parentheses) indicate items on that critic. Some critics (e.g., John Berger, Hugh MacDiarmid, George Orwell) are also authors; criticism on their creative work can be found in section 11.*

Adler, Joyce. 11.139f, 11.139g, 11.139h, 11.139i.
Adorno, Theodor. 2.1, 4.1, 7.1, 11.96b, 14.39, 15.15, 15.27, 15.28, 15.49, 15.78, 15.125, 15.147, 15.148; 4.22 (Buck-Morss), 4.83 (Jameson), 15.39 (Enzenberger), 15.65 (Negt), 15.79a (Waldman), 15.189 (Laing).
Althusser, Louis. 4.2, 5.1, 13.14; 4.3a (Callinicos), 4.3b (Barker), 4.23 (Burniston), 4.112 (Macherey), 13.5 (Bennett).
Aronowitz, Stanley. 4.4, 4.5, 15.25, 15.29, 15.40a.
Arvin, Newton. 9.51, 9.59, 9.61, 11.94b, 11.97b, 11. 186b, 11.217d, 11.228a.
Barker, Francis. 4.3b, 4.177b, 14.5, 14.6.
Barthes, Roland. 13.3, 13.14, 13.17, 13.35, 14.8, 15.31; 13.4a (Jayne), 13.4b (Thody), 13.12 (Coward and Ellis), 13.27 (Jameson).
Baxandall, Lee. 1.4, 2.2, 4.7, 4.8, 4.9, 4.126, 4.145a, 4.146, 5.3, 5.4, 5.5, 9.46a, 11.2b, 11.34a, 11.144b, 15.41.

Beitz, Ursula. *See* LeRoy, Gaylord.
Benjamin, Walter. 2.1, 4.13, 4.14, 4.15, 4.16, 5.11a, 15.32; 4.1 (Adorno), 4.17a (Jacobs), 4.17b (Witte), 4.17c (Burns), 4.22 (Buck-Morss), 4.83 (Jameson), 15.39 (Enzenberger), 15.65 (Negt), 15.154 (Berger).
Berger, John. 7.17a, 15.31, 15.154; 4.104 (Long).
Birchall, Ian. 4.18, 4.19, 6.22b, 14.73a; 15.189 (Laing).
Brecht, Bertolt. 2.1, 5.9, 5.10, 7.3; 4.6 (Arvon), 4.13 (Benjamin), 5.1 (Althusser), 5.3 (Baxandall), 5.11a (Benjamin), 5.11b (Lunn), 5.11c (Hermand), 5.11d (Zimmerman), 5.11e (Bruggemann), 5.41 (Williams), 15.65 (Negt), 15.98 (Greene).
Bronowski, Jacob. 7.4, 11.19c, 11.19d.
Buhle, Paul. 9.11, 11.124a, 15.156.
Burgum, Edwin Berry. 6.3, 7.5, 9.77, 9.78, 11.61c, 11.66a, 11.88c, 11.96a, 11.102e, 11.144a, 11.187a, 11.200b, 11.201b, 11.233a, 11.235b, 11.237a.

Burke, Kenneth. 9.40, 9.50, 9.51; 9.41a
(Jameson), 14.12 (Duncan).
Calverton, V. F. 9.3, 9.34, 9.42, 9.56,
9.65, 11.4a; 9.8 (Hicks).
Cantarow, Ellen. 4.46, 8.26, 12.4, 12.18.
Cantwell, Robert. 11.97c, 11.118b,
11.194b.
Caudwell, Christopher. 4.24, 4.25, 4.26,
8.98, 11.113c, 11.114a, 11.190b,
11.222b, 14.68; 4.27a (Margolies),
4.27b (Mulhern), 4.27c (Sypher), 4.27d
(Pradhan), 4.27e (Thompson), 4.27f
(Draper), 14.61 (Maxwell).
Clark, J. Wilson. 10.2, 10.20, 10.21,
10.22, 11.129c.
Cowley, Malcolm. 9.35, 9.36, 9.43, 9.50,
9.51, 9.53, 9.65, 9.72, 11.60a, 11.165a.
Craig, David. 2.3, 4.29, 4.30, 4.31, 8.3,
8.15, 8.28, 8.67, 11.58q, 11.62d, 11.63o,
11.113l, 11.126c, 11.126d, 11.193c,
12.6, 15.14; 4.9 (Baxandall).
Danby, John E. 8.29, 11.13a, 11.192a,
11.236a, 11.236b.
Day-Lewis, Cecil. 8.83, 8.84, 8.85, 8.88.
Delany, Paul. 11.102g, 11.113b, 11.189u,
13.3.
Delany, Sheila. 8.30, 8.31, 8.32, 11.40b,
11.40c, 11.40d, 11.104a, 11.170a,
12.18, 13.15.
Diakonova, Nina. 6.7, 11.31c, 11.188c.
Eagleton, Terry. 2.1, 4.39, 4.40, 4.41,
4.42, 4.43, 4.44, 4.45, 4.115a, 4.204c,
6.29, 8.33, 8.68, 11.7k, 11.21a, 11.36a,
11.48e, 11.48f, 11.63n, 11.80b, 11.85d,
11.92a, 11.113i, 11.162f, 11.208b,
11.221a, 13.12; 4.203 (Williams).
Egan, Michael. 4.30, 4.31, 8.67, 11.217c.
Egbert, Donald Drew. 8.4, 9.5, 14.13.
Enzenberger, Hans Magnus. 15.39; 15.32
(Benjamin), 15.40a (Aronowitz), 15.65
(Negt).
Ellis, Kate. 4.46, 12.18, 15.19.
Engels, Frederick. See Marx, Karl.
Fairley, Margaret. 10.3, 10.4, 11.125a,
11.132a.
Farrell, James T. 9.44, 9.50, 9.72, 9.80.
Fekete, John. 4.47, 4.48, 11.71c, 11.130c,
11.173a.
Finkelstein, Sidney. 4.50, 4.51, 4.52, 9.6,
9.82, 11.2c, 11.2d, 11.16d, 11.60e,

11.63m, 11.66h, 11.68e, 11.130a,
11.133a, 11.134a, 11.145c, 11.161c,
11.185e, 11.189e, 11.206b, 11.218a.
Fischer, Ernst. 2.3, 4.53, 4.54, 4.165; 4.20
(Bisztray), 4.104 (Long).
Franklin, H. Bruce. 6.6, 9.7, 9.19,
11.139l, 12.12, 12.18.
Freeman, Joseph. 9.47, 9.50, 9.51, 9.53,
9.57.
Garaudy, Roger. 4.56, 4.57.; 4.20 (Bisztray).
Geismar, Maxwell. 9.83, 9.84, 11.4c,
11.16b, 11.38d, 11.53b, 11.60d, 11.61d,
11.66b, 11.68a, 11.76a, 11.88d, 11.97a,
11.111a, 11.118c, 11.123e, 11.140a,
11.157a, 11.185a, 11.201c, 11.206a,
11.233b, 14.20, 14.21, 14.22, 14.23.
Giles, Barbara. 11.66a, 11.68c, 11.76b,
11.185b.
Girard, René. 14.8, 14.24, 14.25, 14.26.
Gitlin, Todd. 15.19, 15.41, 15.97.
Gold, Michael. 9.49, 9.53, 9.57, 9.58,
9.65, 9.72; 9.54 (Madden).
Goldmann, Lucien. 4.59, 4.60, 4.61, 4.62,
4.63, 4.64, 4.65, 4.66, 4.124a, 6.11,
13.35, 14.2, 14.8, 14.71, 15.43; 4.67a
(Rodriguez and Zimmerman), 4.67b
(Rudich), 4.67c (Leenhardt), 4.67d
(Routh), 4.156 (Sanders), 4.201 (Wil-
liams), 14.24 (Girard), 14.51 (Lauren-
son and Swingewood), 14.67 (Sam-
mons).
Goldstein, Leonard. 8.34, 11.39a, 11.39b,
11.146f.
Goode, John. 8.52, 11.44a, 11.75b,
11.75c, 11.75d, 11.97f, 11.97g, 11.113j,
11.141b, 11.150k, 11.150l.
Gramsci, Antonio. 4.69, 4.70; 4.23
(Burniston and Weedon), 4.71a
(Boggs), 4.71b (Thibaudeau), 4.71c
(Davidson), 4.71d (Mercer), 15.68
(Sallach).
Gray, Nigel. 8.70, 11.14a, 11.90a,
11.154a, 11.193d, 11.205a, 11.220a,
12.6.
Hall, Stuart. 4.18, 4.73, 11.113f, 14.5,
15.45, 15.102, 15.178, 15.198.
Harap, Louis. 4.74, 4.132, 11.169a,
11.169b, 11.169c.
Harold, Brent. 6.12, 11.661, 12.8, 12.13.

Harrison, John R. 11.63k, 11.113h, 11.119c, 11.171b, 11.239d, 14.29.
Hart, Henry. 9.50, 9.51, 9.58.
Hawthorn, Jeremy. 4.76, 11.235a, 12.6; 4.9 (Baxandall).
Heinemann, Margot. 5.20, 11.131a, 11.189d, 12.6.
Henderson, Harry B. 9.21, 11.50b, 11.139j.
Henderson, Philip. 8.90, 8.91, 8.92, 8.95, 11.135a, 11.150e.
Hicks, Granville. 8.51, 9.8, 9.50, 9.51, 9.52, 9.53, 9.57, 9.61, 9.65, 9.72, 11.30c, 11.38b, 11.85a, 11.150g, 11.165b, 11.183a, 11.230a
Hill, Christopher. 8.35, 11.136a, 11.146a, 11.177c.
Hoggart, Richard. 11.7b, 11.7c, 14.31, 14.32, 14.33, 14.34, 15.47, 15.202.
Hohendahl, Peter U. 4.22, 4.79, 4.80, 4.81.
Horkheimer, Max. 15.28, 15.48, 15.49; 15.39 (Enzenberger), 15.65 (Negt), 15.79a (Waldman).
Howard, David B. 8.52, 11.50a, 11.86b, 11.141c.
Howard, Milton. 11.88e, 11.158a, 11.162d.
Howe, Irving. 9.22, 9.87, 11.16e, 11.48c, 11.61e, 11.70b, 11.72a, 11.75e, 11.97d, 11.97e, 11.114b, 11.162e, 11.168b, 11.171c, 11.179b, 11.182b, 11.203a, 11.225a, 14.35, 14.36, 14.37, 14.38, 14.39.
Inglis, Fred. 14.42, 15.13, 15.182, 15.183.
Jackson, T. A. 8.5, 8.88, 8.95, 11.58a.
Jameson, Fredric. 2.1, 2.9, 4.6, 4.83, 4.84, 4.85, 4.86, 6.13, 9.41a, 9.88, 11.119a, 13.25, 13.26, 13.27, 15.19, 15.25; 14.67 (Sammons).
Johnson, Roy. 6.14, 11.20a, 11.74e.
Kampf, Louis. 4.89, 12.2, 12.15, 12.16, 12.17, 12.18, 15.19.
Kettle, Arnold. 4.42, 4.90, 4.204a, 8.6, 8.7, 8.53, 8.54, 8.73, 8.74, 11.8b, 11.17a, 11.21d, 11.30d, 11.37a, 11.48a, 11.48b, 11.56b, 11.56c, 11.58f, 11.58g, 11.58h, 11.58i, 11.62a, 11.69c, 11.80a, 11.85b, 11.102f, 11.188b, 11.190d, 11.209a, 11.219a, 12.6.
Kogan, P. 4.91, 4.92, 4.93, 11.71a, 12.19.

Krieger, Elliott. 11.40f, 11.189s, 11.189t.
Landor, M. 11.16c, 11.66f, 11.66g, 11.68h, 11.206c, 11.215a, 11.218b.
Lawford, Paul. 1.5, 11.116f, 13.1
Lawson, John Howard. 5.22, 9.6, 9.58, 9.91, 11.161b, 11.165c, 15.114.
Lenin, V. I. 4.96, 4.97, 4.98; 4.20 (Bisztray), 4.82 (James), 4.99a (Morawski), 4.194 (Williams).
LeRoy, Gaylord. 2.7 (with Ursula Beitz), 4.100, 4.101 (with Ursula Beitz), 4.188, 8.8, 8.56, 9.23, 9.73 (with Ursula Beitz), 9.92, 11.5a, 11.35a, 11.102g, 11.181a, 11.183b, 11.211a, 11.230b, 12.23, 12.24; 4.9 (Baxandall).
Lindsay, Jack. 2.3, 4.103, 5.23, 7.9, 7.10, 7.11, 7.12, 7.13, 9.6, 11.19a, 11.19b, 11.26a, 11.46b, 11.58b, 11.58c, 11.74c, 11.100a, 11.102i, 11.113p, 11.141a, 11.150c, 11.150d, 11.158c, 11.195a.
Lowenthal, Leo. 14.56, 14.57, 14.58.
Lucas, John. 8.52, 8.57, 8.97, 11.58k, 11.73a.
Lukács, Georg. 2.1, 4.105, 4.106, 4.107, 4.108, 5.25, 5.26, 5.27, 6.17, 6.18, 6.19, 6.20, 6.21, 11.188a, 14.8, 14.71, 15.117; 4.6 (Arvon), 4.17b (Witte), 4.20 (Bisztray), 4.23 (Burniston and Weedon), 4.27c (Sypher), 4.35 (Demetz), 4.83 (Jameson), 4.103 (Lindsay), 4.109a (Murphy), 4.109b (Lowy), 4.109c (Schmidt), 4.109d (Markus), 4.109e (Orr), 4.149 (Rieser), 4.169 (Steiner), 5.11b (Lunn), 6.10 (Fruchter), 6.22a (Fehér), 6.22b (Birchall), 6.22c (Crow), 6.26 (Shor), 8.58 ("Marxism and Romanticism").
Lunacharsky, Anatoli V. 4.110, 11.10a, 11.31a; 4.111a (Lebedev).
MacDiarmid, Hugh. 4.116, 11.28b; 8.75 (Kocmanova).
Macherey, Pierre. 4.112, 4.113, 4.114; 4.115a (Eagleton), 4.115b (Mercer and Radford).
Marcus, Jane. 11.235h, 14.40, 14.69.
Marcuse, Herbert. 4.118, 4.119, 4.120, 4.121, 4.122, 4.123, 15.58, 15.59; 4.83 (Jameson), 4.124a (Goldmann), 4.124b (Schoolman), 15.65 (Negt).
Marx, Karl. (Includes items for Engels,

Frederick.) 2.3, 2.6, 2.15, 4.126, 4.127, 13.14; 4.18 (Birchall), 4.20 (Bisztray), 4.35 (Demetz), 4.102 (Lifshitz), 4.106 (Lukács), 4.129 (Mehring), 4.133 (Morawski), 4.146 (Prawer), 4.147 (Rader), 4.152 (Rose), 4.181 (Von Staden), 4.182 (Von Staden), 4.194 (Williams), 5.26 (Lukács), 8.58 ("Marxism and Romanticism"), 14.61 (Maxwell).

Mathews, Robin. 10.1, 10.8, 11.6a, 11.32c, 11.82b, 11.129e, 11.147a, 11.148a, 11.178a, 12.25.

Matthiessen, F. O. 9.25, 9.94, 9.95, 11.61a, 11.64a, 11.86a, 11.139c, 11.212a, 11.228e; 9.26a (White), 9.64 (Ruland).

Mehring, Franz. 4.129, 11.58d; 4.35 (Demetz).

Mercer, Colin. 4.71d, 4.115b, 4.130.

Mitchell, Jack. 8.59, 8.77, 11.158d.

Mitchell, Stanley. 4.18, 4.131, 8.15.

Morawski, Stefan. 4.99a, 4.126, 4.132, 4.133, 4.134, 4.135, 4.136, 4.137, 4.138, 4.139; 14.67 (Sammons).

Morton, A. L. 7.19, 8.2, 8.10, 8.11, 8.12, 11.10b, 11.10c, 11.19f, 11.21e, 11.41a, 11.42a, 11.56a, 11.63j, 11.69a, 11.69b, 11.93b, 11.106a, 11.116b, 11.149c, 11.150h, 11.184a, 11.207a.

Mulhern, Francis. 4.27b, 4.39, 4.42, 4.66, 11.116a.

Musselwhite, David. 8.60, 11.21j, 14.5, 14.6.

O'Flinn, Paul. 8.13, 11.48i, 11.58s, 11.69e, 11.78c, 11.85f, 11.162g, 11.162h, 11.189r.

Ohmann, Carol. 11.21g, 11.185g, 11.235d.

Ohmann, Richard. 11.7g, 11.185g, 12.8, 12.9, 12.18, 12.27, 12.28, 13.37, 13.38.

O'Neil, Wayne. 12.2, 12.18, 13.31, 13.39.

Orr, John. 4.109e, 11.48l, 11.162j, 14.64.

Orwell, George. 8.14, 11.58e, 11.145a, 13.40, 14.68.

Phillips, William. 9.53, 9.59, 9.61, 9.62; 9.48 (Gilbert).

Plekhanov, George. 4.143, 4.144; 4.35 (Demetz), 4.145a (Baxandall).

Rahv, Philip. 9.53, 9.59, 9.61, 9.62, 9.63, 11.63c; 9.48 (Gilbert).

Raskin, Jonah. 8.78, 11.37b, 11.48h, 11.69d, 11.107b, 11.117a, 11.213e.

Rickword, Edgell. 8.85, 8.95, 8.97, 8.103, 11.7e, 11.12a, 11.45b, 11.119b.

Robinson, Lillian S. 4.150, 12.18, 15.67.

Rodriguez, Ileana. See Zimmerman, Marc.

Rubinstein, Annette T. 4.118, 8.16, 9.14, 11.56e, 11.64c, 11.88g, 11.97h, 11.189d, 11.212e, 14.63, 14.69.

Rudich, Norman. 2.13, 4.67b, 4.154, 11.46g, 11.79a.

Sanders, Scott. 4.156, 6.24, 8.79, 11.113a; 11.113o (Efron).

Sartre, Jean-Paul. 4.158, 4.159, 4.160, 4.161, 4.162, 4.163, 4.164, 4.165, 5.36, 11.60c, 11.66e, 14.39; 4.56 (Garaudy), 4.83 (Jameson), 4.166a (Willcox), 4.166b (Chiodi), 4.166c (Lawler), 4.166d (Aronson), 4.166e (McGuigan).

Schlauch, Margaret. 7.22, 8.38, 8.39, 8.40, 8.41, 11.40a, 11.102c, 11.171a, 13.48, 13.49, 13.50, 13.51, 13.52; 8.42a (Niecko).

Shor, Ira. 4.168, 5.5, 6.26, 12.31.

Siegel, Paul N. 4.176, 6.27, 7.23, 9.101, 11.17b, 11.109b, 11.123f, 11.162i, 11.189c, 11.189k, 11.189l, 11.189m, 11.189n, 11.199a, 11.237c.

Sillen, Samuel. 11.25a, 11.212b, 11.228b.

Smith, Bernard. 9.15, 9.53, 11.22a, 11.94a, 11.165a.

Solomon, Maynard. 2.15, 11.53c; 4.9 (Baxandall).

Southall, Raymond. 8.17, 8.43, 11.8d, 11.26c, 11.46h, 11.59a, 11.62g, 11.78b, 11.91a, 11.99b, 11.101b, 11.143b, 1.146e, 11.149d, 11.197b, 11.207e, 11.236h, 11.238a.

Spender, Stephen. 8.100, 8.101, 11.7e, 11.93a.

Swingewood, Alan. 4.170, 4.171, 4.172, 6.29, 6.30, 11.48j, 11.75f, 11.117c, 14.51, 15.73.

Thompson, E. P. 11.45a, 11.150a, 11.150b.

Thomson, George. 4.174, 5.38, 7.25, 7.26, 13.56, 13.57.
Trotsky, Leon. 4.175, 4.176, 7.27; 4.169 (Steiner), 4.177a (Deutscher), 4.177b (Barker), 4.177c (Geras).
Van Ghent, Dorothy. 11.8c, 11.56d, 11.58j, 11.128a, 11.177a, 14.74.
Vásquez, Adolfo Sánchez. 4.111b, 4.180; 4.9 (Baxandall).
Vicinus, Martha. 7.28, 8.62, 12.18.
Watt, Ian. 6.31, 11.56f, 11.67a, 11.177b, 14.8.
Way, Brian. 11.68d, 11.113g, 11.145b, 11.185c.
Weimann, Robert. 4.188, 4.189, 6.32, 6.33, 11.153a, 11.189c, 11.189d, 11.189h; 4.190a (Lennox).
West, Alick. 8.19, 8.20, 8.21, 8.63, 11.26b, 11.56g, 11.63e, 11.63f, 11.102b, 11.113m, 11.120a, 11.163b, 11.166a, 11.172a, 11.174a, 11.175a, 11.190a, 11.207d, 11.230c, 13.59.
Weston, Jack. 8.47, 8.48, 12.8.
Whipple, T. K. 9.38, 9.67, 11.1a, 11.4b, 11.38a, 11.60b, 11.61b, 11.70a, 11.118a, 11.121a, 11.123c, 11.161a, 11.179a, 11.186a, 11.201a.
Williams, Raymond. 4.193, 4.194, 4.195, 4.196, 4.197, 4.198, 4.199, 4.200, 4.201, 4.202, 4.203, 5.39, 5.40, 5.41, 5.42, 5.43, 6.34, 8.22, 8.23, 8.24, 8.64, 8.65, 8.66, 8.81, 11.5b, 11.21f, 11.35b, 11.48g, 11.58l, 11.58m, 11.62e, 11.63h, 11.63i, 11.85c, 11.113d, 11.113e, 11.116c, 11.143a, 11.161d, 11.162a, 11.175b, 11.231a, 14.8, 15.14, 15.75, 15.76, 15.77, 15.141, 15.142, 15.202; 4.204a (Kettle), 4.204b (Siegmund-Schultze), 4.204c (Eagleton), 4.204d (Watkins).
Wilson, Edmund. 9.59, 9.68, 9.69, 9.70, 10.43, 11.32a, 11.63b, 11.200a.
Wojcik, Manfred. 11.46c, 11.46d, 11.46e, 11.46f, 11.191f.
Zimmerman, Marc. 4.67a (with Ileana Rodriguez), 4.151 (with Ileana Rodriguez), 4.205, 4.206, 4.207, 5.11d.
Zipes, Jack. 4.128, 5.44, 6.35, 9.30, 9.31.
Zollman, Sol. 9.104, 11.32b, 11.168a.

B. TOPIC INDEX

This is a listing of topics that are treated in at least three items in the Guide.

Aesthetics. (*S.a.* Marxism and Art.) 1.10 (Raina), 2.1 (*Aesthetics and Politics*), 2.6 (Lang and Williams), 2.16 ("Symposium on Marxist Aesthetic Thought"), 4.6 (Arvon), 4.16 (Benjamin), 4.17b (Witte), 4.26 (Caudwell), 4.27a (Margolies), 4.27b (Mulhern), 4.38 (Dunham), 4.50 (Finkelstein), 4.55 (Fokkema and Kunne-Ibsch), 4.87 (Jauss), 4.103 (Lindsay), 4.106 (Lukács), 4.107 (Lukács), 4.118 (Marcuse), 4.124b (Schoolman), 4.127 (*Marx/Engels*), 4.131 (Mitchell), 4.132 (Morawski), 4.145a (Baxandall), 4.147 (Rader), 4.153 ("Round Table on the Arts"), 4.154 (Rudich), 4.162 (Sartre), 4.167 (Scanlan), 4.180 (Vásquez), 8.27 (Colley).
Alienation. 4.51 (Finkelstein), 5.12 (Caute), 9.6 (Finkelstein), 9.29 (Simpson), 9.90 (Langford), 11.2c (Finkelstein), 11.40d (Delany), 11.60e (Finkelstein), 11.66h (Finkelstein), 11.145c (Finkelstein), 11.156a (Gervais), 11.161c (Finkelstein), 11.185e (Finkelstein), 11.206b (Finkelstein).
Allegory. 8.26 (Cantarow), 8.31 (Delany), 8.89 (Harris), 11.40f (Krieger).
American Indian. 9.17 (Barnett), 11.139f (Adler), 15.146 (Wright).
Ballads. 7.19 (Morton), 8.3 (Craig), 8.10 (Morton), 9.1 (Ames).
Black Literature. 9.1 (Ames), 9.19 (Franklin), 9.75 (Brown), 11.66b (Geismar), 11.66c (Kroner), 11.66k (Kent), 11.237e (Robinson).
Censorship. 4.135 (Morawski), 4.137 (Morawski), 4.152 (Rose).
Character. 6.21 (Lukács), 8.87 (Fox), 11.97g (Goode).
Children's Literature. 5.44 (Zipes), 6.35 (Zipes), 12.10 (Dixon), 12.22 (Leeson).
Class. 4.125 (Markiewicz), 8.61 (Thompson), 10.7 (Mandel), 10.22 (Clark),

11.57a (Alsen), 11.210a (Smith),
11.217c (Egan), 12.10 (Dixon), 14.11
(Daiches), 15.62 (Murdock).

Class and Language. 13.6 (Bernstein),
13.7 (Bisseret), 13.30 (Lawton), 13.42
(Rosen), 13.53 (Sinha).

Classical Literature. 4.181 (Von Staden),
4.182 (Von Staden), 5.23 (Lindsay),
5.38 (Thomson), 5.39 (Williams), 7.25
(Thomson), 7.26 (Thomson), 13.57
(Thomson).

Commitment. 4.40 (Eagleton), 4.158
(Sartre), 5.12 (Caute), 8.72 (Katona).

Culture. (S.a. section 15.) 2.2 (Baxandall),
4.1 (Adorno), 4.4 (Aronowitz), 4.26
(Caudwell), 4.48 (Fekete), 4.61 (Goldmann), 4.69 (Gramsci), 4.72 (Gross),
4.73 (Hall), 4.85 (Jameson), 4.119
(Marcuse), 4.130 (Mercer and Nawrat), 4.173 (Tax), 4.194 (Williams),
4.195 (Williams), 4.196 (Williams),
5.28 (Mayer), 8.3 (Craig), 9.73 (Bonosky), 9.89 (Jerome), 9.91 (Lawson),
9.97 (Newman), 10.5 (Fine), 11.24a
(Harper and Kenny), 11.116b (Morton), 11.116d (Anderson), 12.17
(Kampf), 14.7 (Bradbury).

Decadence. 4.165 (Sartre), 8.67 (Craig
and Egan), 9.99 (Riche), 11.39a
(Goldstein), 11.63g (Ames), 11.66a
(Burgum).

Detective Fiction. 9.28 (Reilley), 11.84a
(Hulley), 15.210 (Visnevskaya).

Existentialism. 4.164 (Sartre), 4.166c
(Lawler), 9.6 (Finkelstein), 11.2a
(Bigsby), 11.2d (Finkelstein), 11.133a
(Finkelstein).

Feminist Literary Criticism. See Women
and Literature.

Frankfurt School. 4.22 (Buck-Morss),
4.88 (Jay), 15.65 (Negt).

Genres. 2.6 (Lang and Williams), 2.10
("Marxist Alternatives to the Traditions"), 12.8 (Davis), 14.53 ("Literature and Society").

Hegemony. 4.70 (Gramsci), 6.30
(Swingewood), 11.85g (Bromley),
11.166b (Oakley), 15.68 (Sallach),
15.140 (Tuchman).

Ideology. 2.4 ("Ideology and Literature"), 2.14 ("Socio-Criticism"), 4.2
(Althusser), 4.8 (Baxandall), 4.11
(Bell), 4.23 (Burniston and Weedon),
4.32 (Crews), 4.39 (Eagleton), 4.42
(Eagleton), 4.47 (Fekete), 4.54 (Fis-
cher), 4.58 (Girnus), 4.62 (Goldmann),
4.70 (Gramsci), 4.84 (Jameson), 4.112
(Macherey), 4.130 (Mercer and Naw-
rat), 4.179 (Truitt and Meehan), 4.191
(Werkmeister), 7.22 (Schlauch), 8.26
(Cantarow), 8.46 (Turner), 9.4 (Dur-
and), 9.26a (White), 9.28 (Reilley),
9.41a (Jameson), 9.88 (Jameson), 10.8
(Mathews), 11.8f (Lovell), 11.11a
(Stratman), 11.191 (Fauvet), 11.48f
(Eagleton), 11.110a (Aers), 11.171d
(Rabate), 11.180a (Lecourt), 11.189f
(Shanker), 11.237e (Robinson), 12.7
(Davies), 12.9 (Dieterich), 12.25 (Ma-
thews), 13.7 (Bisseret), 13.27 (Jame-
son), 13.28 (Kress and Hodge), 13.43
(Rossi-Landi), 15.16 (Camargo), 15.20
(Mattelart and Siegelaub), 15.44
(Gouldner), 15.109 (Kellner), 15.130
(Renault), 15.180 (Hart), 15.203 (Sul-
livan), 15.207 (Todd).

Imperialism. 8.14 (Orwell), 8.78 (Ras-
kin), 11.48o (Hawkins), 11.129c
(Clark), 11.168a (Zollman), 15.20
(Mattelart), 15.72 (Schiller).

Literary Form. 4.40 (Eagleton), 4.41
(Eagleton), 4.42 (Eagleton), 4.83
(Jameson), 4.84 (Jameson), 4.94 (Kö-
peczi), 4.100 (LeRoy), 4.144 (Plek-
hanov), 5.9 (Brecht), 8.69 (Egri), 9.40
(Burke), 9.77 (Burgum), 11.29a
(Adam), 11.48f (Eagleton).

Literary History. 4.29 (Craig), 4.66
(Goldmann), 4.81 (Hohendahl), 4.188
(Weimann), 4.189 (Weimann), 10.21
(Clark).

Literary Production. 4.112 (Macherey),
4.115a (Eagleton), 4.141 (Naumann),
4.207 (Zimmerman), 5.11d (Zimmerman), 10.1 (Cappon), 14.16 (Escarpit).

Literature and History. 4.21 (Bisztray),
4.30 (Craig and Egan), 4.40 (Eagleton),
4.148 (Richter), 6.19 (Lukács), 6.26
(Shor), 9.21 (Henderson), 9.69 (Wil-

son), 10.2 (Clark), 11.171d (Rabate), 11.188d (Swann), 11.210a (Smith), 14.6 (Barker), 14.59 (McRobbie).

Little Magazines. 8.80 (Wall), 10.14 (*Alive* collective), 10.19 (Castro), 10.45 (Zwicker), 11.116a (Mulhern), 11.116d (Anderson).

Marx and Engels as Literary Critics. *See* Marx, Karl.

Marxism and Art. (*S.a.* Aesthetics.) 2.2 (Baxandall), 2.15 (Solomon), 4.3b (Barker), 4.9 (Baxandall), 4.53 (Fischer), 4.57 (Garaudy), 4.75 (Harrington), 4.77 (Hess), 4.78 (Hess), 4.90 (Kettle), 4.95 (Laing), 4.97 (Lenin), 4.102 (Lifshitz), 4.110 (Lunacharsky), 4.117 (Mao Tse-Tung), 4.126 (*Marx & Engels*), 4.134 (Morawski), 4.140 (Morris), 4.143 (Plekhanov), 8.4 (Egbert), 9.5 (Egbert), 14.2 (Albrecht), 14.13 (Egbert), 14.15 (Enzer), 14.30 (Hauser), 15.32 (Benjamin), 15.48 (Horkheimer).

Medieval Literature. 8.26 (Cantarow), 8.27 (Colley), 8.30 (Delany), 8.31 (Delany), 8.32 (Delany and Ishanian), 8.37 (Lawton), 8.38 (Schlauch), 8.39 (Schlauch), 8.40 (Schlauch), 8.41 (Schlauch), 8.42a (Niecko), 11.40c (Delany).

Modernism. 4.89 (Kampf), 4.100 (LeRoy), 4.101 (LeRoy and Beitz), 4.105 (Lukács), 4.186 (Wasson), 5.9 (Brecht), 8.8 (LeRoy), 11.16f (Bullock), 11.133b (Nikolyukin), 11.225a (Howe), 13.3 (Barthes), 14.37 (Howe), 14.39 (Howe).

Nature and Landscape. 4.199 (Williams), 8.1 (Barrell and Bull), 8.23 (Williams), 8.46 (Turner), 11.43a (Barrell), 11.112a (Lever), 11.127a (Hopwood), 11.236g (Friedman), 11.236h (Southall).

New Criticism. 4.37 (Di Salvo), 4.47 (Fekete), 4.156 (Sanders), 7.7 (Graff), 9.82 (Finkelstein), 9.85 (Graff), 11.79a (Rudich).

Politics and Culture. 4.4 (Aronowitz), 15.14 (Bigsby), 15.15 (Casty), 15.39 (Enzenberger), 15.51 (Jones), 15.64 (Murdock and Golding), 15.96 (Furhammar and Isaksson), 15.113 (Lang), 15.139 (Tracey).

Politics and Literature. 4.163 (Sartre), 4.198 (Williams), 4.204c (Eagleton), 5.12 (Caute), 6.16 (Levine), 6.25 (Schwartz), 6.35 (Zipes), 7.8 (Laska), 7.13 (Lindsay), 8.27 (Colley), 8.31 (Delany), 10.8 (Mathews), 10.30 (Mundweiler), 10.36 (Stanley), 11.7e (Rickword), 11.74e (Johnson), 11.81a (Wolff), 11.109a (Harrington), 11.208b (Eagleton), 11.239b (O'Brien), 11.239c (O'Brien), 12.10 (Dixon), 12.18 (Kampf and Lauter), 12.24 (LeRoy), 13.21 (Hoyles), 13.33 (McCaffery), 13.36 (Mueller), 13.40 (Orwell), 14.9 (Cole), 14.35 (Howe), 14.40 (Hynes), 14.48 (Laqueur and Mosse).

Praxis. 4.170 (Swingewood), 4.183 (Wartofsky), 6.30 (Swingewood), 15.197 (Piccone).

Proletarian Literature and Culture. 4.109c (Schmidt), 4.175 (Trotsky), 6.14 (Johnson), 8.59 (Mitchell), 9.13 (Rideout), 9.34 (Calverton), 9.53 (Hicks), 9.54 (Madden), 9.92 (LeRoy), 10.46 (Birney), 10.52, (McKenzie), 11.20a (Johnson), 11.21c (Wilson), 11.196a (Crepon), 11.214d (Mitchell), 14.14 (Empson), 14.44 (Kahn).

Realism. (*S.a.* Socialist Realism.) 4.20 (Bisztray), 4.25 (Caudwell), 4.105 (Lukács), 4.113 (Macherey), 4.121 (Marcuse), 6.10 (Fruchter), 6.20 (Lukács), 6.34 (Williams), 8.6 (Kettle), 8.41 (Schlauch), 9.86 (Green), 10.40 (Wayman), 11.16f (Bullock), 11.62b (Milner), 11.62c (Milner), 11.133b (Nikolyukin), 11.207c (Kott), 14.4 (Auerbach), 14.25 (Girard), 14.49 (Larkin), 14.64 (Orr).

Reception Theory. 4.55 (Fokkema and Kunne-Ibsch), 4.80 (Hohendahl), 4.141 (Naumann), 4.182 (Von Staden), 4.189 (Weimann).

Revolution. 2.8 ("Literature and Revolution"), 4.111b (Vásquez), 4.122 (Marcuse), 4.155 (Rühle), 4.204a (Kettle), 5.6 (Beck), 5.7 (Blankfort), 6.27 (Siegel), 6.29 (Swingewood), 7.6 (Cudjoe), 7.17a (Berger and Bostock), 8.84 (Day-Lewis), 10.14 (*Alive* collective), 11.62h (Swann), 11.150l (Goode), 11.155a (Nelson), 11.162h (O'Flinn), 13.17 (Ehrmann), 14.52 ("Literature and Revolution"), 15.105 (Henny), 15.118 (Macbean).

Romance. 4.25 (Caudwell), 6.13 (Jameson), 8.6 (Kettle), 11.77b (Kuczynski), 11.150i (Munby), 11.192a (Danby), 15.159 (Cawelti).

Romanticism. 8.8 (LeRoy), 8.15 (Pearson), 8.19 (West), 8.58 ("Marxism and Romanticism"), 8.63 (West), 8.82 (Brown), 9.18 (Charvat), 11.46h (Southall), 11.150b (Thompson), 11.151a (Pearson).

San Francisco Mime Troupe. 5.5 (Baxandall), 5.13 (Davis), 5.14 (Davis).

Science Fiction. 6.4 (Burgum), 6.6 ("Change, SF and Marxism: Open or Closed Universe?"), 6.9 (Fitting), 6.28 (Suvin), 9.100 (Shaftel), 14.1 (Angenot).

Semiology/Semiotics. 13.1 (Lawford), 13.12 (Coward and Ellis), 13.20 (Hawkes), 15.86 (Caughie), 15.92 (Denkin), 15.95 (Fiske and Harley), 15.131 (Rustin), 15.145 (Wollen).

Sexuality. (*S.a.* Women and Literature.) 7.15 (Matthews), 11.113g (Way), 11.113o (Efron), 11.170a (Delany), 11.208b (Eagleton), 12.10 (Dixon), 15.17 (Friedman), 15.108 (Kaplan).

Socialist Realism. 2.7 (LeRoy and Beitz), 4.33 (Cultural Theory Panel), 4.82 (James), 4.95 (Laing), 4.100 (LeRoy), 4.105 (Lukács), 4.149 (Rieser), 5.33 (O'Casey), 7.14 (Markov), 8.7 (Kettle), 11.214d (Mitchell), 13.3 (Barthes).

Soviet Literary History. (*S.a.* Socialist Realism.) 2.7 (LeRoy and Beitz), 4.2 (Althusser), 4.6 (Arvon), 4.82 (James), 4.96 (Lenin), 4.97 (Lenin), 4.98 (Lenin), 4.99a (Morawski), 4.110 (Lunacharsky), 4.143 (Plekhanov), 4.144 (Plekhanov), 4.175 (Trotsky), 6.20 (Lukács), 7.16 (Mayakovsky), 9.16 (*20th Century American Literature: A Soviet View*), 13.1 (Lawford),

13.5 (Bennett), 13.18 (Ehrlich), 13.25 (Jameson), 14.5 (Barker), 15.92 (Denkin), 15.94 (Eisenstein), 15.121 (Mayne).

Structuralism. 4.55 (Fokkema and Kunne-Ibsch), 4.142 (Neilson), 4.188 (Weimann), 4.205 (Zimmerman), 4.206 (Zimmerman), 4.207 (Zimmerman), 13.1 (Lawford), 13.2 (Bann), 13.13 (Culler), 13.14 (DeGeorge), 13.19 (Ehrlich), 13.20 (Hawkes), 13.25 (Jameson), 13.45 (Rutherford), 13.47 (Schaff), 15.74 (White).

Tradition. 2.10 ("Marxist Alternatives to the Traditions"), 10.38 (Waddington), 11.126b (Arundel), 11.165c (Lawson), 13.4b (Thody).

Tragedy. 5.15 (Figes), 5.40 (Williams), 11.82b (Mathews), 11.161b (Lawson), 14.64 (Orr).

Utopia, Utopian Literature. 2.9 ("Marxism and Utopia"), 5.11c (Hermand), 8.11 (Morton), 9.5 (Egbert), 9.27 (Pfaelzer), 11.78b (Southall), 11.96b (Adorno), 11.123h (Beauchamp), 11.124a (Buhle), 11.149d (Southall), 11.222b (Caudwell).

Women and Literature. 4.46 (Ellis), 4.49 (Ferrier), 4.68 (Goode), 4.150 (Robinson), 8.13 (O'Flinn), 8.50 (Beardon), 9.9 (Martin), 11.8g (Newton), 11.21g (Ohmann), 11.21i (Gubar), 11.21m (Marxist-Feminist Collective), 11.23a (Marxist-Feminist Collective), 11.40c (Delany), 11.62i (Showalter), 11.235d (Bell and Ohmann), 11.235g (Barrett), 11.235h (Marcus), 14.60 (Maglin), 14.63 (Moers), 14.69 (Showalter), 15.17 (Friedman), 15.89 (Citron), 15.185 (Jones), 15.200 (Rossi).

Work. 8.3 (Craig), 12.31 (Shor), 12.32 (Voight), 14.60 (Maglin), 14.62 (Meakin), 15.29 (Aronowitz).

Working-Class Literature. 7.28 (Vicinus), 8.9 (Gallacher), 8.62 (Vicinus), 8.70 (Gray), 8.71 (Jones), 8.77 (Mitchell), 8.93 (Jones), 8.104 (Thomas), 10.53 (M.M. and V.L.J.), 11.47a (Webb), 11.108a (Duran), 11.214e (Webb), 14.43 (James), 15.47 (Hoggart).